Disputed Issues

Contending for Christian Faith in Today's Academic Setting

Stephen T. Davis

BAYLOR UNIVERSITY PRESS

Cover Design by Joan Osth

Library of Congress Cataloging-in-Publication Data

Davis, Stephen T., 1940-
Disputed issues : contending for Christian faith in today's academic setting / Stephen T. Davis.
p. cm.
Includes index.
ISBN 978-1-60258-151-7 (pbk. : alk. paper)
1. Apologetics. I. Title.

BT1103.D38 2009
230--dc22

2008010613

Printed in the United States of America on acid-free paper.

Disputed Issues

Contents

Introduction

Attacks on orthodox Christian beliefs and practices originate from many quarters. Those of us who are professionally located in secular academia find criticisms coming from three main academic locales—biblical studies, theology, and philosophy. (Some also arise out of the sciences, of course, but they will not be my focus in the present book.) Many of these attacks are from intelligent and serious people. Throughout my career, I have found myself from time to time defending religious belief and especially Christian belief from assaults from all three sources. This book brings together some of those writings. Some of the essays have not been previously published; others have appeared in other settings and have been revised for this occasion. The book does, however, constitute a coherent overall argument. Its conclusion is that orthodox Christian belief can be defended against the attacks that are coming its way.[1]

Part I deals with issues that have arisen in recent years from New Testament studies. The issues here have to do with texts, history, and believability. Chapter 1 deals with the Jesus Seminar, a group of New Testament scholars who achieved real notoriety in the last few years of the twentieth century. They saw themselves as cut off entirely from any sort of churchly or religious authority, and they reached rather startling conclusions, among other things, about the authenticity of the teachings of Jesus. I conclude in chapter 1 that both the methods and conclusions of the Seminar are flawed. Chapter 2 deals briefly with recent research on the source that scholars call Q, a hypothetical source that was apparently used by the writers of the gospels of Matthew and Luke but not Mark. Located primarily in my own hometown of Claremont,

California, researchers on the International Q Project also make rather startling claims that are, I believe, unfounded.

Also local to Claremont, Professor Dennis MacDonald has recently argued that much of the material in Mark's gospel was mimetically copied from Greek classics such as the Iliad and the Odyssey. This thesis appears to have rather dramatic implications for the historical accuracy of claims that are made about Jesus in Mark, although MacDonald does not spell out those implications. Chapter 3 is my response to his argument. Chapter 4 deals with a controversial issue among New Testament scholars, viz., whether Jesus claimed for himself the authority to forgive sins, as the Gospels claim. Since an affirmative answer to this question has long been used by theologians and preachers to support the notion that Jesus was God incarnate, this issue has important theological implications. Chapter 5 is, in effect, a long book review. Recently a group called "Internet Infidels," who publish mainly on the Internet and in an avowedly antireligious philosophical journal called *Philo*, has been raising harsh criticisms of Christian belief in the resurrection of Jesus. Their book, *The Empty Tomb: Jesus Beyond the Grave* (Amherst, N.Y.: Prometheus, 2005), raises a whole series of criticisms, mainly from people who think clearly and have done their homework. Chapter 6 concerns exegesis, the art or science of reading and interpreting the Bible. Since the time of Bultmann, scholars have asked whether it is appropriate for exegetes to approach the Bible with certain presuppositions. This chapter presents and defends my own views on this matter.

Part II deals with theological issues that mainly relate to Christian doctrines. Chapter 7 takes up the issue of relations between the religions and asks whether orthodox or evangelical Christians ought to embrace religious pluralism. I argue that they should not do so; I also try to say what sort of attitude Christians ought to have toward other religions. Chapter 8 specifically concerns relations between Jews and Christians. A recent movement in some Christian circles promotes rethinking Christian theology in the light of the Holocaust. This often involves the recommendation that Christian theses that can be offensive to Jews—e.g., the claim that Jesus was the Messiah and the Son of God—be revised or rejected. A recent impetus to further thinking about this subject was the appearance in 2004 of Mel Gibson's movie, *The Passion of the Christ*. In chapter 8, I present my own views on this subject.

Having lived and worked in Claremont, California—the world center of Process Theology—for many years, it is natural that I have had to engage in dialogue with Process thinkers on many occasions. While I admire the accomplishments of Alfred North Whitehead—I consider his great book *Process and Reality* to be one of the major intellectual achievements of the twentieth century—I have always been correctly perceived here as an opponent of Process Theology. Chapter 9, in a brief way, is an attempt to say why. A second recent theological movement is called theological nonrealism. A hallmark of this approach, which comes in many versions, is a reductionist understanding of such theological claims as "God exists" and other crucial theological statements. In chapter 10, I try to come to grips with and refute some versions of theological nonrealism. Chapter 11 deals with the relationship between Christian eschatology and the notion of resurrection. On both topics, there are viewpoints out there in the contemporary world with which I strongly disagree. This chapter is my attempt to understand the two notions correctly.

Part III deals with various issues in the philosophy of religion, a subfield of philosophy that has enjoyed a renaissance in recent decades. That revival is due primarily to the excellent work of such philosophers of religion as William Alston, John Hick, Alvin Plantinga, Eleonore Stump, Richard Swinburne, and others. Chapter 12 deals with the question of hope and despair in the light of human suffering and especially the phenomenon of genocide. Using two stories from the book of Genesis, I argue that hope is possible, even in the light of murder and genocide, if God exists. Chapter 13 involves arguments that Antony Flew has been making, in one form or another, since the 1950s. He argues that the notions of "surviving death" or "living forever" are incoherent, and accordingly that Christian belief in an afterlife should be abandoned. I again argue against his claim.

With the late D. Z. Phillips as a longtime friend and Claremont colleague, I have had to think a great deal in recent years about what is called Wittgensteinian philosophy of religion, of which Phillips was the most noted representative. While wanting to be true to the language and experience of actual religious believers, I believe that this way of doing the philosophy of religion presents a deep challenge to religious belief and Christian faith. I try to say why in chapter 14. Chapter 15 is a response to criticisms of the famous ontological argument for the existence of God. The criticisms were presented by Michael Martin, a talented and respected philosopher who, in a series of books and articles, has argued strongly against virtually all aspects of religious belief, Christian doctrine, and theistic proofs. Finally, chapter 16, is an attempt to argue against classical Thomist conceptions of God and (at the other extreme) the so-called Open View of God in favor of what I call the neoclassical view of God.

The title of this book, *Disputed Issues*, requires comment. One of the great opportunities that my career has presented to me is living and working in Claremont. Some world-renown scholars are or have been also located here—John Cobb, John Hick, James M. Robinson, and D. Z. Phillips have all been colleagues of mine—and it has been a marvelous opportunity for me to have interacted with them. Moreover, it seems that, at one time or another, almost every notable scholar in biblical studies, Christian theology, or the philosophy of religion arrives in Claremont to participate in a conference or give a paper. And on many such occasions I have found myself criticizing or defending aspects of their work. Several of the chapters of this book came to life in such settings.

A few years ago, my friend, former teacher, and former colleague John Hick produced a book called *Disputed Questions* (Yale University Press, 1993). Like the present volume, it reflects and continues the habit of medieval thinkers who wrote books or essays that they called Questiones Disputatae. In those writings they took up issues in philosophy or theology that were being debated by scholars who were their contemporaries or near contemporaries. The difference (as Hick points out) is that the various medieval Questiones Disputatae mainly argued about points that were considered somewhat secondary in importance. The issues that I deal with in the present volume (like the issues that Hick deals with in his book) are, in my opinion, crucial for Christian philosophy and theology. So although John Hick and I disagree on very many points in theology and the philosophy of religion, I happily point out that his book has been something of a model for this one. The crucial difference, of course, is that I am defending Christian orthodoxy.

Part I

New Testament Issues

1

Should We Believe the Jesus Seminar?

I

The so-called Jesus Seminar (JS) was much in the news in the 1990s, and its work had the effect of confusing and troubling many Christian laypersons. It is, in my opinion, a good example of biblical scholarship that has lost its way. First I will tell you what it is and what it tries to do; then I will offer four criticisms of its work.

The JS was headed by Professor Robert W. Funk and was sponsored by his Westar Institute, a scholarly think tank located in Sonoma, California. Its first meeting was in 1985. At one time or another over two hundred scholars were members of the JS, but at the time its book, *The Five Gospels: The Search For the Authentic Words of Jesus* (New York: Macmillan, 1993), was published, there were seventy-four members.

II

The JS continues a work in which various New Testament scholars have been engaged for some two hundred years, that is, the attempt to arrive at the facts about the life and teachings of Jesus. The so-called quest for the historical Jesus is generally said to have begun with German theologian Herman Samuel Remarius (1694–1768). His aim was to disregard the theological teachings of the church and the assumption of divine intervention in the

The present chapter, which is published here for the first time, was originally a talk I delivered on one or two occasions in 1996.

world; he wanted to find the truth about Jesus based entirely on naturalistic assumptions. But the heyday of the quest was undoubtedly the nineteenth century, during which scholar after scholar tried to separate the historical Jesus from what they called "the Christ of faith." David Friederich Strauss' *The Life of Jesus Historically Examined* (1835) was one of the major works.

Albert Schweitzer brought this first quest to a close with his 1906 book, *The Quest of the Historical Jesus.* (Yes, this is the same Schweitzer who was the famous musician and medical missionary to the Congo.) Although most scholars today reject Schweitzer's own picture of Jesus, he made a trenchant point that is widely accepted: the nineteenth-century "questers" about whom he wrote all seemed to end up with a Jesus who was very much in their own image. I will return to that point later in connection with the JS.

I have no problem with the idea of scholarly research about the historical Jesus. It is true that there are four canonical gospels and that they are not always in perfect agreement. Did the centurion himself ask Jesus to heal his servant (Matt 8:5-13) or did he send Jewish elders to Jesus to do so (Luke 7:1-10)? Was the cleansing of the temple early in Jesus' ministry (as in John's gospel) or during Holy Week (as in the synoptics)? Did the women arrive at the tomb of Jesus while it was still dark (John 20:1) or after sunrise (Mark 16:2)? These (and others) are legitimate questions.

Furthermore, the Gospels are the result of a complicated forty-or-more-year process of redaction and recontextualization, and in many cases it is not easy to see whether a given saying that is attributed to Jesus is intended as a word-for-word quotation, a loose paraphrase, an interpretation, or what. This, especially since some of Jesus' sayings seem to reflect later times, for example, note the use of the word *ecclesia* (church) in Matthew 18:17: "If the member refuses to listen to them, tell it to the church."

In *The Five Gospels*, the members of the JS try to decide which sayings were actually said by Jesus and which were not. There are some fifteen hundred sayings attributed to Jesus in the JS's inventory, that is, from Matthew, Mark, Luke, John, and the Gospel of Thomas, a Gnostic gospel about which I will say more later. One of the major emphases of the JS is that its work is completely unencumbered by church or dogma; they are just scholars (so they keep declaring)—no church controls or even influences them. The JS, however, is not a group of ivory-tower scholars shut up in university offices—they are highly publicity conscious individuals. They constantly promote their work in newspapers, on talk shows, and in syndicated news releases.

Probably the JS's most famous methodological innovation was voting with color-coded beads. When considering a given saying attributed to Jesus, JS scholars who thought it was actually said by Jesus voted with a red bead. Those who thought it was possibly said by Jesus but probably not in the recorded form voted with a pink bead. Those who thought it was probably not said by Jesus although something like it may have been said by him voted with a gray bead. Those who firmly denied that Jesus said it or anything like it voted with a black bead.

These votes correspond to the colors of print used for alleged sayings of Jesus in *The Five Gospels*. In JS meetings, the votes were tabulated as follows: three points for each red bead; two for each pink bead; one for each gray bead; and zero for each black bead. The total points were added up and then divided by the number of voters present. If a saying received over 75 percent of the possible points, it is colored red in *The Five Gospels*. By consensus of the JS, Jesus actually said it. If a saying received between 50 and 75 percent of the possible points, it is colored pink. Jesus possibly said it or at least an earlier version of it. If a saying received between 25 and 50 percent of the possible points, it is colored gray. Jesus probably did not say it, although something said by Jesus may be in back of it. If a saying received 25 percent or less of the possible points, it is colored black. The members of the JS hold that Jesus definitely did not say it.

What do we find when we read *The Five Gospels?* There are explanatory essays, detailed notes that amount to a full commentary on *The Five Gospels*, a roster of JS members, and other assorted indices and tables. The main body of the book is taken up with a new translation (called the Scholars' Version) of the four canonical gospels plus Thomas. As noted, the sayings attributed to Jesus in those sources are colored red, pink, gray, or black. The first impression one gains from the book is that the members of the JS are extremely skeptical about the authenticity of those sayings.

For example, nothing whatever in the Gospel of John is colored red, although John 4:44 is colored pink. The JS translates this verse as, "a prophet gets no respect on his own turf," which is typical of the colloquial, somewhat "with it," style of the Scholars' Version. Only one saying from Mark is colored red; it is Mark 12:17: "Give to Caesar what is Caesar's and to God what is God's" (NIV). All told, only fifteen sayings of Jesus from the five gospels are colored red, and seventy-five are colored pink. We notice right away that all fifteen red sayings are short, pithy aphorisms, and so are most of the pink sayings (a few parables, or fragments of parables, pass muster for pink). Some 82 per cent of the sayings attributed to Jesus by Matthew, Mark, Luke, John, or Thomas are considered inauthentic by the JS (i.e., are colored either gray or black), and most of the sayings from the remaining 18 percent are pink.

These highly skeptical conclusions reflect in part the JS's methodological commitment to the notion that a saying is guilty till proven innocent. That is, unless a given saying attributed to Jesus in the inventory can be shown to be authentic, it must be judged inauthentic. The burden of proof is on the one who accepts authenticity.

III

Let me now turn to four criticisms of the work of the JS.

1. *The JS makes eccentric use of sources and dating.* Let's talk about dating first, because that is the point where the JS would best be able to defend itself. To sum up briefly a hotly contested point, the JS dates all the synoptic gospels as having been written after the destruction of the temple in A.D. 70, and John's Gospel as having been written in the 90s at the earliest. Although I disagree with this conclusion (as do most conservative biblical scholars who hold that the synoptics, and especially Mark, reached final form before A.D. 70), many biblical scholars outside the JS would agree.

What is odd is that the JS holds that the Gospel of Thomas, a gnostic gospel discovered (in a Coptic translation) in Nag Hammâdi in Egypt in 1946, antedates Mark and thus is a more reliable source of the sayings of Jesus than Mark. Gnosticism was a mainly second- and third-century philosophical and religious movement. It came in many varieties but was typically characterized by: (1) a cosmic dualism between good and evil, body and spirit, light and darkness; (2) denigration of bodily existence; and (3) salvation through higher knowledge (*gnosis*) or secret lore.

Gnosticism was recognized by the church fathers as heretical, despite the fact that several ostensibly Christian writers and communities during that period were more or less influenced by Gnosticism. It was known prior to 1946 that there was such a thing as the Gospel of Thomas, but we did not have a full manuscript of it until then, when a gnostic Christian library, including the Gospel of Thomas, was discovered at Nag Hammâdi.

Thomas consists of 114 sayings of Jesus; there is virtually no narrative structure—no stories of Jesus' birth, death, or resurrection, and virtually no life setting for the sayings that are recorded. The gnostic library in which it was found dates from (and was buried during) the fourth century A.D.; however, it is clear that Thomas is older than that. But the point is that the vast majority of non-JS biblical scholars would date Thomas from the mid-second century, arguing that it depends on the canonical gospels as literary sources. (About fifty of the sayings of Jesus recorded in Thomas have parallels in the canonical gospels; that is, about sixty-five of them are unique to Thomas—and they are, of course, the most gnostic-sounding ones.) So it is odd that the JS dates Thomas so early, and there is (I believe) a hint of scholarly dishonesty in the fact that *The Five Gospels* makes no reference to the current scholarly controversy over the dating of Thomas. The book gives the clear impression that a first-century dating of Thomas is the consensus of all competent scholars.

Why do most scholars contend that Thomas is a second-century document that quoted from or alluded to the canonical gospels rather than (as the JS would have it) a first-century document that influenced the canonical gospels? There are several reasons, but I will cite one. The sayings attributed to Jesus in Thomas have parallels in all four canonical gospels as well as all commonly recognized literary strata of the Gospels. There are parallels with material found only in Matthew, with material found only in Luke, and with material from Q. (Q comes from the German word *Quelle* or source and refers to the large amount of material—mainly sayings of Jesus—that is found in Matthew and Luke but not in Mark.) It is much more probable, then, that Thomas knew and relied upon the canonical gospels (which would have been quite possible in the middle of the second century) than that every canonical gospel, with all of their sources, independently depended upon a mid-first-century Thomas.[1]

A late dating of Mark would mean that by the time it was written, few eyewitnesses to the life of Jesus would still be living, and thus few who could correct false claims about what he had said during his lifetime. Accepted by the JS, this late dating accordingly makes it easier for the JS to reject most of the sayings in Mark as nonauthentic. Furthermore, it makes room for acceptance of an assumption that is crucial to the JS's work, viz., that the early church felt free to "invent" sayings out of whole cloth and attribute them to Jesus. Indeed, if we are to believe the JS, the vast majority of the sayings attributed to Jesus in the synoptics were products not of Jesus but of the later Christian church.

For myself, I think it undeniable that many sayings of Jesus were embellished, reinterpreted, and recontextualized until the time that the Gospels were written. But the idea that the church felt free simply to invent sayings and attribute them to Jesus is one that I entirely reject. There is in my opinion no hard evidence for this at all—indeed, the great respect for oral traditions (often memorized and passed on) that we see in ancient cultures like first-century Judaism argues against the claim of the JS.

There are powerful arguments against the claim that the early church felt free to invent sayings of Jesus out of the blue, and the JS has not taken them into account. First, had the early Christians engaged in such a practice, it is highly probable that sayings would have been placed in the mouth of Jesus that were relevant to the central concerns and controversies of the church in the second half of the first century. But notice that there are no sayings attributed to Jesus in the canonical gospels that are directly relevant to such burning issues in the late-first-century church as the proper use of spiritual gifts, whether male Gentile converts were obliged to be circumcised, whether Christians should divorce their non-Christian spouses, the proper practice of the Lord's Supper, how churches ought to be governed, etc.

Second, notice that the church preserved and passed on "difficult" sayings of Jesus—sayings that it would have been convenient for the church to forget—for example, sayings about the human failings of some of the church's greatest leaders (e.g., Peter, in Mark 14:66-72), sayings about Jesus' apparent lack of omniscience (Mark 13:32), sayings about his inability on one occasion to work any miracles because of the people's lack of belief (Mark 6:5-6), etc.

Third, notice that Paul makes a careful distinction between his own teachings—which he regarded as authoritative for the churches and individuals to whom he wrote—and the teachings of the Lord, which he regarded as even more authoritative (1 Cor 7:10-12).

All of these arguments show, I believe, the respect that the church had for the actual teachings of Jesus—I believe they were reliably preserved and passed on rather than amended or even made up. And this stands to reason. After all, the early church, centered in and in some sense governed from Jerusalem, was concerned that its faith be preserved and communicated properly. So the leaders exercised a degree of control over what was taught (Acts 8:14; 11:1-3; 15:1-2; 21:17-25). I believe the Jerusalem leadership would have immediately corrected any distorted Jesus traditions or invented sayings.

2. *The JS used flawed criteria of authenticity.* How did the JS go about deciding whether a given saying attributed to Jesus is authentic? Well, the answer is that the members voted. But the deeper epistemological question is: what criteria did the individual members of the JS use in order to help them decide how to vote in the case of a given saying? The answer is that several criteria were used, and some of them were criteria that would be accepted by many New Testament scholars. I want to focus on just one of them, the so-called criterion of dissimilarity.

This criterion, which I believe has some usefulness as a positive criterion (i.e., one that helps us be sure that a given saying was in fact said by Jesus), holds that a saying is to be attributed to Jesus if it is dissimilar to what would or could have been said by others around the time Jesus lived. For example, if a certain saying is attributed to Jesus by, say, Luke, it almost certainly was said by Jesus if it cannot be found in the Old Testament, would not have been said by first-century Jews as part of their common fund of cultural lore, and does not bear any marks of the theological interests of the Christian church in the 60s or 70s. Dissimilarity thus becomes a strong piece of positive evidence.

The problem is that the JS turned the criterion of dissimilarity into negative evidence. Its view is that a saying can only be considered authentic if it is dissimilar in the above sense. That is, only sayings that are dissimilar are to be judged authentic and printed red. But this produces an absurd consequence: the arrived-at "authentic" sayings of Jesus will be entirely disconnected from the historical and cultural and religious milieu in which Jesus lived.

Suppose that for some reason certain scholars in the late twenty-first century decide to engage in an attempt to discover which of the sayings attributed to Mao Tse-Tung in the famous little red book from the 1960s, *The Sayings of Chairman Mao*, are authentic. And suppose they decided to exclude anything that was similar to colloquial Chinese wisdom of the time, anything that could have been said by Marx or Engels, or anything that reflected actual conditions in China in the 1940s, 1950s, or 1960s. Isn't it obvious that the "Mao" that these scholars would arrive at would be absurdly disconnected from his historical situation? That is, isn't it obvious that such a procedure would be, well, ridiculous?

Most of the sayings attributed to Jesus in the canonical gospels are excluded by the JS on the grounds that they are too Jewish or too Christian or too self-centered (the members of the JS believe that Jesus never made claims about himself) or too eschatological (they also deny that Jesus made any "bombastic and threatening" statements about the end of the world or the coming judgment). Not all of these conclusions are based on a wrong use of the criterion of dissimilarity (some are based on an ideological view of Jesus shared by the members of the JS, about which I will say more), but some are.

So the "Jesus" of the JS turns out to be an eccentric iconoclast, quite unconnected to Judaism, to Jewish apocalypticism, to the Old Testament, or to the later concerns of the Christian church. The only sayings that are colored red are highly idiosyncratic. This is odd and unscholarly in at least two ways: First, it is not easy to see why such a totally disconnected

"Jesus" was even taken seriously by his contemporaries. Second and most important, two conclusions that the vast majority of New Testament scholars today would accept are that Jesus was an apocalyptic proclaimer of the kingdom of God and that Jesus was through-and-through Jewish. The JS denies both.

3. *An a priori, ideological view of Jesus controls the findings of the JS.* We have seen evidence of this already. It held that Jesus was not an apocalyptic teacher, so any sayings about the end of history and the kingdom of God are inauthentic. Jesus did not talk about himself, and indeed had no consciousness of himself as the Messiah, so any sayings that attribute statements about himself to Jesus are inauthentic.

Other points are as follows:

1. The JS rejects any idea of divine intervention in history, so any apparently supernatural predictions by Jesus (e.g., about his upcoming passion, death, and resurrection) are unauthentic "retrojections" by the early church placed in the mouth of Jesus decades later.
2. The JS also holds that Jesus never made long speeches, so all such speeches attributed to Jesus in the Gospels are inauthentic. What he did offer, according to the JS, were either terse and provocative maxims or a few slightly longer parables. Jesus was, they say, a kind of laconic, itinerant sage, like the Cynic philosophers of the Greco-Roman world.
3. The JS holds that there was no big controversy between Jesus and the Jewish religious leaders, so all the denunciations of "the scribes and the Pharisees" by Jesus in the Gospels are inauthentic.

As I noted earlier, Albert Schweitzer correctly accused the nineteenth-century "questers" of arriving at a Jesus made in their own image. Whatever view of Jesus the quester wanted to find was, lo and behold, exactly what emerged after all the scholarly exertions. I believe that exactly the same point can be made about the "Jesus" of the JS. Just as the JS would want him to have been, its Jesus is a bland and tweedy guru who spouts obscure profundities, heavy gems of original wisdom, and Zen koans.

4. *The JS wrongly gives the impression that its results constitute the consensus of contemporary New Testament scholarship.* As noted, this is far from true, even if you exclude evangelical biblical scholars from consideration. Indeed, many mainline scholars take the work of the JS to be an embarrassment. They are profoundly skeptical about the methodology and conclusions of the JS, and they consider it something of an idiosyncratic

splinter group. For the JS to give the impression that its conclusions represent the "assured results" of contemporary scholarship is misleading. It is also somewhat off-putting that the JS likes to give the impression that its conclusions are based on new evidence that has just recently been discovered. This, too, is far from the truth.

It also does not wash for the members of the JS to give the impression, as they do, that their views represent the only alternative to fundamentalism. "Either you're a literalist or you're with us," they seem to say. But that implicit claim is quite deceptive. The JS does not represent a balanced cross section of New Testament scholars, and there are all sorts of possible views of the sayings of Jesus that are to the left of fundamentalism but to the right of the JS.

IV

I have always felt that one crucial way of testing any theory of Jesus is to ask whether it can account for the crucifixion and the rise of the church. It is undeniable that Jesus was crucified, and it is undeniable that he was and is the central figure of a movement that came into existence soon after the crucifixion. How does the JS fare in explaining these two points?

First, I confess to great difficulty seeing how the "Jesus" of the JS could have made certain religious and political leaders so upset with him that they crucified him. The Jesus of the JS seems a nonthreatening, self-effacing guru who eschewed controversy and whose main claim to fame was producing puzzling and surprising bits of religious wisdom. Why would anybody—Jew or Roman—find such a Jesus at all offensive, let alone so offensive as to be hated, let alone so hated as to be executed?

Second, I confess to having equal difficulty seeing how the "Jesus" of the JS could have inspired the church. It is true that in reading all the passages printed red in *The Five Gospels,* one finds amazing bits of spiritual and ethical wisdom. They are inspiring, uplifting, puzzling, challenging. Who would deny that? But would these sparse bits of wisdom, however wise they are, be enough to inspire people to begin a new religion? Would they inspire people to risk their lives on behalf of a movement committed to Jesus? No, something much more radical than Jesus the laconic sage must be posited to explain the rise of the Christian church.

In the end, the JS does not make a convincing case. It is sad that so many laypersons—and some journalists—have been confused by what amounts to the implausible claims of a scholarly subgroup whose main gift seems to lie in the area of generating publicity.

My central conclusion is that the traditional picture of the words and deeds of Jesus as recorded in the four canonical gospels is holding quite well despite all the current scholarly controversies. That is, the portrait of the teachings of Jesus found in Matthew, Mark, Luke, and John is reliable. We do not always find there the exact *words* of Jesus. In one sense, we never do—Jesus undoubtedly taught mainly in Aramaic, and the New Testament was written in Greek. But I would argue that we do hear in the canonical gospels the authentic *voice* of Jesus. Contrary to the conclusions of the JS, Matthew, Mark, Luke, and John do, by and large, faithfully represent the authentic teachings of the historical Jesus.[2]

2

Is the Jesus of Q Theory Believable?

I

Since the time of the early church, a curious fact about the synoptic gospels has been noticed. There is a large amount of material—almost all of it sayings of Jesus—that is found in Matthew and Luke, often in word-for-word agreement, but not at all in Mark. But given that most scholars believe that Mark was the first gospel, and given the obvious fact that (on that assumption) Matthew and Luke derived much of the structure and content of their gospels from Mark (i.e., Mark was a source for both of the other synoptic evangelists), it seems to follow that Matthew and Luke had access to a source that Mark knew nothing of.

Accordingly, many scholars believe that there once actually existed a written source of sayings of Jesus. It is called Q after the German word for source (*Quelle*); it is also called the Sayings Source. It is held to be quite early; some hold that Q existed as a document in the 50s, some twenty years after the crucifixion and some twenty years before Mark was written. There is disagreement about whether Q existed originally in Aramaic and was later translated into Greek or was in Greek from the beginning.

Serious research on Q has gone on since the nineteenth century. But in the 1980s and 1990s a group of scholars became interested in studying Q further. They called themselves the International Q Project (IQP) (there

The present chapter appears here in print for the first time. It is based on some letters that I exchanged in 1998 with Professor Patrick Hartin of Gonzaga University. Pat, a Catholic priest and a noted New Testament scholar, had been involved in some of the Q research. He agreed with many, but not all, of the points I made in our exchanges.

are, of course, Q scholars who do not identify with this group). Under the leadership of James M. Robinson, John Kloppenborg, Burton Mack, and others, they began studying the boundaries of Q (trying to decide what verses it actually contained), the theology of Q (what it said about God, Christ, and human beings), and the Q community (its location, social and religious setting in the first century, and especially its Christology). There were also efforts to distinguish earlier and later versions of Q. The IQP has even published what it calls a critical edition of Q. Edited by James M, Robinson, Paul Hoffman, and John S. Kloppenborg, it is called, *The Critical Edition of Q: Synopsis Including the Gospels of Matthew and Luke, Mark and Thomas, with English, German, and French Translations of Q and Thomas* (Minneapolis: Hermeneia-Fortress, 2000).

Some of the conclusions of this team seem acceptable and have advanced the cause of New Testament scholarship. But there is much in its research that I strongly disagree with. In this brief chapter, I will explore some of those points.

II

My main complaint is that much Q research is based on a series of unproved assumptions—so far as I can see, the whole research program collapses if they aren't true—and Q scholars almost never signal readers that they are aware of that fact. Indeed, they act as if there is no need to do so, presumably on the grounds that "everybody just knows" that the assumptions are true.

Let me discuss in turn four such assumptions.

Assumption A: *There existed in the first century an actual document corresponding to what we now call Q.* Although this assumption has not been proved, I am inclined tentatively to accept it. I certainly accept Marcan priority and the two-source theory. The verbal agreements between Matthew and Luke (where Mark is silent) show that either (1) a great deal of memorization of the sayings of Jesus was practiced in the pre-70 period, and Matthew and Luke simply accepted material that had been memorized and passed on orally; (2) Luke got his Q verses from Matthew or vice versa[1]; or else (3) Q existed and was a source for Matthew and Luke. Let me speak briefly about each possibility.

1. *Memorization.* It is highly probable that a great deal of memorization of teachings of Jesus did go on among early Christians. But there is a problem with using this fact to explain the Q material. Jesus presumably taught in Aramaic, and the Q sayings are in Greek. So on the memorization hypothesis, there must have been an early translation of

Jesus' teachings from Aramaic to Greek, which translation Matthew and Luke both had access to and used. They were clearly not doing separate translations themselves since their Greek is identical in most places. So they must have used a single source that was known to both of them. In theory, that source could have been oral, but it does seem doubtful that a purely oral source could have remained virtually identical in wording for some twenty to thirty years. It seems more probable that a written text was the basis for the handing on of early traditions of Jesus' teachings. If this reasoning is correct, memorization alone cannot account for the existence of the Q material in Matthew and Luke.

2. *Matthew was a source for Luke (or vice versa).* It is most probable that Matthew and Luke wrote their gospels quite independently of each other. That is, neither evangelist used the other's gospel as a source.[2] This is because it is otherwise hard to explain why there is so much unique material in each gospel (often referred to as "special M" and "special L" or merely "M" and "L") that the other either does not know or chooses to ignore. Just in the birth accounts, if Luke read Matthew, why does he omit the visit of the Magi? If Matthew read Luke, why does he omit Luke's intimate knowledge of Mary's thoughts and reactions?

3. *Q existed as a written source.* As noted, I am inclined to accept this hypothesis, but with misgivings. What would of course prove that Q existed as a written source would be the recovery of an actual manuscript of Q. But what also gives me pause is not so much that Q has not survived as a distinct document (after all, very many manuscripts from the first century no longer exist), but that there is no clear reference to Q as a separate document in the postapostolic writings. This, to be sure, is an argument from silence, and such arguments at best are less than probative. But it does seem sensible to ask why—if the document existed and played as important a role as the Q project people claim—that we find no unambiguous references to it in the *Didache* or Clement or Polycarp or Ignatius or Justin Martyr. These folks talk about Jesus all the time[3] but never mention (what we now call) Q.

There is a response to this worry that admittedly has some force. This is the fact that there are very few clear references to the four gospels by name before the middle of the second century (although there are references to Matthew in the *Didache*[4]). Perhaps Q had disappeared by the middle of the second century (perhaps because it had by then been recognized that the Q material could be found in Matthew and Luke), when quotations from the four gospels became common. Still, it is (or ought to be) a major embarrassment for Q researchers that we have no hard evidence at all that Q existed as an independent text.

Finally, here is a point that ought to be obvious: the fact that Robinson, Hoffman, and Kloppenborg have succeeded in producing a "text of Q" is not evidence that Q existed. I make this point because the very existence in libraries and on desks of *The Critical Edition of Q* might lend psychological weight to belief in the actual first-century existence of Q.[5] Of course, such an argument would be circular. In fact, the existence of *The Critical Edition of Q* is quite irrelevant to the question whether Q existed.

III

Assumption B: *We can infer roughly what Q contained.* What we might call "classic Q" is just whatever material that we find in common in Matthew and Luke and is not found in Mark. But nobody has ever disproved the possibility that Q—if it existed—was much larger than we believe. Maybe it contained material not found in Matthew or Luke, or material found in Matthew and/or Luke that overlapped with Mark. Perhaps it even contained a passion and resurrection narrative. I do not claim that this last point is probable, since our evidence is that Q was a sayings source. Still, my point is that we do not know.

But I also want to point out that Q, if it existed as a document, might have been smaller than many Q scholars believe. Indeed, it has been interesting to notice what we might call the growth of Q in the past twenty years. What was a hypothesized first-century source whose boundaries were fairly clearly established except at the margins (as noted, whatever is in Matthew and Luke, with striking similarity, but not in Mark) has now grown much beyond its earlier size. Sometimes the reasons for the inclusion of new material in Q seem to be theological, that is, agreement with what is taken to be Q's or primitive Q's theology. I am suspicious that the whole thing is pretty subjective.

I am especially suspicious of the "layers" that some claim to find in Q (sometimes called Q1, Q2, and Q3), as well as the supposed problems and tensions in the Q community that are said to have led to the later editions. I can admit that some of the stated criteria of "primitiveness"—items like being less polished in grammar or style, being less elaborate, etc.—have some minimal usefulness. But I get worried when the operative criteria seem to be agreement or disagreement with a theology that is taken to be primitive, for example, anything that does not reflect a "wisdom" theology must be a later accretion. The largely nonapocalyptic, non-Jewish Jesus who emerges from the "earliest stage" of Q is, in my opinion, a scholarly myth. And apparently no two Q scholars agree on the contents of Q.

Despite the possibility that Q might have been larger, or smaller, than scholars think, it seems clear that we must limit ourselves to what can be reconstructed from the agreements between Matthew and Luke and not go beyond them. When we consider the use that Matthew and Luke made of (not Q but) Mark, it is clear that they used virtually all of it. There is very little in Mark that cannot also be found in Matthew and/or Luke. So it seems probable that the same would be true of their use of Q. This is how they apparently dealt with their sources.

A final point: in the work of the International Q Project, one gets the impression that deciding on the contents and limits of Q is less like gospel source criticism and more like biblical textual criticism. But reconstructing the original text of Q is not like reconstructing the original text of, say, Matthew. With Matthew we possess actual ancient texts that we have good reason to think agree for the most part with the autograph. We do not have before us any ancient texts of Q; Q is merely a hypothetical text. Moreover, the people in the first few centuries who made copies of New Testament texts had a very different and much more conservative attitude toward those texts than, say, Matthew and Luke did toward Mark or Q.[6]

IV

Assumption C: *There was a Q community.* Now of course if there were a document, then in one sense almost by definition there must have been a community—a person who was or a group of persons who were responsible for the research, writing, and preservation of the document. But the term, "the Q community," as used by at least some Q scholars, means a great deal more than that. It means a social group, an ongoing worshipping community for whom Q was its sacred book about Jesus and that saw itself as distinct from other extant Jesus communities. But despite the best efforts of Q scholars, I don't think anybody has ever come close to establishing this assumption.

Now what I claim has not been ruled out is the possibility that there was no Q community. Perhaps Q was composed by an individual[7] or a very small group of people who were not particularly motivated by any partisan desire to separate themselves, either sociologically or theologically, from other early Christian groups. But if there did exist a Q community in some robust sense (which I doubt), it might be possible to deduce some things about their community from Q, for example, that the Q community was Jewish, economically poor, antagonistic to the Pharisees, and believed in the authority of Jesus. Fair enough. But many

Q scholars go far beyond this, as we will see below. In the end, it is highly questionable whether there ever was a Q community.

V

Assumption D: *Q exhausts what the Q community believed about Jesus, that is, it contains (without remainder) their Christology.* Thus, for example, since Q contains little or nothing about the crucifixion and resurrection of Jesus, it follows that there was a Jesus community in the first century (by now sadly wiped out by the forces of orthodoxy) that did not believe that Jesus was crucified or else believed that the crucifixion was unimportant and did not believe in his resurrection (Crossan and Mack). All that mattered to them—so it is concluded—was his teachings. Again: how do we know this is true? There is, in my opinion, no evidence whatsoever for assumption D.

As noted above, perhaps it is possible to induce a few things about the Q community (again, assuming that such a community existed) from reading Q. Possibly we can even induce a few things from Q about the community's Christology, for example, its belief that Jesus was the Son of Man. But to conclude that it did not believe in the resurrection because it is not mentioned in Q is absurd and says more about the agenda of the people who are drawing the conclusion than it does about the Q community. No piece of writing, no matter how extensive (and we know that Q is hardly exhaustive of Jesus' teachings) verbalizes every thought of the person or community that produced it.[8] Moreover, as a list of Jesus' teachings, we would hardly expect Q to contain narratives of Passion Week and its outcome.

VI

Doubtless Q scholars would say, in response to my objections, something like this: Yes, these are unproved assumptions, but they are based on scholarly consensus, and it is perfectly legitimate for scholars to make inferences based on scholarly consensus. But I deny that there exists a scholarly consensus that the above four assumptions are all true. Possibly such a consensus exists among the scholars of the International Q Project themselves but hardly in the guild of New Testament scholars. Moreover, the whole research program reminds me of a house of cards. It consists of assumption based on assumption; it does not constitute a firm foundation for the speculation that is engaged in. In other words, in scholarly discussions of Q, standards of evidence, truth, and verification seem amazingly loose and flexible. Hypothesis and speculation abound.[9]

But my deepest disquiet about Q research is that much of it seems to be done in aid of a theological agenda. It is designed to support the idea that the earliest and thus best Christologies were nothing like the orthodox ones that emerged later and, sadly, eventually won out. Since I see myself as a defender of orthodox views of Jesus, I resist this aspect of Q scholarship. Orthodox Christologies did win out, but that fact does not sadden me.

3

Did Mark Copy Homer?

I

Nothing is more important for Christians than Jesus. Christian faith begins with Jesus, with narratives about who he was and what he did. We believe that our salvation depends on the truth of certain claims about the life, death, resurrection, and person of Jesus. That is why Christians take an active interest in contemporary Jesus scholarship. Intellectual fads seem to come and go in that world with amazing rapidity (in fairness, this is probably true in most academic disciplines today). The most recent movement—one that seems to be growing in influence—tries to place the Gospels in a Greco-Roman historical and literary context.

This chapter is a response to recent work by Professor Dennis R. MacDonald of the Claremont School of Theology. He is involved in a research program that aims to detect the influence of the *Iliad*, the *Odyssey*, and other ancient Greek and Roman classics on early Christian literature. I will focus on MacDonald's book, *The Homeric Epics and the Gospel of Mark* (Yale University Press, 2000; citations from this book are placed in parentheses in the text), as well as his recent conference paper, "Did Luke Know His Stories Were Fictions? Luke-Warm Attitudes to History in Luke-Acts."[1]

MacDonald's highly original and rather startling claim is that very many of the episodes, motifs, and characters in Mark and Luke/Acts were mimetically "borrowed" from the Homeric epics. MacDonald further claims that

The present chapter is a slight revision of my "Mark and Luke: History or Imitative Fiction? A Response to Dennis MacDonald," Philosophia Christi *6, no. 2 (2004).*

Mark wanted his readers to recognize the Homeric influence and see Jesus as greater than the Homeric heroes like Ulysses. I will call MacDonald's overall theory "The Homer Thesis" (THT).

Producing new and surprising theories of Jesus is a thriving industry among New Testament scholars these days. MacDonald's book, which is attracting considerable attention in those circles, is allied with a growing movement. As noted, this is the effort to read New Testament texts in the context of Greco-Roman literature. This movement in itself is not threatening to traditional Christian views of Jesus (indeed, some evangelical scholars participate in it), not at least as long as the intrinsic and essential Jewishness of Jesus is not eclipsed. But MacDonald's thesis seems to be the logical outcome of pushing the connections of the New Testament to Greco-Roman literature as hard as possible.

Unfortunately MacDonald does—as I will explain—end up with a Jesus that orthodox Christian believers of all stripes will fail to recognize. One (but only one) aspect of this point is that, along with several other contemporary revisionist views of Jesus that have nothing to do with THT, he very much deemphasizes the influence of the Hebrew Scriptures on the New Testament's picture of Jesus. For those reasons, his arguments need to be countered.

II

MacDonald argues that the *Iliad* and the *Odyssey* were read by and influenced writers throughout the Roman world in the first century. And so far as Greek and Latin speakers are concerned, this claim is obviously true. He then argues that their influence can be demonstrated in the Gospel of Mark. And this is the part of THT that concerns me.

The two strong points of THT are doubtless the many parallels that McDonald cleverly finds between the works in question and his skill in placing those parallels in the context of the ancient educational and cultural tradition of *mimesis*. (This term means "imitation" and refers to the ancient educational and literary practice of imitating or emulating styles and themes from recognized literary masters such as Homer.)

In his book, although MacDonald is clear that Mark was not writing historical biography, he largely avoids the issue of the historicity of the events that Mark narrates. Nevertheless, MacDonald's readers will naturally wonder whether THT is an entirely literary claim, or whether it also has implications for history. For example, suppose we are convinced with MacDonald that there are striking similarities between Homer's account of the death of Hector and Mark's account of the death of Jesus and that

Mark borrowed from the *Iliad* in writing his passion narrative: [136, ("Mark seems to have created much of the Passion Narrative in imitation of Homeric Epic.")]. Question: Is Mark's account accordingly untrue or unreliable or invented? Did Jesus *not* die on a cross? Naturally, this is an important question for Christians, the vast majority of whom accept that Jesus did die on a cross in (at least roughly) the way Mark describes and insist on the importance of that truth.

That Jesus did not die in the way Mark claims is surely a sensible inference to draw from THT. MacDonald certainly holds that Mark is historically unreliable at many other points. At times in his book he seems (somewhat grudgingly) to accept that some point or other in Mark may be attributable to "tradition" or even to the historical Jesus, rather than to borrowing from Homer or the LXX. For example, he allows as how the historical Jesus probably was baptized by John the Baptist and probably did have a controversy with Jewish leaders (33, 196). But his main thesis is that Mark was not writing history but fiction or myth; his gospel is "a novel, a prose anti-epic of sorts" (7).

On the other hand, it seems possible, almost anywhere we might look, to find striking similarities between accounts of vaguely similar but quite separate events. Consider, for example, Plato's account of the death of Socrates in the *Apology*, *Crito*, and *Phaedo* (see E. Hamilton and H. Cairns, eds., *The Collected Dialogues of Plato* [New York: Pantheon, 1961]) and the account of the death of John Adams, the second president of the United States, in David McCullough's recent work, *John Adams* (New York: Simon and Schuster, 2001); references to Plato or McCullough are placed in parentheses in the text). As Plato and McCullough describe the lives of Socrates and Adams, here are some parallels:

- Both Socrates and Adams were well-known public figures.
- Both Socrates (*Phaedo* 118a) and Adams (470) were men of integrity who achieved greatness despite opposition.
- Both Socrates (*Apology* 23c) and Adams (103, 170–71, 222–24, 259–60) had strong opinions about education and enjoyed helping to educate young people.
- Both Socrates (*Apology* 23d, 24b–28b) and Adams (425, 462–63) had bitter enemies who brought serious charges against them.
- Both Socrates and Adams were subject to public ridicule and lampooning.
- Both Socrates (*Crito* 50–54, *Apology* 29e) and Adams (20) were patriotic men who emphasized the welfare of their nations.

- Both Socrates (*Phaedo* 61c) and Adams (19) participated in and enjoyed philosophy.
- Both Socrates and Adams (17, 19, 260, 591–92) could read Attic Greek.
- Both Socrates (*Apology* 17d) and Adams (649–51) died in old age, Socrates at age seventy and Adams at age ninety.
- Both Socrates (*Phaedo* 115–18) and Adams (641–51) received visits from friends at the end of their lives.
- Both Socrates (*Phaedo* 115–18) and Adams (641–49) spent their last days giving advice to friends and loved ones.
- Both Socrates (*Apology* 35d) and Adams (625) believed in and trusted a good God or gods.
- Both Socrates (*Apology* 40b-c, 41d) and Adams (617, 624) ruminated about death and the afterlife during their last days and looked forward to a good afterlife.
- Both Socrates (*Apology* 41d) and Adams (650) spoke about virtue and goodness during their last hours.
- Both Socrates (*Apology* 28d–29b, *Phaedo* 58e, 63e) and Adams (628) remained in good spirits, professed no fear of death, and faced death with equanimity.
- Both Socrates (*Crito* 49b-d, *Phaedo* 69e) and Adams (632, 637) died without hatred of their enemies.
- Both Socrates and Adams died in their respective hometowns.
- Both Socrates and Adams died on, or just after, a national holiday.

Suppose that one is impressed, as I was when I discovered them, with these parallels between Plato's dialogues and McCullough's book. What do we make of these amazing similarities? Four possibilities come to mind:

1. McCullough consciously borrowed from Plato.
2. McCullough unconsciously or unintentionally borrowed from Plato.
3. There are certain settled patterns in narratives of the lives and deaths of great heroes, which Plato and McCullough both quite naturally followed.
4. The similarities are merely, or mainly, coincidental.

Doubtless there are others. But which is the best explanation? Or is it some combination of the four? And how do we decide?

MacDonald provides six criteria, which, when satisfied for any two texts, constitute a cumulative case for borrowing (8–9). Let's call the two texts A (the prior one) and B (the latter one). The more of the criteria that are satisfied, MacDonald says, the stronger the case. Here are the criteria:

- *Accessibility*. A was widely distributed at the time of the writing of B and was probably available to the author of B.
- *Analogy*. A had been imitated in other writings prior to B.
- *Density*. There are many parallels between A and B.
- *Order*. Many of these parallels exhibit similar sequence.
- *Distinctive traits*. There are intertextual markers, that is, atypical features that set A and B apart, where the feature in A is a distinctive contribution of its author, and the same feature is included in B in order to indicate its reliance on A.
- *Interpretability*. It is possible to explain why the author of B imitated and tried to improve upon or (as MacDonald says) make a "transvaluation" of A.

Surely these criteria make a powerful case for McCullough's imitating Plato. *Accessibility*: the Socratic dialogues of Plato were obviously available to McCullough. *Analogy*: the life and death of Socrates, of which Plato's writings constitute our most credible source, have always been considered fit objects of imitation. *Density*: the many parallels just noted between Plato's account of the death of Socrates and McCullough's account of the death of Adams are impressive indeed. *Order*: both men were born, then lived fascinating and admirable public lives, then got old, then drew near to death, then had long conversations with friends, and finally died, and afterward lived on in honored memory.[2] *Distinctive traits*: three of the parallels listed above can easily and naturally be interpreted as intertextual markers: the fact that both Socrates and Adams were subject to public ridicule and lampooning (Socrates in Aristophanes' *Clouds* and Adams in the Antifederalist newspaper *Aurora*); the fact that both Socrates and Adams died in their respective hometowns (Socrates in Athens and Adams in Quincy, Massachusetts); and the fact that both died on, or just after, a national holiday (Socrates died when the Athenian state galley returned from its annual religious mission to Delos, and Adams died on the Fourth of July). *Interpretability*: it seems quite possible that McCullough wanted to present John Adams as a Socrates-like hero, whose main values were political, democratic, and American rather than Greek and purely philosophical or moral. This seems a fine reason why McCullough might have wanted to imitate and offer a "transvaluation" of Plato.

So apparently five, and perhaps even all six, of MacDonald's criteria are or can be satisfied here. Accordingly, it seems that the case for McCullough's imitating Plato is strong. This especially since MacDonald occasionally argues for mimesis on the basis of the satisfaction of as few as three or even two of the criteria (93–95, 101).

But wait a minute: isn't this conclusion problematical? Notice that if we accept it, we could naturally infer that McCullough's account of the death of John Adams is not historically reliable (being largely borrowed from the account of the death of another person). But the trouble with that inference is that the events that McCullough describes really did occur. That is, they are confirmed by other accounts of the life and death of John Adams, confirmed about as well as any historical event ever is.

Naturally, like any historian, McCullough has his own point of view and his own biases, but the fact remains that his book largely describes known historical events. Accordingly, borrowing—at least to the extent that it impugns historical reliability[3]—does not seem plausible in this case after all, despite the satisfaction of most of MacDonald's criteria.

Suppose we know that what McCullough writes is, in the main, verifiable history. And suppose this convinces us that McCullough did not "borrow" the episodes in his book. Then it seems that anyone like MacDonald who thinks that the story Mark tells is largely borrowed (in this case, from Homer) has already formed an opinion about the genre of Mark. Such a person must hold, as MacDonald does, that whatever Mark was writing, it was not factually true statements about the past. The genre of his gospel must be more like myth or fable or fiction.

III

Well then, is there reason to consider Mark historically reliable? Of course Mark was not writing neutral, facts-only history. He had a theological purpose in mind and shaped his material accordingly. But that does not entail that he was not also trying to write true claims about the past, for example, that Jesus died on a cross.

Virtually all Christians accept a doctrine of Scripture that entails at the very least a presupposition of historical reliability as to central points. I take it that most mainstream Protestants and Catholics do so, let alone fundamentalists and evangelicals (who would of course make the point even more strongly). But belief in the trustworthiness of the Bible will not carry much weight with those, like MacDonald, who do not hold such a presupposition. So the question is: are there historical-critical reasons for holding that Mark is, in the main, historically reliable (and isn't just based on borrowing from Homer)?

I will present two such reasons.

1. *Agreement with Paul.* It is often said that the apostle Paul knew and cared little about the life of Jesus. But that is far from the truth. What is correct is that as far as we know, Paul never wrote a gospel; his extant letters were all occasional pieces that responded to various needs that he saw in the churches and individuals to whom he wrote.

But clearly the life and teachings of Jesus were important to Paul. This is not difficult to establish. He stressed the need for believers to obey and even imitate Jesus (1 Cor 11:1; 2 Cor 4:10-12; 10:5; 1 Thess 1:6) as he himself did. But it is difficult to see how that could be done or even attempted without at least some knowledge of Jesus' life. Moreover, Paul made a careful distinction between Jesus' teachings and his own teachings (1 Cor 7:7-16; cf. 2 Cor 11:17; 1 Thess 4:2, 15). And again, it is hard to see how Paul could do that without knowing what Jesus' teachings were. Note also that Paul accused his enemies of preaching "another Jesus" (2 Cor 11:4), as if knowledge of the real Jesus were crucial.

And in broad outline, we can piece together a credible "life of Jesus" by noting scattered references in the seven letters that even nonevangelical New Testament scholars accept as authentically Pauline (Romans, 1 and 2 Corinthians, Galatians, Philippians, 1 Thessalonians, and Philemon). And this broad outline largely confirms what is said in Mark.

Here is what we can find: His name was Jesus (1 Cor 1:1); he was a man (Rom 5:15), born of a woman (Gal 4:4); he was Jewish, a descendent of Abraham (Gal 3:16) and David (Rom 1:3); he had brothers (1 Cor 9:5); and he was brought up under the Law (Gal 4:4). He was sent by God to take on human form (Rom 8:3; Phil 2:6-11); he was poor (2 Cor 8:9) and humble (Phil 2:6-11); he suffered (Rom 8:17); he was loving and compassionate (Phil 1:8); and he lived an exemplary life, aiming to please God rather than himself (Rom 15:3, 8; Phil 2:6-8).

Jesus gathered disciples, including Cephas, James, and John (Gal 1:19; 2:9), and taught people on various religious subjects (1 Thess 4:2), including marriage and divorce (1 Cor 7:10), the way in which those who preach the gospel should make their living (1 Cor 9:14), and his own ultimate triumphal return (1 Thess 4:15-17). On the night Jesus was betrayed he took bread, broke it, gave thanks, and said: 'This is my body that is for you. Do this in remembrance of me.' Then he took a cup and said: "This cup is the new covenant in my blood. Do this, as often as you drink it, in remembrance of me" (1 Cor 11:23-26).

There are many other echoes in Paul of Jesus' teachings in the Gospels. For example, Romans 12:17-20 contains several phrases that seem to be taken from what we now call the Sermon on the Mount (Matt

5–7). Indeed, the topics are listed in the same order in both places: not to return evil for evil, to live at peace with everyone, to avoid revenge, and to love one's enemy. Paul's teaching in Romans 12:14—about blessing those who persecute you—seems to echo Jesus' teachings (Luke 6:27b-28a) in Luke's Sermon on the Plain (Luke 6:17-49).[4]

Jesus was betrayed (1 Cor 11:23), was killed by "the Jews" (1 Thess 2:14) by crucifixion (1 Cor 1:18, 23; 2:2), and was buried (1 Cor 15:4). On the third day (1 Cor 15:4) God raised him from the dead (Rom 1:4; 4:25; 6:4; 8:34; 1 Cor 15:4; 2 Cor 4:14 Gal 1:1; 1 Thess 4:14). He appeared to Peter, then to "the twelve," then to more than five hundred people, then to James, and then to all the apostles (1 Cor 15:5-7). Finally, as the gospel writers do, Paul insists that Jesus will one day return (1 Thess 4:16-17) to be revealed (1 Cor 1:7) and to judge all people (Rom 2:16). Indeed, this last point constitutes a major theological innovation shared by Paul and Mark: the idea of a suffering messiah who dies on a cross and will one day return in victory over his enemies.

I do not claim that the canonical gospels or even Mark are simply reproduced in Paul; indeed, some items just mentioned are not in Mark at all (e.g., resurrection appearances only occur in that gospel's inauthentic "long ending"); and many items from the Gospels (e.g., miracle stories, parables) are not mentioned in the Pauline letters. But the basic outline is there.

The importance of this point about agreement with Paul is obvious: the authentically Pauline epistles were all written well before Mark, well before the Jewish war, and indeed within twenty to thirty years of the death of Jesus. Thus what Paul said about the life of Jesus is much more likely to be reliable on purely historical-critical grounds than something written, say, after the Jewish war. And this confirms the accuracy of later texts (like Mark) that largely agree with Paul on the life of Jesus. This argument does not rule out Marcan borrowing from Homer. But it does rule out the kind of extensive borrowing that MacDonald argues for and that is inconsistent with historical reliability. Mark does not appear to be myth or fable or fiction.

2. *The Ring of Truth.* This is hardly the place for a major apologetic effort in favor of the reliability of Mark's picture of Jesus.[5] But I will make a gesture toward two reasons for considering Mark generally historically trustworthy, for considering his "life of Jesus" to have "the ring of truth." It needs to be remembered that virtually whatever sensible date is accepted for the Gospel of Mark, it was written at a time when the events it records were within the living memory of at least some individuals. (There seems to be wide scholarly agreement, even among nonevangeli-

cal biblical scholars, that Mark was written in the late 60s or early 70s. MacDonald himself allows that Mark was written "in the war's immediate aftermath" [15], which would mean a few years after 70.)

(a) One obvious but seldom-remarked-upon point is that Mark's Gospel was convincing to the first-century church and to the other synoptic evangelists. Luke, who claimed to have consulted sources carefully (Luke 1:1-4), simply adopted Mark's outline of the life of Jesus, as well as almost every specific event that Mark recorded. He added a great deal to Mark, and consistent with his own theological purposes, he worded, ordered, and interpreted certain events differently than Mark did. But it cannot be gainsaid that Luke basically accepted Mark. Matthew, too, simply adopted Mark's outline and most of the events Mark recorded.

(b) A second point: certain aspects of the Gospel of Mark indicate trustworthiness. I will mention just two of them. The first, a point I do not have space to explore thoroughly, is that Mark's Jesus says little that seems relevant to many of the burning issues that were facing the Christian churches in the 70s and 80s (Jewish versus Gentile Christianity, incipient Gnosticism, charismatic gifts, church order, etc.), which is not what we would expect if Mark were an unreliable product of that era.

The second is a point that was recognized early in the history of the church, for example, by Eusebius:

> Mark writes these things, and through him Peter bears witness, for the whole of Mark is said to be a record of Peter's teaching. Note how scrupulously the disciples refused to record those things that might have given the impression of their own fame. Note how they handed down in writing numerous charges against themselves . . . which no one in later years would ever have known about unless hearing it from their own voice. By thus honestly reporting their own faults, it is reasonable to view them as relatively void of false speaking and egoism. This habit gives plain and clear proof of their truth-loving disposition. . . . If it was their aim to deceive, and to adorn their master with false words, they would never have written these demeaning accounts of his pain and agony and that he was disturbed in spirit, that they themselves forsook him and fled, or that Peter the apostle and disciple who was chief of the apostles denied him three times, unless they had an extraordinarily high standard of truth-telling. (*Proof of the Gospel*, 3.5)

Few scholars now hold, as Eusebius did, that the gospel writers were all members of "the twelve," and some doubt that Peter was Mark's main source. Still, Eusebius' central argument holds: unless the evangelists had determined to tell the truth, they would never have recorded events that must have been embarrassing to Peter and the other disciples who were, at the time Mark was written, pillars or deceased former pillars of the church.

MacDonald, of course, has his own explanation for Mark's criticisms of the disciples: the evangelist was emulating Homer's less-than-flattering depiction of the crew of Ulysses. But that does not refute the point. Even if THT were true in this case, it would still constitute an acute embarrassment for the church in the 70s to hear that its leaders behaved as Mark says they did before and during Passion Week.

IV

Before turning to MacDonald's paper on Luke/Acts, let me mention what I take to be three further difficulties for THT.

The first is that THT would be immeasurably stronger if MacDonald were able to offer historical rather than purely literary arguments, for example, if he were able to point to ancient authors, Christian or non-Christian, who recognized and plausibly explained the dependence of Mark on Homer. Since he is unable to do so, he must rely on his six criteria, most of which (analogy is an exception) are completely internal to the two texts in question. But the Plato/McCullough example shows that the criteria are in themselves inconclusive.

The second point concerns MacDonald's criteria themselves. He presents the six as if they are all equal in weight. But that cannot be the case. For example, unless the first criterion is satisfied, none of the others count for anything. He never says exactly how many of the criteria must be satisfied, or which ones, before borrowing is established. And he never says which of them are necessary conditions and which (or which combinations of them) are sufficient conditions. This point does not refute THT. But clearly MacDonald needs to do much more work in establishing the relative weight and cognitive order of his criteria.

The third is a point of which MacDonald is aware, but I am unsatisfied with what he says about it. Suppose MacDonald is correct that Mark wanted to make it clear to his readers that Jesus was a hero who was similar to, but greater than, Ulysses. Then why did Mark disguise his intention so well? Precisely why was Mark, as MacDonald (rather understatedly) says, "long on concealing, short on revealing" (6; cf. 3)?

After all, neither Luke nor Matthew, who obviously paid close, word-for-word attention to the text of Mark, noticed any Homeric influence. Neither did any of the Eastern church fathers, several of whom were exceedingly well versed in the Greek classics and were at pains to demonstrate the superiority of the Bible to those works. Neither did *anybody*, until MacDonald came along centuries after the fact. Now, I am not accusing MacDonald of excessive hubris; new discoveries are occasionally made, and new and fruitful theories propounded, even about ancient texts. But it is puzzling that Mark hid his intentions as well as MacDonald says he did. Why didn't Mark occasionally mention Homer or quote from Homer or use Homeric vocabulary or make direct allusions to Homer? This is the way we usually show that a given text depends upon an earlier one. And Mark is not at all shy about quoting from or alluding to the Hebrew Bible. So the very novelty of THT is one of its biggest problems: it remains a major challenge to MacDonald to explain why the influence of Homer was not noticed until the twenty-first century.[6]

Moreover, since Homer makes it clear in both epics that Ulysses had character flaws, it seems odd that MacDonald holds that Mark held that Jesus was like Ulysses. Of course, MacDonald's notion is that Mark wants us to see that Jesus was greater than Ulysses; still, this point is troubling to THT. Moreover, MacDonald's reading of Mark's comparative intentions is amazingly flexible: on MacDonald's account, Mark compares Jesus not only to Ulysses but also to Telemachus, Menelaus, and Hector.

I conclude that THT is clever but unconvincing.

V

In his conference paper, MacDonald turns to Luke/Acts. Assuming THT as it applies to Mark, he asks whether Luke knew that his stories were fictional. My problem arises at the outset of MacDonald's argument. There is, I am afraid, an unbridgeable philosophical gap between the two of us at this point. I do recognize that there exists an ongoing scholarly debate over the historical reliability of Luke/Acts. But, to put the point bluntly, I am not impressed when MacDonald gives as a reason for holding that Luke is not writing history the fact that Luke records many miracles.

I do not accept miracles stories blindly. But I do believe in the existence of a God who has both the ability and occasionally the intention to interrupt the natural flow of events and bring about an event that would not otherwise have occurred.[7] That is, I am no deist. Apparently unlike MacDonald (who specifically mentions these very items in his paper), I believe in the Holy Spirit, angels, the devil, and miracles like the resurrection of Jesus. Accordingly, the fact that Luke also believes in them does not tempt me to accuse him of being (as MacDonald says) "credulous" or "hopelessly naive." In other words, MacDonald rejects, a priori, the historical reliability of any text that narrates miraculous occurrences.

MacDonald generously acquits Luke of the charge of deliberately misleading his readers. He argues that Luke intended them to understand that he was not writing history but foundational mythology, like Virgil's *Aeneid.* According to MacDonald, Luke/Acts is a kind of playful, clever, creative theological fiction. But the problems here, in my view, are the many signals that Luke emits that he wanted his story to be believed.

MacDonald claims that Luke signals his readers that he was *not* writing history, but the only signal he mentions is a curious example involving Rhoda/Rose/Aphrodite. The argument goes like this: MacDonald holds that Acts 12 mimetically "borrows" from *Iliad* 24, and he claims that Luke intentionally named the maid who responded to Peter's knocking at the gate of Mary's house "Rhoda." This, he says, was meant to signal Cassandra, because *Iliad* 24.699 relates Cassandra to Aphrodite, who was commonly identified with the rose [= Rhoda]. But this rather convoluted argument is clearly a frail reed with which to buttress the claim that Luke did not want to be understood as writing history. Remember, the issue we are considering is not whether Luke was an accurate historian (I hold that he was, but on that matter, as noted, there is much debate among scholars), but whether Luke wanted his readers to accept what he wrote as true.

There are several such signals. The first is the prologue to Luke (which MacDonald discusses). There Luke claims to have done careful research and to have presented the facts "accurately." I am much inclined to take these words to mean just what they plainly say. The second is the fact that Luke struggles mightily to connect the events he records with secular history and public figures and events (Luke 2:1; 3:1-2; Acts 13:4-12; 16:35-40; 18:12-17; 19:31; 25:10-11; 26:32). The third is the accuracy of the titles Luke gives to municipal and imperial officials in Acts, as well as his detailed knowledge of the boundaries and alignments of Roman districts and provinces in the 50s (Acts 13:12; 17:6; 18:12; 19:31, 35).[8]

Again, as arguments that Luke wrote accurate history, these points are not probative. Luke-like prologues were known in antiquity, and the other two points could be dismissed as attempts to provide "local color." But as arguments that Luke wanted his readers to believe what he wrote, they seem rather telling.

I conclude that MacDonald has much work to do in order to make the argument of his paper convincing. There exists a strong *prima facie* case that Luke intended to be believed. Of course he was also trying to strengthen the faith of Theophilus and other believers who read his books. But those of us who accept the basic reliability of Luke's narrative will be much inclined to say that the best way for Luke to have done that was to have written, as he himself claims to have done, an accurate narrative.

VI

We began by noting that nothing is more important for Christians than Jesus. Ours is a religion of history, not a dropped-from-the-sky set of laws, rituals, or spiritual practices. We believe that God has acted in human history and preeminently so in Jesus Christ. So questions about who Jesus was and what he said and did are crucial to us. One of the reasons evangelicals look with suspicion on much contemporary Jesus research is its puzzling diversity. Aside from the claim that there was a religious teacher and healer named Jesus who lived and died in first-century Palestine, contemporary Jesus scholars agree about almost nothing. Another reason evangelicals are suspicious is the strong impression that contemporary nonevangelical Jesus scholars are eagerly willing to entertain almost any ideas about Jesus, however bizarre they are, except orthodox ones.

Many will consider MacDonald's largely fictional Jesus to be just the latest effort of this ongoing antitraditional research program. It is incumbent upon evangelical scholars to show that conceptions of Jesus like MacDonald's are themselves fictional and that a convincing case can be made on purely historical-critical grounds that the traditional Christian picture of Jesus is the true one.[9]

4

Did Jesus Claim to Forgive Sins?

I

This chapter is a piece of theological and philosophical exegesis. It concerns the concept of forgiveness of sins, and especially Jesus' apparent willingness in the New Testament to offer forgiveness. I will deal primarily with Mark 2:1-12.

Section II lays some philosophical groundwork with a brief discussion of the phenomenon of forgiveness of one person by another. Section III deals with divine forgiveness and, more specifically, with a recent argument by philosopher Anne C. Minas to the effect that God, a perfect being, *cannot* forgive sins. Then in Section IV we will turn to the Mark text, where Jesus seems to dispense forgiveness to a paralytic. My concerns will be both exegetical and theological, that is, I will try to deal both with the text itself and with its place in the church's theology. In Section V, I will discuss two large ways of interpreting the text christologically, the first of which I will call the traditional reading. The second—which comes in different varieties—I will call christologically minimalist ways of interpreting the text. I will argue that those interpretations are unconvincing. Finally, in Section VI, I will argue that Jesus' offer of forgiveness to people is one of the materials from which a coherent Christology should be constructed.

An earlier version of this chapter appeared as "'Who Can Forgive Sins but God Alone?': Jesus, Forgiveness, and Divinity," in The Multivalence of Biblical Texts and Theological Meanings, *ed. Christine Helmer (Atlanta, Ga.: Society of Biblical Literature, 2006).*

II

In order to forgive, one must have a certain moral standing. If you were to ask me to forgive some offense that you once committed against, say, your brother, I would have to reply that I am unable to do so. I do not have the necessary moral standing. In general, the person who has the moral standing and thus the logical opportunity to forgive is the person against whom the offense was committed. In this case, your brother is the person to whom you should apply for forgiveness.

Forgiveness presupposes that something morally wrong has been done and that the perpetrator is responsible. Forgiveness is inappropriate in cases where the alleged wrongdoer did not really do the deed or cause it to occur, or where she did the deed but under the cover, so to speak, of a legitimate excuse or justification. Only those who are truly guilty can be forgiven. So forgiveness is not the same thing as *justification* (which argues for no wrongdoing), *excuse* (which argues for no moral responsibility), *mercy* (which may or may not be involved in forgiveness and which may be granted by those who do not have the moral standing to forgive), or *reconciliation* (which can occur without forgiveness and is often a result of forgiveness).

Forgiveness usually involves the forgiver voluntarily: (a) having a change of heart toward the evildoer, for example, giving up anger and resentment toward her; (b) giving up the desire for punishment of the wrongdoer (although forgiveness can be consistent with punishment still being administered); and (c) reconciliation, that is, restoration of the old relationship between the two parties (assuming that there was one). Forgiveness is rarely morally required. Since it presupposes the guilt of the wrongdoer, forgiveness also assumes the legitimacy of both the resentment felt by the offended person and punishment of the wrongdoer. Accordingly, forgiveness is normally morally allowed but not normally required.

Taken to extremes, forgiveness can have an unsavory aspect. Lest forgiveness slide over into servility, condoning of evildoing, or lack of self-respect on the part of the offended person,[1] certain acts are its normal prerequisite. They include contrition (or apology), repentance, and some degree of reparation (where possible) on the part of the wrongdoer.[2] This is not to deny that there can be cases where forgiveness is possible and even desirable quite apart from the satisfaction of some of these prerequisites.

As Jean Hampton argues, forgiving is not the same thing as condoning. Condoning a given act entails accepting it, taking it as morally allowable. Forgiveness, on the other hand, entails that the forgiver continues to hold that the forgiven deed was morally wrong.[3]

In some traditions, for example, the Christian tradition, forgiveness is a virtue. Christians are encouraged to forgive those who commit offenses against them. Harboring grudges instead of forgiving can be damaging to the soul. Indeed, according to Scripture (Matt 18:22; Luke 17:4), Christians are to forgive people an unlimited number of times, since that is how God forgives them. In places in Scripture the point is made so strongly as to constitute a virtual prerequisite for receiving forgiveness. "Forgive us our debts," Jesus taught the disciples to pray, "as we also have forgiven our debtors" (Matt 6:12; cf. also 6:14-15). In other words, those who do not forgive will not be forgiven.

III

Suppose that God exists. And suppose, as Christians hold, that all sins are offenses against God. Then it would seem that in the case of any sin or offense whatsoever, God has the moral standing to forgive it (of course, so do the people who are harmed by it). If wrongdoing amounts to breaking moral laws, and if God is the author of the moral laws that have been transgressed, then God (unlike most human judges) has the right simply to forgive the guilty sinner.

Christian teaching holds that all human beings are guilty before God (Rom 3:23; Jas 2:10). We are called to be obedient to God's command and are accountable to God for our failures to do so. Guilt is simply the moral state of someone who has done something morally wrong. Feeling guilty and being guilty are to a certain extent correlated in normal human beings but are not the same thing. It is possible to be guilty without feeling guilty, as we see with people who are unaware of their being responsible for an evil deed or unaware of its moral wrongness. It is also possible to feel guilty without being guilty, as we see with people who are overscrupulous, who blame themselves inordinately.

Christianity also teaches that God not only can but does forgive sins. "God in Christ has forgiven you" (Eph 4:32). "I will remember their sins and their lawless deeds no more" (Heb 10:17). Virtually all human beings are troubled by guilt. There are secular ways of dealing with guilt, but Christianity teaches that in forgiving our sins, God makes our guilt disappear, no longer exist. "As far as the east is from the west, so far he removes our transgressions from us" (Ps 103:12). Accordingly, divine forgiveness is not the same thing as *clemency* (where one is punished more mildly than one deserves) or even *pardon* (where one is not punished at all): in both cases, the person's guilt remains. In divine forgiveness, on the other hand, sinners are not just pardoned but cleansed (Col 2:13; 1 John 1:9; 2:12).

Let me try to be more precise as to the meaning of "divine forgiveness." Let us say that the statement, "God forgives act X committed by Smith" entails the following five statements:

1. Smith is morally responsible for the occurrence of X.
2. X is morally wrong.
3. Accordingly, Smith is guilty and deserves punishment.
4. Smith sincerely repents and asks God for forgiveness.
5. God cleanses Smith from the guilt of committing X and does not punish Smith for doing X.

So in forgiveness, God sets the sin and guilt aside and restores the old fellowship and friendship between God and the sinner. There is no more enmity between them.

But philosopher Anne C. Minas has recently argued that God's perfection is logically inconsistent with God's granting forgiveness. God's perfection, she points out, entails that God has "a perfect moral sense, a perfect moral will, perfect knowledge, and perfect benevolence."[4] Minas discusses various possible senses of the word *forgive* and argues in each case that a perfect being cannot offer that sort of forgiveness. And Minas is surely correct in several such cases:

1. She points out that forgiveness sometimes amounts *to revising or retracting an adverse moral judgment about an act.* She correctly argues that a reversal of moral judgment of that sort is never in order for a perfect being. None of the judgments of a perfect being are subject to reversal.
2. She points out that forgiveness at other times amounts to *deciding that a certain moral rule is defective in the special circumstances of a given case* (stealing is wrong, to be sure, but maybe not to feed one's starving children; killing a person is wrong, but maybe not in self-defense). And again, it is hard to see how a perfect being could forgive in this sense: no perfect being will entertain faulty moral rules.
3. She notes that forgiveness sometimes amounts to *a decision simply to overlook or condone someone's moral wrong,* especially if the offense was minor. But it is hard to see how a morally perfect being can condone anything that is genuinely morally wrong.
4. Minas also argues that forgiveness usually involves *giving up a feeling of resentment held against the evildoer* because of the harm

> his evil deeds have done; sometimes this involves an attitude of "forgive and forget" or "no longer taking the offense personally" on the part of the injured person. But, she argues, it is hard to see how a perfect being could be harmed or injured, let alone how a perfect being could forget anything.

So far Minas appears to be on firm ground. But she then argues that forgiveness might amount to something akin to *clemency exercised by a judge or pardon by a high official.* But, she asks, how could a perfect being simply remit justified punishment? Won't that make God something like a practical joker, she asks, assigning punishments God knows (with his perfect foreknowledge) he is going to remit? If the punishment was morally justified, and if a perfect being is perfectly just, she says, no perfect being can forgive in this last sense.[5]

Let me stray from Minas' argument for a moment and ask: is divine forgiveness *unjust*? In one sense, yes it is. Christian teaching holds that all human beings are guilty of sin and that the just penalty is eternal separation from God. Because of God's grace, however, we can be forgiven. What sinners must hope for, then, is something different from justice. If we were to be treated only according to the canons of justice, we would be condemned. Grace is, so to speak, different from and better than justice. But in another sense God's mercy is not unjust. Since God has certain rights over his creatures, rather than duties to them imposed from the outside, God may compassionately forgive sinners, if God wants to do so, without being accusable of injustice.

To return to Minas, she is correct that a perfect being will never forget a fact that it once knew. It is also true that a perfect being, understood in the broadly Thomistic way that her argument presupposes, cannot be harmed or injured. But the valid point that our sins do not damage or injure God does not entail that they do not do wrong to God. Indeed, that is just what they do. Just as you do me a moral wrong if you tell me a lie (without, let us suppose, the lie's harming me in any way), so we do God a wrong whenever we disobey any of God's commands, even though God, a perfect being, has not been damaged or lessened in any way.

I conclude that the type of divine forgiveness defined above in the fourth paragraph of this section (Section III) of the chapter is not refuted by Minas' argument.[6] Divine forgiveness need not involve changing a judgment about a moral issue, need not have anything to do with defective moral rules, need not entail condoning evil deeds, and need not have anything to do with feelings of resentment.

IV

Mark 2:1-12, the story of the paralytic who was let down through the roof and was forgiven and then healed by Jesus, is a fascinating text for many reasons: (1) form critics have discussed the history of this pericope in great detail;[7] (2) with parallels in both the other synoptic gospels (Luke 5:17-26; Matt 9:1-8), redaction critics have also mulled it over[8] (I will not discuss the possibly related but quite different story of the healing in John 5:1-18); (3) the story plays a crucial narrative role in Mark's Gospel, as the first serious indication in Jesus' ministry of controversy with the religious leaders; (4) the story is dramatic and arresting as a piece of literature; and finally (5) the story appears to have theological ramifications, or at least so Christians have usually thought.

I will not discuss the interesting question of whether this story really occurred as told by Mark or even largely as told by Mark. That is, I will not offer any arguments on the general historicity of the text or the more specific question of whether the words attributed to Jesus in this pericope constitute the *ipsissima verba* or even capture the *ipsissima vox* of Jesus. I want to ask rather what theological implications the story has as it stands in Mark (which of course Christians have always taken as part of sacred Scripture).[9]

The most obvious implication has to do with Jesus' offer of forgiveness to the paralytic. This offer has traditionally been taken as an implicit claim to divinity or at least to divine prerogative on Jesus' part.[10] As we have seen, we all have the right to forgive sins that have been committed against us, but only God has the right to forgive sins *simpliciter*. This point is made clear in the Hebrew Bible (Exod 34:6-7; 2 Sam 12:13; Pss 32:1-5; 51:3-4, 9-11; 103:3; 130:4; Isa 43:25; 44:22; Dan 9:9; Zech 3:4).

Accordingly, the church fathers saw Mark 2:1-12 as proof of Jesus' deity; they pointed to: (1) Jesus' clairvoyant ability to read the thoughts of the scribes (that only God can know the minds and intentions of human beings is attested to in 1 Sam. 16:7; 1 Kings 8:39; 1 Chron 28:9; Ps 139:1-2, 6, 23; Jer 11:20; 17:9-10); (2) his ability to heal the paralytic; and most importantly (3) his forgiveness of the paralytic's sins. On this third point, Irenaeus asks: "How can sins be rightly remitted unless the very One against whom one has sinned grants the pardon?"[11] Novatian declared: "If Christ forgives sins, Christ must be truly God because no one can forgive sins but God alone."[12]

There appears to be no evidence that the messiah, as most first-century Jews understood that figure, would have had the ability to forgive sins.[13]

This is also true of such figures as the Suffering Servant and the eschatological High Priest. Carefully surveying the evidence, Robert A. Guelich concludes: "No evidence has emerged to indicate that the Jews expected even the Messiah, regardless of how one defined this expectation, or any other eschatological figure, to have the right to forgive sins."[14]

The point then is that Jesus was accused of blasphemy because in this text and others he assumed the right to forgive sins that were committed against God rather than personally against him.

V

As noted, there seem to be two possible ways of interpreting Jesus' willingness to offer forgiveness. The traditional interpretation is that Jesus, the incarnation of God in our midst, had, as God, the full divine authority to forgive sins. Jesus himself was the agent who was dispensing forgiveness of sins.

But some argue for what I call a christologically minimalist interpretation of the text. There are several ways in which this is done. Some say that in Mark 2:1-12 and similar texts Jesus was not forgiving people (so to speak) on his own initiative, but was rather *speaking on behalf of God, relaying (as it were) God's own decision to forgive to the person.* On this reading, Jesus was not explicitly claiming to be divine but to have, as we might say, God's power of attorney. On this theory, Jesus certainly had special status but not necessarily divine status. He was more like God's spokesperson or representative.

Others argue that Jesus was simply *conveying the news that God had forgiven the guilty person.* Like Nathan in his confrontation with King David (2 Sam 12:1-15), Jesus was simply assuring the guilty party of God's forgiveness. John Hick (following E. P. Sanders) opts for this interpretation. In his *The Metaphor of God Incarnate*, Hick argues that Jesus was not usurping God's prerogative to forgive sins, but was only pronouncing forgiveness, "which is not the prerogative of God, but the priesthood."[15] On this interpretation, Jesus had little special status other than that of a passer-on of assurance or good news from God. He certainly did not have divine status.

But it seems to me that this second way of interpreting the text cannot be sustained. Let me now make a case for that claim.

It must initially be admitted that there are some texts that can possibly be read in a christologically minimalist way. One would be Luke 7:36-50, where the woman's tears can perhaps be read as contrition for her sins and even repentance; maybe, in this case, Jesus' saying "Your sins are forgiven" amounted to no more than Jesus' performing a priestly role, viz., declaring that a sinner who had truly repented would be forgiven by God. But there are problems with this reading: What qualified Jesus to function as a Levitical priest? And the central point on this issue is that in Mark 2:1-12 the paralytic is reported as having done none of the acts that were normally requisite for receiving divine forgiveness. There is no evidence of sorrow for his sins, confession of them, repentance from them, or of any sacrificial act at the temple or anywhere else.

It must also be admitted that Mark 2:1-12 may appear to be somewhat anomalous because there is only one other occasion in the synoptic gospels where Jesus explicitly pronounced forgiveness, and that is Luke 7:36-50, the text just mentioned. But there are other narratives in the Gospels where forgiveness of a sinner is implicit (Luke 19:1-10; John 8:1-11). Moreover, Jesus had frequent table fellowship with sinners (e.g., Mark 2:15-17; Luke 15:1-2). Finally, Jesus offered many figurative expressions of forgiveness (e.g., Matt 18:27; Luke 7:42; 15:10, 11-32; 18:14). These texts certainly seem to reinforce the idea that Jesus explicitly offered forgiveness.

One theologically minimalist reading of Mark 2:1-12 is provided by the Jesus Seminar. In *The Five Gospels*, it argues that either Jesus said the words attributed to him, assuming the power to forgive, or he did not. If he did (which the Seminar raises as a possibility but ultimately rejects), then "v. 10 may represent a bold new claim on Jesus' part that gives authority to forgive sins to all human beings." But if he did not say them, then "the early church was in the process of claiming for itself the right to forgive sins and so would have been inclined to claim that its authorization came directly from Jesus."[16] In either case—so the Seminar seems to be saying—Jesus was claiming no divine prerogative here. Now, as noted, in the present chapter I am not interested in debating whether the historical Jesus actually said the words attributed to him in our text. But I think it ought to be rather obvious that the "bold new claim" that the Seminar attributes to Jesus on their first reading of the text is implausible in the extreme.[17]

The crucial point is this: the violent reaction of the scribes in Mark 2:7 ("Why does this fellow speak in this way? It is blasphemy! Who can forgive sins but God alone?") seems to belie minimalist readings. It would hardly amount to blasphemy simply to assure repentant sinners that God had forgiven them. It seems that any priest, or any believer in the God of Israel, could do that. But suppose the point is pressed that since the paralytic did not repent or offer temple sacrifice for his sins, the charge against Jesus must have been something like: falsely assuring a man who did not deserve it of divine forgiveness. But would that charge have amounted to blasphemy? It seems that if the scribes thought that Jesus was guilty of that offense, what was called for was correction of his error, not execution (the sanction for blasphemy).

Moreover, in 2 Samuel Nathan explicitly names God and attributes the forgiveness of David to God. But Jesus did neither. He appeared to dispense forgiveness on his own initiative. He didn't just assure people that forgiveness had occurred; he seemed to act as the agent of forgiveness. He seemed to the scribes to be blaspheming because he was claiming to be able to do what only God can do. That this is a serious charge indeed (Lev 24:14-16 calls for the death penalty for blasphemy) is revealed by the fact that it was invoked at Jesus' trial (Mark 14:64).

One point that might be taken in favor of minimalist readings is the claim of Jeremias[18] and others that the words, "Your sins are forgiven" (*aphientai sou hai hamartiai*) (Mark 2:5), constitute a "theological passive," which would indicate that the act of forgiving was done by God, not Jesus. If this is true, then perhaps Jesus' declaration was similar to that of a Levitical priest, who makes atonement for the sins of a person, and then "he shall be forgiven" (Lev 4:26, cf., 4:31). The issue, then, is this: was Jesus in Mark 2:1-12 forgiving sins, or was he declaring on behalf of God that God had forgiven sins?

A point from John Chrysostom seems telling here: "Whenever Christ had to do any of these much greater things [like forgive sins or make laws], you will not characteristically find him praying or calling on his Father for assistance. All these things, as you discover in the text, he did on his own authority."[19] In short, Jesus seems to be doing more here than simply offering encouragement or assurance to people on the grounds that God has forgiven them or even declaring that God had forgiven them. He certainly seems to be doing something, acting as an agent.

That Jesus had authority to forgive sins is consistent with another New Testament notion: that Jesus, the Son of Man, will be the eschatological judge (Matt 25:31-46; Mark 8:38; John 5:22). As Gary Shogren argues,[20] this means that even in advance of the final judgment, Jesus is able to pronounce acquittal and judgment (Matt 11:20-24; Luke 10:13-15).

Whether or not Mark 2:5 is a theological passive (and the active voice in 2:7 and 2:10 casts doubt on the idea that Jesus was not acting on his own initiative), it surely seemed to the scribes in the story that Jesus was doing more than simply announcing what God had already done. As Guelich insists: "Whereas the scribes might have questioned Jesus' right in 2:5b to pronounce forgiveness in God's name apart from the cult and without demanding repentance, or even to pronounce God's forgiveness of sins now rather than in the eschaton, their implicit charge does not arise from the divine passive in 2:5b. Rather it focuses on the issue expressed in 2:10, Jesus' usurping God's authority to forgive sins. The answer to the scribes' question, 'Who except God . . . ?' is clearly, 'the Son of Man' (2:10)."[21]

VI

It seems then that the first and more traditional reading of Mark 2:1-12 is the most sensible. Indeed, the others are hard to reconcile with the climactic statement of our text, "The Son of Man has authority on earth to forgive sins" (Mark 2:10). Of course Jesus was not going about declaring, "I am God." But he does seem to be claiming to be able to do something that only God has the right to do. Accordingly, the church fathers were right in holding that our text has christological ramifications.

There is of course nothing in this text that expresses the language of later creedal orthodoxy. There is nothing here about persons or natures or essences or hypostatic unions. Not everything that Christians want to say about Jesus is implicit in this text. Still, it is clear that Mark 2:1-12 is and ought to be one of the texts that Christians take into consideration in doing Christology. In this text Jesus seems to be giving himself such authority as to be setting himself on a par with God. His willingness to offer forgiveness was surely one of the things about Jesus that made such an impression on early believers that they reached the conclusion that he was divine.[22]

5

Have the Infidels Refuted the Resurrection?

I

This chapter is a critical review of the recent book *The Empty Tomb: Jesus Beyond the Grave* (Amherst, N.Y.: Prometheus: 2005), edited by Jeffery Lowder and Robert Price.[1] The word *Infidels* in the title of this chapter reflects the fact that the contributors to this book call themselves the "Internet Infidels." They operate a web site, the Secular Web (www.infidels.org), that serves as home base for their program. *The Empty Tomb* is an important book, written by intelligent and informed scholars, that attacks the Christian claim that God raised Jesus from the dead.[2]

After some introductory observations, I respond to the essays of each of the book's ten contributors and close with a few overall comments. My remarks on the essays vary in length, and in the interest of saving space, I do not restate in detail the arguments that I intend to criticize. *The Empty Tomb* (TET)[3] constitutes a serious assault on one of the most important doctrines of the Christian faith. As a believing Christian, I have occasionally written in defense of the resurrection,[4] so it will surprise no one that I will be critical of the book.

On the other hand, I am happy to note the emergence of a somewhat-new philosophical genre. Pioneered by Prometheus Press, the Secular Web, and the journal *Philo*, it consists of contemporary secular philosophers and other scholars answering the arguments of those increasingly pesky and aggressive philosophers who are believers. I consider this a positive development, especially when compared with the situation that existed when I was a

An earlier version of this review appeared in Philosophia Christi *8, no. 1 (2006).*

graduate student in the late 1960s and early 1970s. Then, as now, most philosophers were atheists. But in those days, we students were scarcely allowed even to mention words like "God" or "theology," and claims like, "God raised Jesus from the dead" were dismissed with disdain, scorn, and knowing looks. Now—as this book shows—our arguments are being taken seriously. And that, I suggest, is a good thing.

I do not hold that nonbelief in the resurrection of Jesus must be irrational. Although I strongly disagree with the overall thesis and many of the arguments given in TET, I can usually appreciate where the authors are coming from, given the assumptions that they make. Indeed, if I were a naturalist,[5] I, too, would reject the resurrection and would probably be justified in doing so. (Whether naturalism is defensible is a question that I will not address here.) What I do hold is that belief in the resurrection of Jesus is completely rational from a Christian supernaturalist perspective.[6]

II

Greg Cavin is associate professor of philosophy and religious studies at Cypress College in California. His contribution to TET is called, "Is There Sufficient Historical Evidence to Establish the Resurrection of Jesus" (TET, 9–41). He and I discussed the central thesis of his paper years ago in my office. He correctly points out that Christians typically believe not just that God raised Jesus from the dead, but also that the risen Jesus had a resurrection body with new and unusual properties. Cavin describes those properties as including the ability to move instantaneously from place to place and inability to become ill, be injured, or die. So Cavin argues that a Christian logically cannot prove that Jesus was raised without also having to prove that the risen Jesus had these properties (TET, 33). And the chances of doing that, he says, are remote.

But it seems to me a perfectly sensible position to argue for Cavin's proposition—(1) Jesus died and afterward he became alive once again, (or, as I would prefer, "God raised Jesus from the dead")—and also believe some version of Cavin's propositions (8)–(12) (these are various claims to the effect that the risen Jesus had these new and unusual properties[7]), but *not* attempt to argue for (8)–(12). Indeed, one might happily admit that one is unable to prove (8)–(12). Similarly, a historian may feel able to prove that Caesar crossed the Rubicon and also believe (maybe even equally firmly) that Caesar got his shoulders wet crossing the Rubicon, but not be able to prove this latter point.[8] Likewise, a believer in the resurrection may hold that Cavin's (1) is provable or can be shown to be a rational belief, but hold that the rest of what Christians believe about the resurrection of Jesus must be taken on faith. That is, it is not necessary to establish (8)–(12) in order to establish (1).[9]

It is quite true, as Cavin says, that the Christian doctrine of the resurrection includes propositions like (8)–(12). So if we were to try to prove a statement like, "Jesus died and afterward was restored into a living supernatural body," we would have to try to prove items like (8) – (12). But it seems to me that most Christian apologists for the resurrection, like me, are only trying to establish the rational credibility of belief in (1), which of course describes a miracle that is big enough in itself.

In his internet response to my initial review, Cavin claims that I misinterpreted him; he was not insisting that proof of (1) requires proving (8)–(12) but rather that proof of (2) does.[10] And I entirely agree with that point. But then where did I get the idea that in his essay Cavin was saying that any Christian who wants to prove (1) will have to shoulder the burden of trying to prove (8)–(12)? Well, in his opening paragraph, Cavin in effect claims that you cannot establish "the historicity of the resurrection" apart from establishing that the resurrected Jesus had a "supernatural body," which Cavin interprets as including (8)–(12). Now if by the phrase, "the historicity of the resurrection," Cavin means the historicity of the entire Christian doctrine of the resurrection, he would certainly be correct. But I believe that most contemporary apologists try to argue for the historicity of the resurrection in terms of propositions like (1), which require no such thing.

Moreover, a bit later in his original essay (TET, p. 22), Cavin argues as follows: "Correlatively, it is clear that those who claim that the New Testament Easter traditions are sufficient to establish the resurrection hypothesis are claiming not merely that there is sufficient evidence to establish (1) but, quite significantly, that this evidence is sufficient to establish the much stronger hypothesis (2). . . ." Well, the truth of this claim depends on what is meant by "the resurrection hypothesis." If it means the entire Christian doctrine of the resurrection, Cavin is right. But if it means something like, "God raised Jesus from the dead," it is not true. I think the New Testament Easter traditions are sufficient to establish that claim.

Cavin further supports his point by claiming that the Christian position on the resurrection *entails* (8)–(12). Not so: it certainly *includes* something like (8)–(12); indeed, it is true that (8)–(12) capture fairly well what most Christians mean by, "God raised Jesus from the dead." Still, I cannot see how anybody would claim that this statement (or Cavin's [1]) logically entails (8)–(12). If A implies B, it is not logically possible for A to be true and B false. Although God in fact did not do so, it certainly seems logically possible for God to have raised Jesus from the dead without granting him any of the new and unusual properties that Cavin discusses.

III

Michael Martin (professor emeritus of philosophy at Boston University) and I have already argued, at some length, about the issues that come up in his essay, "The Resurrection as Initially Improbable." (TET, 43–54)[11] So on this occasion, I will simply mention five points where I disagree most crucially with the arguments that he raises in this essay in TET.

(1) Again, my notion is that belief that God raised Jesus from the dead is rational from the perspective of Christian supernaturalism. I agree with Martin that even from that perspective, miracles will be highly unusual. Neither in Scripture nor in Christian experience does God constantly perform miracles. Yet suppose we take someone who believes what Christians believe about God and God's actions in history, but for some reason does not believe that God raised Jesus from the dead. That is, this person believes things like:

- God exists and has the ability, and occasionally the intention, to interrupt the natural order and bring about events that would not otherwise have occurred.
- God wants to redeem human beings and that includes redemption from death.
- Life after death is promised in the Old Testament (e.g., Dan 12:1-3).[12]
- Jesus predicted his own death and resurrection (Mark 8:31; 9:9-10, 31; 10:33-34).[13]

I hold that it could well be rational for such a person to come to believe that God raised Jesus from the dead. That is, given the points just noted, the initial probability of that proposition for a Christian supernaturalist is nowhere near as low as Martin alleges.

(2) I do not accept Martin's epistemological claim that the probability of a given hypothesis H must be greater than .5 for belief in H to be rational. Normally, this is indeed the case. But suppose we are in a situation where (a) there are four mutually exclusive alternatives to belief in H (call them A, B, C, and D); (b) each of A, B, C, and D has a probability of .15 (and thus the probability of the falsity of H is .6, and the probability of the truth of H is .4); (c) it is necessary to choose among H, A,

B, and C; and (d) H, A, B, C, and D exhaust all the possibilities. In such a case, believing H is the most rational alternative.

(3) Martin's argument that God would never want to perform a miracle is feeble. Miracles might indeed confuse or mislead certain people, but they surely can be powerful ways of getting points across to others. But then—so Martin asks—why can't an omnipotent being get his point across "without misleading anyone"? But the answer is that given human freedom and our tendency toward self-centeredness, there may be no way for even an omnipotent being to accomplish that. There is probably no method of divine revelation that cannot be misconstrued or garbled by morally free human beings.

And I deny that miracles—as long as they are rare, as Christians insist that they are—would impede "scientific understanding of the world" (TET, 46). It is true that a miraculous event cannot be explained scientifically, but the vast majority of events—all the nonmiraculous ones—still can. Notice that the work of science is not impeded by the fact, admitted by all, that there are very many phenomena that science cannot now explain (even if perhaps some day it will be able to do so). There are even contemporary secular philosophers who argue that explaining things like consciousness and qualia is permanently beyond the pale of science. Mental properties, they say, resist scientific explanation and form a limit to scientific understanding.[14] In his internet response, Martin argues that "a necessary condition of finding a scientific explanation is to assume there is one to be found and to act accordingly." Not so. You can find a scientific explanation for a phenomenon by looking hard for one, even if you are not sure there is one. Theistic scientists have made many such discoveries despite their being theoretically open to the possibility of miracles.

(4) Is it a priori highly unlikely, given God's freedom of choice about when and where to place it, that the incarnation would occur at the particular time and place that Christians say it did? Martin argues that it is. However, the trouble with that claim is that it renders extremely unlikely virtually any hypothesis about the time and place of any past event. Suppose Jimmy Carter was trying to establish that exactly three years ago today at 3:17 P.M. in his back yard in Plains, Georgia, he for the first time drank a glass of tomato juice. Think how initially improbable that putative event would be in relation to all the other places and times that it could have occurred. Imagine that for some reason it was important for Jimmy to prove in a court of law that the event happened when and where it did. And imagine further a lawyer on the other side

giving Martin-like arguments to the jury: "Think of all the other times and places that the event of Jimmy Carter's first drinking tomato juice could have occurred," the lawyer might say, "so it is highly improbable that it occurred when and where Jimmy Carter alleges." Such an argument would convince no one. Moreover, Martin's argument is irrelevant to the debate about the resurrection of Jesus because he and the apologists have already agreed on the question of where and when Jesus' putative resurrection occurred. It occurred in or around Jerusalem some time in the very late twenties or very early thirties of the first century. This argument from Martin goes nowhere.

(5) I had earlier objected to Martin's assumption that the rarity of miracles entails that such events have a low probability.[15] Suppose, I said, that I enter a used-car lot that has a thousand cars for sale.[16] What is the probability that I will buy the one and only red car in the lot? I argued that the answer to that question will not depend merely on considerations of rarity (which might make one erroneously believe that the probability is .001) but also on consideration of preference. Maybe I have always wanted to own a red car. Martin objects that that analogy fails because we do not know God's preferences. But contrary to Martin, Christians believe that we do "know God's preferences" (or at least many of them), because God has revealed them to us. Among other things, we believe we know that God wants to redeem human beings, that redemption from death is a crucial aspect of redemption, and that Jesus promised that he would be raised from the dead. Accordingly, my used-car-lot illustration still stands. It is entirely possible that God decided to use the vehicle of resurrection in order to vindicate and exalt Jesus in part precisely because of the rarity of resurrections.

Martin's other essay in TET, "Swinburne on the Resurrection" (TET, 453–68), contains very many arguments, often only suggested rather than fully developed. Many of them relate specifically to other points in Swinburne's thought beside resurrection, for example, the nature of God, the problem of evil, and theories of atonement. There are points where I, too, depart from Richard Swinburne's approach. For example, I think he relies too heavily on the notion of simplicity; I am dubious of his emphasis on quantum events as allowing for human free will; and I affirm that God foreknows the results of future free decisions.

I will simply list two crucial points where I disagree with Martin.[17] (1) I do not accept that the concept of God is incoherent. I have read Martin's arguments to this effect in his other writings,[18] and, frankly, I think all of them can be answered, some fairly easily. But since TET is not about the concept of God, apart from one illustrative point, I will explore this issue no further. Take Martin's claim that if God is disembodied, God cannot be all-knowing. A disembodied God cannot, for example, know how to swim (Martin says). But in reply, it need only be said that an all-powerful God can surely decide to take on human form, as Christianity insists that God did do, and learn how to swim. Moreover, given divine foreknowledge, God had this knowledge from eternity, and not just after he became incarnate. And why must everything that God knows be known by acquaintance (so that God is all-knowing, as Martin claims, only if God has experienced the pleasure that sadists get from torturing children)? If God is omniscient, God knows everything that the sadist knows, but obviously not in the same way that the sadist knows it.

(2) As other contributors to TET admit, it is not true that "given Roman crucifixion customs, the prior probability that Jesus was buried is low" (TET, 464). In point of fact, the Romans almost always allowed for local burial customs, and this included Jewish customs, which emphasized quick burial of corpses. The one big exception was during time of war: we know that both during the Jewish war that culminated in A.D. 70 and during the Bar Kochba revolt some sixty-five years later, the Romans left crucified corpses on their crosses for days and weeks. In times of peace (and there was no war in Palestine during the time when Jesus would have been crucified[19]), the Romans allowed executed criminals to be buried. This does not prove that Jesus was buried, of course, but it does render it probable.[20]

IV

I once told Ted Drange (professor emeritus of philosophy at the University of West Virginia) that he appears to know the Bible as well or better than any of the other contemporary philosophers of religion who argue against Christianity. However, I believe the argument of his "Why Resurrect Jesus?" (TET, 55–67) is wrecked by mistakes in theology. For example, he curiously claims that the Christian gospel merely "maintains . . . that Christ's atonement was successful" (TET, 57). I would have thought that it maintains far more than that. And although this next point can be disputed, I disagree strongly with Drange's claim that resurrection has nothing to do with atonement (TET, 57, 58). My own view is that what redeemed humanity was the entirety of the incarnation event—the life, teachings, death, and resurrection of the Son of God.

But most importantly, I have no idea why Drange chose to take on Charles Hodge. Indeed, most of his essay is a critique of one argument from this nineteenth-century American theologian. Hodge was a fine theologian in his day, and I suppose there are points that Christians can still learn from him. But few Christians today read or are influenced by Hodge. The argument from Hodge that Drange attacks essentially (and rather carelessly) says: if God raised Jesus from the dead, it logically follows that the Christian gospel is true, that Christ is the Son of God, and that Christ is equal with the Father, the savior of human beings, the Messiah, etc. This argument is, as Drange points out, a non sequitur. I am unable to defend it. There is indeed a connection between Jesus' resurrection and these other points but not a connection of logical entailment. It is possible for God to raise from the dead (via resurrection, not just resuscitation) people who are not the Son of God. Indeed, I and other Christians believe that God will one day do that very thing.

On the other hand, it is Ted Drange, and not any Christian theologian of whom I have ever heard, who apparently thinks that Christian atonement must require that Jesus die and then stay dead forever. Does Drange think that *he* gets to decide this question? The orthodox Christian position is rather that in order to accomplish our redemption, Jesus had to die (1 Cor 15:3). Well, he did die. It was a genuine death; there was a time when Jesus did not exist. That God subsequently raised him from the dead does not affect the fact that he truly died. However, in answer to a question from Drange, I do not hold that there was any logical or a priori necessity that Jesus die in order to accomplish our redemption. That was simply the method that God, in his sovereign will, chose. Drange asks: did God have to raise Jesus in order to accomplish human redemption and communicate that fact to Christians? No (so I would reply): that is simply the method that God did, in fact, choose.

Drange also asks whether survival of death, in Christian terms, must involve bodily resurrection. Again I would say no: this is simply the method that God chose for placing human persons in the afterlife. Now, on all these points that I am attributing to God's sovereign choice, I want to note that they were not arbitrary choices, as if God, say, flipped a coin in order to decide between bodily resurrection and immortality of the soul. They were appropriate choices, given human nature, God's nature, and God's past actions, as revealed in the Hebrew Bible.

But Drange's deepest question is why God (according to Christians) raised Jesus from the dead in the first place? Was such an event salvifically necessary? It was indeed necessary, so Christians hold. Here are two reasons. First, the resurrection was a way of distinguishing Jesus from all the other gurus, spiritual teachers, prophets, and religious founders in the world's history. Jesus is the true way to God. Paul (through Luke) makes this point clear in his speech in Athens: "And of this [God] has given assurance to all by raising him from the dead" (Acts 17:31). Second, resurrection was God's way of defeating the power of death, from which humans need redemption. Paul makes this clear in I Corinthians 15, where he argues that "if Christ has not been raised, then our proclamation has been in vain and your faith has been in vain" (15:14). By one man (Adam) death entered he world—so Paul goes on—and by another man (Christ) resurrection from the dead and thus life beyond death for human beings are established (15:20-22). In the resurrection of Christ, death, our "last enemy," is defeated (15:50-57).

V

As well as coediting TET, Robert M. Price (professor of scriptural studies at the Johnnie Colemon Theological Seminary) has contributed three essays, starting with the book's Introduction (TET, 9–18). And in that essay, in my opinion, the desire to be clever and even sarcastic in attacking the resurrection causes him to lose his way. Maybe Lazarus is still alive today! Belief that Jesus is alive and has a personal relationship with every Christian is like a child's belief in Santa Claus! Even more seriously, Price directs derisive questions at those who believe that Jesus is still alive ("Has Jesus grown older and wiser all these years? Is he immune from senility? Does he ever forget a face?"), which are nothing but gross caricatures of Christian belief.

Price also argues that Christian apologists unknowingly evacuate "the phenomenon of all its miraculous character" (TET, 13) when they try to give arguments in favor of the resurrection. He appears to hold that if it's a miracle, you can't argue for it. But that is nonsense. Suppose that last night for seven minutes Pitzer Hall levitated two feet off the ground. It seems perfectly possible for someone to argue that God raised the building (i.e., that it was a miracle) without the event ceasing to be a miracle. (Whether this person's argument could possibly be successful is another matter.) To explain the event (tell, in scientific terms, how it happened) would be to take away the miraculous character of the event. However, just saying (or even establishing, if that could be done) that God caused the event does not necessarily do that.

Finally (so far as the Introduction to the book is concerned), I think Price tips his hand when he suggests that for "serious biblical critics" (and it is clear that believers in the resurrection do not count as members of that august group[21]), "the real issue of debate ought to be whether there was a historical Jesus at the core of all the mythology" (TET, 15). Of course, if there was no historical Jesus, then there was no resurrection of Jesus. Q.E.D.

Fortunately, in Price's second essay, "Apocryphal Apparitions: 1 Corinthians 15:3-11 as a Post-Pauline Interpolation" (TET, 69–104), he presents a serious piece of scholarship rather than an exercise in mockery. But, unfortunately for him, his attempt to argue that the list of resurrection appearances, etc. in 1 Corinthians 15:3-11 is a post-Pauline addition to the text is hardly convincing. I cannot contest every point with which I disagree; I will concentrate instead on six points that seem to me important.

(1) In one sense, I am somewhat indifferent to Price's conclusion. This is because I believe that Christian theology ought to be done on the basis of those texts that the Christian church takes to be canonical, including verses 3-11 of 1 Corinthians 15. Theology ought not be done on the basis of hypothesized literary ancestors of canonical texts (as some Q scholars try to do) or on the basis of their hypothesized original versions (as, I assume, Price wants to do[22]). On the other hand, I disagree strongly with Price's thesis (i.e., I consider 1 Corinthians 15:3-11 to be authentic), so I will now respond to the case he makes.

(2) Price honestly admits that there is no textual evidence that supports his claim, that is, all the manuscripts of 1 Corinthians that we have contain the passage in question (TET, 69–70). I will only observe that if there were any text-critical evidence at all in favor of Price's thesis, even a hint in a minor and late manuscript, he would make much of it. Indeed, he would no longer have to argue, along with William O. Walker (TET, 71, 92), that powerful and sinister forces in the Great Church around the year 300 made sure to suppress earlier texts of 1 Corinthians that did not include 15:3-11.[23]

(3) Contra Price, there are, in fact, quotations and clear allusions to 1 Corinthians 15:3-11 in the Apostolic Fathers, that is, well before the third century. Ignatius, who died c110–112 unmistakably alludes to 1 Corinthians 15:8-9 in chapter 9 of his "Epistle of Ignatius to the Romans." *The Shepherd of Hermas*, usually dated between 140 and 155, clearly alludes (in a different context) to 1 Corinthians 15:6. And Irenaeus, who flourished from about 180 to 199, quotes 1 Corinthians 15:8 in 8:2 of his "Against Heresies."

Price dismisses this evidence on the grounds that (a) these citations are indecisive, since "writers like Tertullian and Irenaeus are too late to make any difference" [concerning Tertullian, I agree], and (b) "the date and genuineness of 1 Clement and the Ignatian corpus are open questions" (TET, 93) [and I have not cited 1 Clement]. But this is surely special pleading. Price himself is the one who set the "beginning of the third century" cut-off date (we have, he says, no manuscripts from before that date and that is why we have no evidence of texts of 1 Corinthians 15 sans verses 3-11). Moreover, Ignatius was definitely second century and his "Epistle to the Romans" is widely accepted as authentic.[24] This looks like a case of simply brushing aside inconvenient evidence.

(4) I have never been impressed with the idea that there is a contradiction, or even much of a tension, between Galatians 1:11-12 and 1 Corinthians 15:1.[25] Galatians 1:12 does not say or imply that Paul learned the entirety of his understanding of Christianity, without remainder, by private revelation.[26] On the contrary, he must have learned at least some things from the people who cared for and baptized him in Damascus immediately after his conversion. Indeed, in Acts 9:17 Ananias of Damascus specifically gives Paul some words of instruction. Are we to imagine that the Damascus Christians who baptized Paul had nothing to say to him prior to the ceremony or that Paul refused to listen to them when they tried to speak to him about the movement that he was joining?[27]

Surely the fact of Jesus' resurrection and the list of people to whom the risen Jesus appeared were items that Paul leaned from others. Paul's "gospel," which he insisted he learned "by revelation" and not from those who were apostles before him, would, I believe, have consisted in part of such items as: (a) Christ died for our sins (1 Cor 15:3) and was raised by God, (b) justification before God is by faith in Christ and not by "works of the law" (Gal 2:15), and (c) the meaning of Jesus' resurrection (as expounded by Paul in 1 Cor 15:12-58).

Some of these items were of course accepted by non-Pauline Christians from the earliest period, which is not surprising; James, Cephas, and John would hardly have offered Paul the "right hand of fellowship" (Gal 2:9) had his views been radically at odds with theirs. The crucial bit of "Paul's gospel," I believe, was the thesis that was apparently unique to him at the outset and that got him in such trouble with his enemies in the Christian movement, viz., the doctrine of justification by faith and not works (and accordingly no circumcision for Gentile converts).[28]

(5) Unlike Price, I do not think 1 Corinthians 15 makes much sense without verses 3-11. (If Price is correct, what exactly would Paul be making known to the Corinthians?) Moreover, unlike Price, I think 1 Corinthians 15 makes perfect sense with verses 3-11 included. He claims that there is "an apparent lack of congruity between the formula [i.e., 3-11] and the argument of the rest of the chapter" (TET, 91). Not so, I say.[29] The formula establishes, in Paul's view, the *fact* of the resurrection

of Jesus, and the rest of the chapter explains, in Paul's view, the *implications* or *meaning* of the resurrection of Jesus, especially in terms of the general resurrection. Moreover, Paul shows both here (1 Cor 15:20, 23) and elsewhere (e.g., Rom 6:5; 8:11; Phil 3:10-11, 20-21; 1 Thess 4:14) that he closely connected the two. Jesus' resurrection was the first fruits or promise or guarantee of our resurrection.

(6) Price sympathetically quotes Bart D. Ehrman (in Price's footnote 7, TET, 97), who says: "theologically motivated changes of the text are to be anticipated particularly during the early centuries of transmission, when both the texts and the theology of early Christianity were in a state of flux, prior to the development of a recognized creed." If we were talking about the church's theology of the incarnation or the Trinity, this claim might have some plausibility. But when we are talking about the assertion that God raised Jesus from the dead, Ehrman's argument is hardly convincing. I would have thought that virtually everyone recognizes that this claim was bedrock in the Christian movement from the very beginning. At that point, there *was* a recognized creed.

Accordingly, I think the case that Price makes for the nonauthenticity of 1 Corinthians 15:3-11 is flawed and unconvincing.

I was sorry to note that in his third essay in TET, Robert Price returns to polemics and sarcasm. It is titled, "By This Time He Stinketh: The Attempts of William Lane Craig to Exhume Jesus" (TET, 411–31) Let me say first that to the best of my knowledge I have never met Robert Price, and I know virtually nothing of his history. But there is a degree of hostility and animus here against both William Craig[30] and apparently all evangelicals, that is surprising and disappointing. For example, Craig's strategy is compared to that of the O.J. Simpson defense team (TET, 416). He accuses Craig of "scurrilous mudslinging" like "Creationist stump speaker Duane Gish" who charges that evolutionists "must want society to become a den of murderers and pornographers" (TET, 418). Craig, Price says, uses "every rhetorical trick in the book, since all means are justified by the end of making new converts" (TET, 418)[31] Craig's arguments, Price says, "smack of priestcraft and subterfuge" (TET, 426). One of Craig's arguments is called "downright comical" (TET, 428). And there are, in Price's chapter, several quite gratuitous references to the late Bill Bright, the founder of Campus Crusade for Christ (TET, 415, 417, 419, 420).

Price seems upset that Craig has made up his mind that God raised Jesus from the dead. But hasn't Price made up his mind that God did not raise Jesus from the dead (or maybe even that there is no God and there was no Jesus, so, obviously, God did not raise Jesus from the dead)? Is the problem that Price thinks Craig is close-minded on this point? Then it would become an interesting question whether Craig is more close-minded or personally invested in his view than Price is for his. So far as I can see, both are doing what Price calls "engaged scholarship." In any case, the tone of Price's third essay is so insulting and off-putting that I have no desire to comment on it further.

VI

I will discuss Evan Fales' second essay, "Reformed Epistemology and Biblical Hermeneutics" (TET, 469–89), before considering his first, and more radical, one. (Fales is associate professor of philosophy at the University of Iowa.) Although there are many other points that I disagree with in his second essay, let me concentrate on just two.

Along with Plantinga and much of the Christian tradition, I hold that Scripture is perspicuous. Like any complex and ancient text, written in languages and settings that are foreign to us, the Bible can be extremely difficult to understand. The notion that Scripture is clear does not dispute that fact. Scripture is perspicuous in that, as I myself have seen on many occasions, even children and the uneducated can understand it and be influenced by it. It is intelligible to careful and earnest readers.

Of course I do not hold that everything in the Bible can be easily understood, or understood at all. There are doubtless passages that we will never understand, not in this life anyway. But Christians believe that all that human beings need to know for their salvation is clear in Scripture to educated and uneducated alike. The only requirement is that it be read Christianly, that is, according to what the church fathers called the rule of faith.[32] Now, Fales hints in this chapter (TET, 482, 484) and specifically argues in his other chapter that the Bible was not meant to record history; the apparently historical parts are pure myth from beginning to end. If he is correct, it follows that Scripture is radically unclear.[33] Apparently, virtually nobody has ever understood the Bible until Evan Fales.

Fales lists several assured results of historical biblical criticism (HBC). Some of them are beyond reproach, but others are debatable. (I think he must mean HBC as practiced by nonevangelical scholars or HBC as practiced by scholars who are not orthodox Christians.) There surely is a seven-headed dragon in Sumerian mythology, but I do not accept that the seven-headed dragon mentioned in Revelation "is derived from it" (TET, 476). I do not agree that there is a consensus that the Gospels were all composed after A.D. 70. I believe that Mark is pre-70, and so do many other scholars. Finally, I agree that every purported biblical prophecy of some future event has been disputed by scholars, but I do not accept the claim that "there appears to be not a single biblical prophecy that meets minimal conditions for being genuinely prophetic, and whose fulfillment can be independently confirmed" (TET, 476). In order to falsify this claim, I will submit just one such prophecy. In Matthew 24:5, Jesus says: "Many will come in my name, saying, 'I am the Messiah!' and they will lead many astray." That, surely, is a true statement.

Fales objects to this argument on three grounds. First, how do we know that Jesus actually made this prediction (as opposed to it being a later interpolation)? And it is true that I cannot prove that Jesus himself made this prediction, but it appears that Fales could deploy this objection against *any* putative counterexample to his very strong claim, thus putting his claim in danger of being unfalsifiable. My question would be: Is there any good reason, apart from the obvious fact that the alleged prophecy came true, to hold that Jesus did not make it? Second, Fales says that even if Jesus did utter these words, the prophecy is rather unsurprising. I agree that "there will be wars and rumors of wars" (the part of the passage that Fales quotes) is rather obvious, but the assertion that there will be people who will claim to be the messiah and "will lead many astray" is only unsurprising in the light of subsequent history. Third, Fales asks what subsequent false messiahs are attested to in ancient extra-Christian sources? Well, there were several in the centuries after Jesus, among them Bar Kokhba, Abu Isa al-Isfahani, Severus, and an anonymous Jew from third century Crete.

Fales' other essay in TET is called, "Taming the Tehom: The Sign of Jonah in Matthew" (TET, 307–48). In it, he uses an analysis of Matthew 12:39-40 to introduce a thesis that he has been working on for years (and about which he and I once corresponded by e-mail). The thesis asserts that the apparently historical parts of the Bible should be understood not as history but as myth, that the biblical writers understood and accepted that mythology was what they were doing, and that biblical mythology was always written in support of political or social goals.

So far as the "sign of Jonah" text is concerned, Fales' argument is based on the apparent inconsistency between Jesus' prediction in that passage that he would be in the heart of the earth for "three days and three nights" (which was obviously a reference to his upcoming death) and the fact that Jesus was in the tomb at most for part of Friday, all of Saturday, and part of Sunday, which hardly amounts to three days. Fales is right that there is a difficulty here, and that none of the available solutions is without problems. But I have always been impressed with the fact that Matthew seems to use the phrase "after three days" (27:63) synonymously with the phrase "on the third day" (16:21; 17:23; 20:19). So perhaps the phrase "after three days and three nights" was meant, despite the implication of seventy-two hours, not to be taken literally, but instead to be taken as meaning the same thing as the other two phrases. Perhaps "three days and three nights" was a Hebrew figure of speech. Note Esther 4:16 and 5:1, where Esther and the Jews of Susa apparently fasted for seventy-two hours, but then it says she appeared before the king "on the third day."[34] As I said, this solution is not entirely satisfactory, but adopting it (so I think) is far better than going where Fales wants us to go. Jesus certainly was in the tomb for parts of three different days.

Fales defines the term *myth* as "a way of conceptualizing and articulating a theoretical understanding of (some features of) human existence in a fictionalized narrative form" (TET, 313). The purpose of biblical mythology (and remember, this includes what Fales calls the Bible's "seemingly historical passages") is to "establish and charter, codify, and/or justify the social and institutional structures that govern the life of the community" (TET, 313). The biblical writers knew that they were writing myth in the guise of history. Religion, Fales says, is actually politics or at least political theorizing.

In any case, as Fales must surely recognize, an enormous burden is placed on the shoulders of anybody who wants to interpret a text in a way that cuts against the grain of that text's plain sense and that overturns the way it has always been interpreted. There are hundreds of passages in the Bible that seem to report what the writer took to be historical facts and wants readers to believe really occurred. When Fales claims that those writers were not trying to do that—that they were trying to write mythology for political and social purposes—he should not be surprised that some of us express both amazement at his courage and puzzlement that he could become convinced of such a thesis. Even the God of Israel for Fales becomes not an actual being, not the creator of the heavens and the earth and the judge of human beings and nations, but some sort of utopian or ideal social-political state of affairs (TET, 316–17). This notion is the lens through which he interprets much of the Bible, including the resurrection texts in the New Testament.

Finally, the rock on which Fales' theory flounders, in my opinion, is the practice of private prayer.[35] Were the ancient Israelites and New Testament Christians so dense as not to see that prayers that included requests for divine forgiveness, intercession for others, and petitions for oneself addressed merely to an ideal socio-political state of affairs were nonsensical? No political situation, however ideal, could be in a position to hear, let alone answer, their requests. An ideal is not a person. Ergo, the ancient Israelites and early Christians, who regularly engaged in such practices of prayer, thought of God as a personal agent, not an ideal socio-political state of affairs. Even if Fales were correct in his Durkheimian conception of God, it would not do to attribute such a conception to the writers of the Bible.

VII

J. Duncan M. Derrett is professor emeritus of oriental laws at London University. I do not have much to say about his essay in TET, which is called, "Financial Aspects of the Resurrection" (TET, 393–409). At many points I am not sure whether I agree with Derrett or not because it is unclear precisely what he is proposing. But I am sure I disagree with him in the following:

1. The mistake of Ananais and Sapphira was not, as Derrett says (TET, 396), to keep back part of the donation that they were making to the community, but to lie about it (Acts 5:3-4).
2. I do not accept Derrett's claim that "people will accept what they want to believe" (TET, 398). I want to believe that terrorism in the world will soon cease, but I do not believe it will. Of course people sometimes think wishfully; probably I do at times. But Derrett's blanket claim is far too strong.
3. This is the first essay from Derrett that I have read, and I am astounded that he apparently wants to revive the swoon theory, that is, the idea that Jesus did not really die on the cross (he only "swooned") but then recovered (TET, 394, 399). I would have thought that this idea has been thoroughly discredited since David Strauss. Even highly skeptical biblical critics do not take it seriously.

But I have no big problem with the project of examining the behavior of the disciples after the Crucifixion in terms of interest and benefit. Indeed, I agree that they were very much looking out for their own interests. The only difference is that, unlike Derrett, I am not thinking of financial considerations. After all, what greater benefit can people ever receive than a message about a person who can explain the meaning of their lives, set them free of what oppresses them, and make possible divine forgiveness? The earliest Christians thought they had found all of that in Jesus.

VIII

Peter Kirby is identified in TET as the founder of the web site Early-ChristianWritings.com. His essay is one of several arguments in TET against the empty tomb. It is titled, "The Case Against the Empty Tomb" (TET, 233–60). The controversy over this point illustrates what I meant when I said that it can be rational either to believe that God raised Jesus from the dead or to deny that claim. I suspect that a coherent case can be made against the empty tomb. Obviously, I find the case in favor of the empty tomb far more plausible. I accordingly think that although Kirby is wrong, he does make an interesting case.

On the other hand, his argument is based on assumptions that are, at the very least, uncertain. He assumes that Mark intended his gospel to end at 16:8 (TET, 239). As we all know, this point has been disputed ad nauseam, and I suspect that the majority of New Testament scholars are on his side. But I have always wondered. Mark makes it clear that at least one resurrection appearance is coming (14:28), and that makes me suspicious that he did indeed write about appearances of the risen Jesus, and that that text has been lost.[36]

Kirby assumes that if a purported event meshes well with an author's redactional themes, then the author made up the event (TET, 238). This assumption is indeed widely made in certain circles of New Testament scholars, but it is unpersuasive nonetheless. Who says that the occurrence of a given actual event cannot dovetail with an author's editorial purposes?

Kirby assumes that John's empty-tomb account is either dependent on Mark or dependent on oral traditions that were influenced by Mark. And I will just note that this point can be and has been disputed. John's account is so different from the synoptic accounts (although I accept that it agrees with them on essential points) that I suspect independence of Mark at this point. And despite their differences from Mark's account, Matthew's and Luke's empty-tomb stories, Kirby argues, are entirely dependent on Mark's. I do not accept this point either, especially since we know that both Matthew and Luke had sources of information about Jesus that were unavailable to Mark. But obviously there is partial dependency, and I will note that the dependency argument can be used to cut the other way (that is, in support of the story): it is significant that Matthew and Luke basically accepted what Mark had to say about the empty tomb. They, at least, thought he had it right.

In my opinion, the weakest part of Kirby's argument is his attempt to argue that Mark's account shows signs of being fiction. The 2 Kings 2:9-18 story (Elijah being carried off to heaven as an instance of looking for and not finding a corpse) is a feeble parallel to the empty-tomb story. Moreover, much of Kirby's puzzlement over the motivation of Joseph of Arimathea in Mark's account (TET, 244) can be answered if Joseph was, as Luke hints (23:51) and John affirms (19:38), a secret disciple of Jesus. Finally, Kirby argues that the consistent use of plural words like "they" and "them" in canonical and noncanonical burial accounts is an indication that Jesus was buried not by Joseph but by his enemies (TET, 247). But of course Joseph would hardly have buried Jesus without any help at all from other persons. As such, the pronouns may refer to Joseph et al. after all.

There are many other points that I could dispute. For example, I think the first appearance was to Mary Magdalene and other women rather than to Peter,[37] but competent people can disagree about that. And I think the first appearance was in Jerusalem not Galilee; and even if (as Kirby claims and I deny) the stories of appearances in Jerusalem "follow on the heels of the empty-tomb story" (TET, 253), it does not follow (as Kirby says it does) that "the empty-tomb story is a relatively recent development in the Gospel of Mark" (TET, 253).

Accordingly, the case that Kirby makes is, in my opinion, unconvincing.

IX

Jeffery Lowder is identified in TET as the cofounder and past president of Internet Infidels, Inc. His essay, "Historical Evidence and the Empty Tomb: A Reply to William Lane Craig" (TET, 261–306) is in my view one of the best in the book. It is generally fair and evenhanded, and despite being a critique of Craig's ten arguments in support of the empty tomb, Lowder occasionally allows himself to admit that Craig has made a good point. In addition, Lowder defends an interesting thesis, viz., that Jesus' body was relocated after its initial burial. A rushed Joseph of Arimathea (rushed because of the fast-approaching Sabbath) first placed Jesus in his own tomb, but then, after the Sabbath (not being a secret disciple, on Lowder's view), moved the body to a criminal's graveyard (TET, 272).

Lowder's scenario is helped by the fact that, as we now know, reburial was common in ancient Palestine. But it is damaged beyond repair, in my view, by the fact that there is no suggestion of any such thing in the texts.[38]

Indeed, Mark 16:6 is inconsistent with it, and so must be explained away. Moreover, what Lowder has in mind is not like the common ancient practice of reburial. Typically, a body was buried for a year until only bones remained, and then those bones were removed and placed in an ossuary. Lowder is suggesting that Joseph relocated the corpse after the Sabbath had passed, not after a year had passed.

Moreover, I do not agree that Jesus' corpse would have been unrecognizable after seven weeks (which Lowder uses to refute the common argument that had Jesus been buried by his enemies, they would simply have put the corpse on display when the disciples started preaching the resurrection). I myself also checked with an eminent pathologist on this point, who told me that when a body is in fact buried, and the climate is dry and fairly cool, a corpse can be readily identified for much longer than that.[39] Moreover, we must note that any body that was found in Jesus' tomb and put on display, even an unrecognizable one, would have spelled disaster for the Christian movement.[40]

I entirely agree with Craig that the silence of the women in Mark was only temporary; Luke 24:22-23 makes it clear that they did speak up. Lowder oddly calls this view the theory that the silence of the women is "legendary" (TET, 282). Not so; it was real but did not last long, as I think we would expect in the circumstances.

Lowder objects to Matthew's guards-at-the-tomb story by saying that "it relates supposedly private conversations among Jews that no Christian could have known about" (TET, 284). And I must ask how Lowder learned that. There are several ways in which Christians could have discovered what had been said.

X

Richard Carrier, a Ph.D. student at Columbia University, has contributed one very long essay and two shorter ones to TET. Indeed, his writings take up over a third of the book. The long essay is called, "The Spiritual Body of Christ and the Legend of the Empty Tomb" (TET, 105–231). In it he argues, in great detail and with broad knowledge of ancient texts, that Paul's theory is that Jesus' body permanently rotted away but God raised him by giving him a second body made of pneuma or heavenly material (the "two-body" theory),[41] and that the empty-tomb stories in the Gospels are a myth invented by Mark (intended by Mark as a kind of symbol or metaphor), and the appearances stories are legends that were originally based on hallucinations. Carrier argues that Paul's view was normative for Christians in the earliest days but was replaced, some time after A.D. 70, by the "one body" theory of resurrection found in the Gospels.

Naturally, I have many criticisms of Carrier's "two body" theory. Unfortunately, I cannot come anywhere near discussing all the points that I would wish to dispute. Surprisingly, given Carrier's vigorous critique of an argument from silence that William L. Craig deploys at one point (TET, 177–79), much of Carrier's case is based, to an amazing degree, on arguments from silence. There is one after another. They are usually of the form, "If Paul had meant X, why didn't he say Y?" Now, to his credit, Carrier does present criteria for what might constitute a convincing argument from silence (TET, 178), nor am I an enemy of all such arguments;[42] sometimes they can be fairly effective (especially where a powerful case can be made in favor of the statement, "if the author had meant X, she would have said Y"). But they are hardly ever probative when standing alone, and the degree to which Carrier deploys them is at least suspicious.

Also, there seems to be in this essay a great deal of what I will call "picking and choosing" among texts. I suppose all of us who study the Bible do a certain amount of this, but one gets the impression that Carrier fastens upon and privileges any texts that can be taken as supporting his theory and rejects all others. For example, he rejects the whole of the book of Acts as "worthless as a source" except the three descriptions of Paul's conversion (Acts 9:1-22; 22:6-16; 25:12-18), which Luke puts in the mouth of Paul. This is because the themes of seeing light and hearing voices (TET, 154) seem to agree with Carrier's vew of the subjective nature of all the Ressurrection appearances of Jesus. Accordingly, he very much likes those bits from Acts.

Carrier argues that "it begs all credulity to maintain that Paul believed in the resurrection of the flesh" (TET, 124). There is an element of truth here: normally (but not quite always), *sarx* for Paul meant the human body as existing under the power of sin. In that sense, Carrier would be right. But I am convinced that Paul's frequent use of the word *soma*, with its heavy connotations of physicality,[43] shows that Paul was talking about bodily resurrection.

As Carrier points out, Paul places great emphasis on the simile of a seed growing into a plant. Carrier sees in this metaphor a confirmation of the two-body theory; after all, he says, the plant is very much different from the seed. Yet I see in the simile proof of the one-body theory. It all depends on what is meant by "the same" (or, alternately, "different from"). Let us say that two things, X and Y, are qualitatively the same if they share all their properties. Notice that I am not qualitatively the same as my body or indeed myself of ten years ago. And let us say that two things, X and Y, are numerically the same if the terms X and Y are two different ways of referring to one and the same thing. I would insist, of course, that I am numerically the same thing or the same person as the Stephen Davis who existed ten years ago. It is certainly true that the seed and the plant are qualitatively different. But they are numerically the same because there is material continuity between them. The one grows, by incremental, measurable, and observable steps, into the other. The second is a new stage of the first. So if Jesus' old body and resurrection body are related, as Paul seems to insist that they are, in the same way as are the seed and the plant, then we have proof of the one-body theory. Jesus' old body is not, as Carrier would have it, replaced by the new one (while the old one decays in the grave); rather it becomes the new body. There is material continuity between the two; the new body, although transformed, is the same body.

I am simply unable to read 1 Corinthians 15 in the way that Carrier does. One minor grammatical point—which is clear both in standard English translations and the Greek—is the repetition in verses 43-44 of what is correctly translated in English as the pronoun "it." Three times Paul says, "it is sown . . . it is raised." What is the intended referent of this word "it"? Surely he means the person's body. Before being transformed, the body is perishable, dishonorable, and weak. After being transformed, it is imperishable, glorious, and powerful. The subject under discussion is numerically the same one thing (referred to by the same English pronoun "it") throughout. This does not sound like the exchange of one body for another.

On the empty tomb, I find the notion that Mark meant his story only as symbol or metaphor (TET, 156–58) to be totally implausible. Whether one judges the story true or false, surely Mark meant his readers to believe that it is a true narrative, just as he wanted them to believe as true everything he recorded about Jesus earlier in his gospel. But the only other point that I will mention is a question addressed to Carrier: in a narrative text from the ancient world (where it is too late for us to look for traces, artifacts, or clues), how do we sensibly distinguish between (1) author B has embellished a story originally told by author A with legendary additions, and (2) author B has added to the story details that A knew but B did not know or did not choose to include? There is no denying that there are details in Matthew, Luke, and John that we do not find in Mark. And I agree that some (not many) of them are extremely hard, maybe impossible, to harmonize with Mark. Nor do I deny a priori that there were legendary accretions (frankly, I have never known what to do with Matthew 27:52-53). But my question remains. It seems entirely possible to me that many of the details added by the later evangelists actually occurred and that is why they included them in their gospels.

Carrier's second essay in TET is "The Plausibility of Theft" (TET, 349–68). It is, as the name implies, a defense of the thesis that Jesus' tomb was empty because the body was stolen. The first half is a reply to six arguments against theft given by William L. Craig. Carrier then argues that Christianity could have continued and thrived even if theft occurred and were found out and that Matthew's story of the guard at the tomb is not believable. My only comment on this essay is that we must distinguish between two quite different questions. First, is it possible for us to imagine a scenario that is not impossible, is not disproved by the available evidence, and that covers all the admitted facts? Second, do we have convincing evidence that that scenario is true?

Believers in the resurrection of Jesus should answer the first question in the affirmative. Of course we can imagine such scenarios. Carrier does so, again and again. So far as the empty tomb is concerned, here is one of my own (of course I do not claim that it is plausible):

> On the day after the crucifixion, three Roman soldiers secretly disposed of Jesus' body by placing it in a hidden cave located ten kilometers from Jerusalem near the road to Jericho, where the body was never discovered; and, on their return to Jerusalem, they were immediately transferred back to Rome, where they eventually died, without ever telling anyone what they had done.

This certainly is a metaphysically possible scenario, but there is no evidence whatsoever for it. That is precisely the case, I believe, for many of the theft scenarios that Carrier creates.

Carrier's third essay, "The Burial of Jesus in the Light of Jewish Law" (TET, 369–92) argues that Jesus' body was taken down from the cross before sunset, was stowed in a temporary location, was legally moved after the Sabbath by Joseph of Arimathea to a criminal's graveyard; not knowing those facts, the disciples found the original location empty and mistakenly believed that Jesus had been raised. Carrier offers a quite learned exposition of all the relevant ancient Jewish legal texts that relate to the burial of corpses. I have no major problems with his analysis of them. I only call attention to a point that Carrier recognizes: scholars of ancient Judaism are familiar with the caveat that the laws (in this case, burial laws) that the rabbis from the late second and third centuries onward wanted Jews to observe might not have reflected actual practice among Jews, even in their own day, let alone centuries earlier.

In addition, Carrier thinks it obvious that the claim that Joseph of Arimathea was a secret disciple of Jesus (John 19:38-40) is a legendary embellishment. I will just say that is not obvious to me. Carrier's theory is based on assuming the truth of what he calls the "core accounts" in the Gospel burial accounts (i.e., "details common to the majority" [TET, 386]). But one cannot help forming the suspicion that Carrier's actual criterion for what details he will accept from the burial accounts is not what is "common to the majority," but what agrees with his theory.

XI

Keith Parsons' essay is titled, "Peter Kreeft and Ronald Tacelli on the Hallucination Theory" (TET, 433–51). (He is associate professor of philosophy at the University of Houston, Clear Lake.) His essay is a point-by-point reply to thirteen arguments given by these two apologists in their *Handbook of Christian Apologetics* (Downers Grove, Ill.: InterVarsity, 1994). Parsons does score some points against Kreeft and Tacelli, but in the end the case he makes is not convincing. For example, for much of his article, Parsons is busy answering the wrong set of questions. Few people, including Christians, will dispute the claim that sane and intelligent people sometimes "believe things that never happened" (TET, 434). Few will dispute the point that group hallucinations occur (although they are rare). The real issue here is whether there is good evidence to believe that this sort of thing happened in the case of the disciples' beliefs about Jesus. I hold, with Kreeft and Tacelli, that the answer to that question is no.

But on the general point (not related to Jesus), I do have a question. Are there cases where A has a hallucination of the deceased B (whether B is a loved one or somebody like Elvis or Jimmy Hoffa), comes to believe that B is alive and kicking here on earth, and A's belief that B is alive has, so to speak, staying power? In other words, A genuinely believes that B is alive and, perhaps, is now in hiding (in Paraguay?). I rather doubt that this occurs, but I confess to being a nonexpert on the psychology of hallucinations.[44]

Contrary to Parsons, the fact that the Gospel of Mark contains no appearance stories in the authentic part of the gospel that we possess does not "indicate that detailed appearances narratives were inventions of the later Gospel writers" (TET, 438). Paul's list of appearances of the risen Jesus is admittedly not embedded in any narrative context in 1 Corinthians, but the list must have been so embedded in the pre-Pauline church. "Okay, tell me about the appearance to Peter" or "Please explain about the appearance to the more than five hundred" are requests that must have been made to the earliest believers by converts and enemies alike. Can we imagine Peter or James replying, "Well, I will happily repeat my recitation of our list of people to whom we say he appeared, but I will not say more than that"?

There are New Testament scholars who are comfortable with the idea, as clearly Parsons is (TET, 443), that the disciples made up out of whole cloth resurrection-appearance stories. I must say that I have always found that point vaguely insulting to Christians. Being sincerely mistaken is one thing; and to be fair, some of the contributors to TET go out of their way to try to find a way to preserve the sincerity and integrity of the early Christians. But Parsons does not. For myself, I cannot read the Gospels without being impressed with the sincerity of the authors. I suppose much of that is because I am a Christian and accordingly approach the Bible with a hermeneutic of trust. I will just leave the point here: nobody, in my opinion, has ever made a convincing case that the evangelists deliberately told falsehoods.

There are also several lesser points where I disagree with Parsons:

- He quotes (TET, 444) Robert Price as asking, "Where in the Gospels or in Acts do we read 'profound, extended conversations' between the risen Jesus and his Disciples?" And I am just wondering why Price and Parsons think John 21 fails to fill that bill.
- The Joseph of Arimathea story does not, contrary to Parsons' assertion (TET, 446), contradict Mark and Luke's claim that the women went to the tomb on the Easter morning for the purpose of anointing the corpse.
- I deny that the Gospels contain "many undeniably fictional elements" and contradict "many known facts" (TET, 439).

Against Parsons, I still think that the resurrection of Jesus looks like an unlikely candidate for hallucination. The considerations here are several: Jesus' followers were not expecting a resurrection; many people saw the risen Jesus; the encounters were located in various places and times; some doubted that it was Jesus, and others only recognized him with difficulty (so they were certainly not *all* hallucinating); there were no drugs, high fever, or lack of food or water mentioned; and longstanding convictions and permanent lifestyle changes were produced. Taken together, these points constitute a powerful cumulative case against hallucination.

XI

By way of conclusion, let me say that TET is a book that apologists for the resurrection should read. The authors have clearly done their homework; they advance interesting theses; and in general they argue skillfully for those theses. I was surprised, however, at how much below-the-surface disagreement there is in the book. Of course one would not expect them to agree on everything. But I found myself at times wondering whether I might just somehow step out of the way and let them duke it out among themselves on such issues as

- whether Jesus ever existed,
- whether Jesus died on the cross,
- whether Joseph of Arimathea existed,
- whether Joseph, if he existed, buried the body of Jesus,
- whether Jesus was buried (by anybody),
- whether the theft-of-the-body thesis is plausible,
- whether the disciples were convinced that Jesus had risen,
- whether Paul learned anything about Christianity from other Christians,
- whether the evangelists were even trying to record actual events, and
- whether any parts of the Gospel accounts of the burial and resurrection of Jesus are either true or were meant to be taken as true.

But the authors certainly are united on the main point of the book: Jesus was not raised from the dead.

In my opinion, Jeffery Lowder is right on the mark when he says of the burial tradition in the Gospels that how one evaluates it depends to a great extent on "what sort of general presumption, if any, one has about the general reliability of the texts which contain this specific evidence" (TET, 265). This point clearly does apply to the claim, made in all four gospels, that Jesus' followers knew the location of the tomb in which he was buried (Matt 27:61; Mark 15:47; Luke 23:55; John 20:1). My only caveat—with which I'm sure Lowder would agree—is that the question of the general reliability of the Bible applies to the entirety of the question of the resurrection of Jesus and not just to the burial tradition.

It is clear that the ten contributors to this book agree in approaching the Bible with a hermeneutic of suspicion. They regard the Bible as no different in kind from any other ancient text. They will accept what it says only when convincing public evidence supports what it says. Those of us who defend the resurrection are practicing Christians[45] who approach the Bible with what I just called a hermeneutic of trust (whether or not we affirm biblical inerrancy). We take the Bible (at least) to be generally reliable; we accept what it says unless convincing public evidence shows that what it says is wrong. And this is not merely a matter of accepting something "on faith"; we believe we can make a powerful case for so regarding the Bible. For myself, I accept the word of all four evangelists that the location of the tomb was known to the earliest Christians. This difference in general attitude toward the Bible seems to me to create an almost unbridgeable gulf between apologists for the resurrection and the contributors to TET. I frankly see no way of adjudicating the dispute.

I must point out that the contributors to TET advance or at least suggest some extremely radical proposals:

- The very concept of God is incoherent.[46]
- The apparently historical parts of the Bible are to be taken as myth in the service of politics.
- Jesus never existed.[47]
- Jesus did not really die on the cross.
- 1 Corinthians 15:3-11 was not written by Paul.

Not all ten authors of TET push these theses. But I must say that these claims seem rather desperate to me. And so I draw this moral: if these are the lengths to which you have to go in order to deny the resurrection, maybe it is better to affirm it. Accordingly, to a certain extent, I believe the authors of TET have shot themselves in the foot. Most scholars will recognize these claims for the eccentricities that they are.

One aspect of the desperation of which I speak is a methodological procedure that unites the essays in TET. I would describe it as having three steps: (1) suggest a naturalistic hypothesis, which, if true, explains some aspects of the New Testament accounts of the resurrection of Jesus; (2) embrace all biblical or extrabiblical ancient texts, phrases, hints, or textual variants that can be interpreted as supporting the hypothesis; and (3) reject all the other biblical texts as late or patently false or apologetically motivated or legendary.

Even so, this book confirms what I mentioned at the outset and have long believed: it is possible for intelligent people to find principled reasons for rejecting the resurrection of Jesus. But it is also possible—as I hope my remarks on this occasion have helped to show—for defenders of the resurrection to respond in kind and answer the arguments given. That back-and-forth debate like this can go on virtually endlessly shows either that one group stubbornly refuses to evaluate the evidence fairly, or that rational belief is possible on either side of the issue. I choose to opt for the latter.

Has TET shown that rational rejection of the claim that God raised Jesus from the dead is possible? I would say yes. Has TET refuted the claim that God raised Jesus from the dead? No: the authors have not even come close to that.[48]

6

Should Exegesis Have Presuppositions?

I

Let me begin with a terse and typically vigorous quotation from Rudolf Bultmann: "Every exegesis that is guided by dogmatic prejudices does not hear what the text says, but only lets the latter say what it wants to hear."[1]

The question of the relationship between philosophical presuppositions and biblical exegesis is a frequently discussed one. It has been analyzed from several angles. Some biblical scholars—recognizing as Bultmann did that the presuppositions of certain exegetes have sometimes distorted their interpretations—have argued for the ideal of presuppositionless exegesis. Others, including Bultmann, have argued that this is impossible; we cannot avoid having presuppositions as we approach the Bible or any other text.

Conservative biblical scholars have discussed this issue as well. Their aim has often been to argue that liberal scholars have been blinded to the Bible's real message by their presuppositions. A great deal of criticism has been heaped on the naturalism or implicit deism of some scholars, especially their acceptance of presuppositions such as: (1) God does not exist; (2) nature is a closed system of causes and effects; or (3) the worldview of the New Testament writers is outmoded and superstitious.

I am going to approach the issue somewhat differently. For it is my view that the holding of certain philosophical positions is essential to interpreting the Bible, at least in Christian exegesis. (I recognize that many scholars who

An earlier version of this paper appeared in a Festschrift. See Julius J. Lipner, ed., Truth, Religious Dialogue, and Dynamic Orthodoxy: Reflections on the Works of Brian Hebblethwaite *(London: SCM Press, 2005).*

are involved in interpreting the Bible do not see themselves as committed in any sense to Christianity or to the church, and my suggestions in the present chapter have little to do with them.) That is, I think it is crucial for biblical interpreters to have the *correct* presuppositions. I will say what I think they are in due time. Some of them are controversial in philosophical circles.

Let me provide a brief roadmap of where we will be going in this chapter. First, I will define the term *presupposition* and contrast it with the term *prejudice*. Second, since I will be using the concept *the meaning of the whole of Scripture*, I need to explain in what sense or senses I consider the Bible to be a unified work that can possess an overall meaning. Finally, I will turn to the task of exploring those philosophical presuppositions that I think are requisite to proper biblical interpretation.

II

What exactly is a presupposition? Philosophers use the word in different ways. I am interested primarily in what are called pragmatic presuppositions. These are claims that a speaker or interpreter takes for granted, that is, she does not state them but takes them to be understood as true. If they are false, the statements made by the speaker or interpreter will be untoward or inappropriate. If I say, "The present king of France is bald," it seems that I am presupposing that "There presently exists a king of France." If that presupposition is false (as it indeed is), my original statement will be inappropriate. More broadly, then, a presupposition is any unstated premise or background belief whose truth is necessary to the truth of another statement or to the soundness of an argument or to the tenability of a position.

Let me emphasize that a presupposition is a belief for which the believer is normally able to give a principled defense. (This does not mean it must be true.) So let me distinguish a presupposition from a prejudice, which is an unstated premise or background belief for which the believer cannot give a principled defense and indeed is usually at pains to hide. As Bultmann pointed out, prejudices are often at work in biblical interpretation as well as elsewhere in life. It is a prejudice when proof-texts are sought out to support a preexisting and unbiblical doctrine (e.g., that slavery is divinely sanctioned). It is also a prejudice when modern views are anachronistically read back into the biblical texts (e.g., the view of some exegetes in the 1930s and 1940s—ironically, exegetes such as Bultmann himself—that existential philosophy is taught in the New Testament).[2]

On the other hand, we have all heard in recent years that there exists no "view from nowhere." And so far as human beings are concerned, that seems to me to be true. There is no such thing as totally neutral, presuppositionless exegesis. Everybody approaches the Bible—or any text—with a network of basic beliefs and attitudes that provide that person's interpretative framework. So, as I say, the task is to approach the Bible with the correct, or most nearly correct, presuppositions. But how do we know what they are? There is no algorithm for finding out. On the present occasion, I will simply suggest a few rules.

- One's presuppositions must be guided by a thorough knowledge of the history of theology and especially of exegesis.
- One's presuppositions must be arrived at not on one's own but in correspondence with the wider Christian and scholarly communities.
- One's presuppositions must be correctable by the Scriptures themselves.

III

Before discussing the unity of the Bible, let me say a word about what scholars call the "hermeneutical circle." This term can mean different things. I take it to be the following phenomenon: in interpreting the Bible, we need to interpret the whole in terms of the parts and the parts in terms of the whole. The first point is that any defensible opinion about the macro message of the Bible, or the overall message of a part of the Bible, must be informed by and consistent with defensible opinions about the meanings of the various smaller texts and pericopes that it consists in. The second point is that any defensible opinion about the meaning of a smaller biblical text or pericope must be informed by and consistent with defensible opinions about the meaning of the Bible as a whole or of large sections of it in which the text is located.

Yet this comment presupposes something that is deeply controversial today among Scripture scholars, viz. the very idea that the Bible is the sort of text that can have a unified meaning. Thus James Barr says: "The Bible is not a unified writing but a composite body of literature."[3] In one sense, this is entirely true. The Bible was written over a very long period of time, by many different authors, and its genre pluralism is staggering. Among other types of literature, the Bible includes: creation stories, historical narratives, law codes, songs, poems, wise saying, prophetic oracles, parables, letters from one person to another, letters from one person to a group of people, and apocalyptic literature.

Reacting against an uncritical assumption of biblical unity in the so-called biblical theology movement of, roughly, 1930–1960, contemporary biblical scholarship has swung mightily in the other direction. Many scholars view the Bible as a library rather than a unified work. Such critics believe that the Bible does not contain a "theology" but rather many competing and mutually inconsistent "theologies." They seek out discrepancies and contradictions in the Bible with inquisitorial zeal. They view any attempt to harmonize two apparently discrepant texts as laughably unsophisticated. For example, many would consider it uncouth to use a text, for example, from the Fourth Gospel to illuminate a Pauline text, or vice versa. At times they give noncanonical texts from the biblical period more weight than canonical ones. It seems to be largely assumed that there is no such thing as "the biblical view" or even "the New Testament view" of this or that. It goes without saying that on this view the Bible is incapable of making normative theological statements.

I will argue against such notions and in favor of the unity of the Bible. I will do so in four ways, the fourth of which is the strongest and most important. In none of these four points, however, will I oppose the notion that the Bible is diverse. I will argue for a complex "unity in diversity" of the Bible. Indeed, I do not rule out a priori the possibility that some biblical texts are simply inconsistent with others. However, I must say that the different and logically inconsistent "theologies" that some contemporary interpreters claim to find in the Bible or even in the New Testament often seem to me to be simply different ways in different contexts of stating similar or complementary theologies.

It will be helpful to explain the sort of biblical unity for which I am arguing. It is not the sort of uniformity that we would expect to find in an article in a scholarly journal in mathematics or philosophy. This is the kind of unity that we expect to find where there is one author who has one topic in mind, who writes in one genre, and all of whose statements are consistent with one another and help contribute to the article's overall aim. Here, as I suppose, the author's intention is the integrating principle of unity. Nor is the Bible's unity the kind that we find in a typical jigsaw puzzle. This is the kind of unity where the various pieces are at first a jumbled muddle rather than a coherent picture, and only after long and patient effort are we able to fit them together and see the picture that was at first hidden. Here the integrating principle of unity is the solution to the puzzle.

I wish to argue for a unity in the Bible that is more like thematic or organic unity. (As my fourth argument below reveals, however, I do not rule out biblical unity as a function of the intention of one divine author.)

Thematic unity is involved in cases where a mass of material, even diverse material, in one way or another advances a certain literary or theological theme or series of related themes. Here the integrating principle of unity, as I suppose, is the theme being advanced. A species of thematic unity is what we might call narrative unity. This is involved in cases where a mass of material, even material diverse as to genre and purpose, is seen when taken together as telling one story. Here the integrating principle of unity is the story.

The issue I am raising is this: does the New Testament, or indeed the Bible as a whole, possess sufficient unity for it to be theologically normative for Christians and to support the hermeneutical circle (which talks about the meaning of the whole)? Is there enough unity to make "agreement of our theological statements with Scripture" a criterion of theological acceptability? I will argue in four ways that the answer is yes.

1. *The Bible as a book inside a cover.* That is, the Bible is a unity simply in virtue of its being published as a single book and accepted as such by the church for nearly two thousand years. This is, of course, a weak sense of unity and is entirely consistent with views of the Bible as a library like those described above. Nevertheless, this is a unity worth noting. Virtually any writings that have been published together and that have a long tradition of interpretation can be considered a unified work in this sense, and discussions about the overall meaning of the book can be quite appropriate.[4]

2. *The Bible as a unity in its basic message.* This is a stronger sense of unity than the first. I am presupposing here the principle that complementary theological claims from various texts of Scripture can be fitted together to form coherent wholes. This point was recognized early in the history of the church: the overall message or meaning of Scripture as a whole was called "the rule of faith." Accordingly, Scripture is the story of the redemptive dealings of the one and only God with human beings. It moves from the creation and the fall of human beings to the choosing of Israel, from the giving of the law to the sending of the prophets, from the birth of the Messiah to the salvation of human beings in the life, death, and resurrection of Jesus Christ, from the creation of the church at Pentecost to the final victory of God in the eschaton. It is the story of God's covenant promises, of the universality of sin and human failure to observe God's covenants, and of God's faithfulness in Jesus Christ in fulfilling God's promises.

The unity of the Bible's two Testaments, despite the diversity that we see there, is seen in their complementary views of God, human nature, the election of a people of God, and God's redemptive purposes for humans. It is evidenced further by the consciousness of the writers of the New Testament of being a continuation of the same people of God as the people of the Old Testament, of their acceptance of the Old Testament as sacred Scripture fit for Christian proclamation, and of their sense of seeing in Jesus Christ the true meaning and goal of the Old Testament.

The unity of the New Testament, despite the many viewpoints expressed there, is a unity provided by Christology—in particular (as James Dunn convincingly argues), by a shared acceptance of the identity of the earthly Jesus with the now-resurrected and exalted Lord and Son of God. The New Testament's unity is also a function of a unified commitment to monotheism, to the Hebrew Bible, to one and the same faith with its promise of forgiveness and salvation, to the notion that the church both continues and fulfills the role of Israel, to baptism and to common meal rites that eventually solidified as the Lord's Supper, to the experience of the Holy Spirit, to love of neighbor as the hallmark of Christian conduct, and to the hope of Jesus' return.[5]

3. *One potential dire consequence of giving up on the unity of the Bible.* Now, this third point can be dismissed as unrelated to the truth of the matter; it is more a pragmatic point about what I see as terrible potential consequences of denying biblical unity. Nevertheless, it is a point I feel deeply. To the extent that interpreters reject both the Old Testament's status as God's word and the firm and unanimous conviction of the New Testament writers of the unity of the two Testaments (among many other texts, see Matt 21:42-44; Luke 24:25-27, 44; John 5:39-46; Eph 1:9-10; 1 Tim 3:16), to that extent the testimony of both Testaments that Israel is the chosen people of God can easily be rejected. The Christian church can then become severed from its Jewish roots; Jews can come to be viewed as a disposable residuum of biblical times; anti-Semitism can become attractive; and even genocide can become slightly more thinkable than it was before. Note the alarming case of those German Old Testament scholars who supported National Socialism and raised no voice against its programs during the Third Reich. Accordingly, in my opinion, Christians must continue to hold that the Old Testament is both divinely inspired and a Christian book. Israel was and is God's chosen people; Christians are shoots grafted on to the branch of the people of God; and Israel has a continuing role to play in the providential plan of God for the human race (Romans 9–11).

4. *Divine inspiration of the Bible.* This argument for biblical unity—the strongest of the four—has been rejected by many scholars today. But most Christians continue to hold that the books of the Bible, and only the books of the Bible, were subject to the inspiration of the Holy Spirit

and were brought together by the church under the influence of the Holy Spirit. This divine inspiration of the books and book writers ceased at the close of the apostolic age. Thus the Bible is unique among all the books in the world's history in having been produced in some strong sense by God (as well as by its human authors).[6] If the Bible is indeed in some strong sense the product of divine inspiration, its unity as the work of a single, divine author (as well as, of course, its many human authors) is to be expected.

It should also be pointed out here that there is a close relationship between the second and the fourth of my arguments for the unity of the Bible. The fourth may be the best explanation of the second. That is, the striking fact that a book with such diverse origins as the Bible displays the overall organic unity noted in my second argument may well be taken as evidence for some kind of divine providential guidance of its writing. The Bible does possess the very sort of "unity in diversity" that we might expect from a book that (1) was written in a great variety of historical, cultural, and religious circumstances; and (2) was intended by God to be a decisive self-revelation, with one message or theme from beginning to end.

My point is that it makes sense to speak of the Bible as a unity, as one work, as the kind of thing that can be said to have a meaning as a whole. Despite its great diversity (of historical content, of authorial concerns, of theological setting, of genre, etc.) the Bible is one book that contains a unified message (along with many different messages). Now, it must be stressed that I have not in any serious sense *proved* in this brief excursion that the Bible is a unity. Beside much further consideration of the four arguments I have raised, this would take detailed exegetical arguments to the effect that various apparently discrepant or unrelated texts actually cohere and help form a unified theological whole. Such a task is beyond my present interests and perhaps my competence as well. Someone else will have to do the detailed work of sorting out apparent inconsistencies and constructing the macro biblical theology sketched out above.

IV

It is time that we turned to those presuppositions that I think proper interpretation of the Bible requires. Like all human beings, Christian philosophers want to know what to believe. And on some issues about which we are curious, both philosophy and Scripture are possible sources of information. Most Christian philosophers see themselves as living under a methodological obligation to make all their beliefs that are relevant to matters on which the Bible speaks consistent with Scripture. I would hold that the Bible is trustworthy and reliable on all matters on which it speaks; Scripture is the source of religious truth above all other sources and the norm or guide to religious truth above all other norms or guides.[7]

If God wants to redeem fallen human beings, it seems sensible to believe that God will communicate the divine method of salvation to those human beings so that they can know and take advantage of it. Christians hold that this is precisely what God has done. Christians affirm that in Scripture God speaks to us. Accordingly, the Bible is unlike all other books; it is revelatory. Our received tradition is that all proposals on any subject that is relevant to Christian thought and practice are to be judged preeminently in the light of Scripture.

The Bible says nothing about many issues that are of concern to philosophers. The Bible is not a work of philosophy or even of philosophy of religion. The concerns and questions of the biblical writers are different from those of contemporary philosophers. But there are certain questions with which Christian philosophers are concerned that are also addressed in the Bible:

- What is the world's origin?
- What is a human being?
- How should human beings live?
- Does God exist?
- Is there life beyond death?

There are of course many others.

It would be taken as the height of absurdity by most secular philosophers if anyone were to suggest—as I am suggesting—that the teachings of the Bible and philosophical conclusions can be relevant to each other. We have all heard in recent years, from Alvin Plantinga and others, that we Christian philosophers should not be afraid to allow biblical and Christian teachings to influence our views as philosophers. I entirely agree with that sentiment. But I also believe that it is acceptable for Christian philosophers in certain instances to allow their philosophical opinions to influence how they approach the Bible. They will be poor exegetes, however, if their philosophical views constrain the Bible, if the Scriptures are not free to speak as the Holy Spirit would have them speak.

In this chapter, I am not arguing (although I believe and think I can demonstrate) that both exegesis and theology require philosophy. Indeed, I think that certain philosophical assumptions and activities are required in order to think coherently about anything at all. Nor will I argue (although I believe and think I can demonstrate) that sound exegesis and theology ought not to be tied too closely to any one philosophical system. That this very thing has occurred in the past and still occurs today almost goes without saying. It is possible to find exegetes and theologians in the tradition whose views are, in my view, too closely tied to various philosophical schools.

Given what the Fathers of the church called "the rule of faith" (as noted above, this is the received and accepted way of interpreting the macromessage of Scripture, which was for them synonymous with the Christian message itself), I believe Christian philosophers are allowed to approach the Bible with certain controversial philosophical theses intact. Let me mention seven of them. I am certainly not arguing that no serious Christian exegete or theologian has ever rejected any of them. I am claiming that no serious Christian exegete or theologian *should* do so.

1. *Metaphysical monism is false.* I take metaphysical monism to be the thesis that there is one and only one reality, and accordingly that all differentiation is illusory. Thus ultimately I am the same thing as my pet African gray parrot, and he and I are both ultimately the same thing as the wall over there, and all of us—parrot, wall, and me—are the same thing as ultimate reality. Metaphysical monism can be found in various places, both in the East and in the West; Advaita Vedanta Hinduism is surely one example of it. But it seems clear that biblical religion is essentially dualist just in this sense: God is one thing and the world, God's creation, is another. God and the world are, as we might say, different things.

2. *Metaphysical materialism is false.* I take metaphysical materialism to be the thesis that the only reality is matter. The physical universe exhausts reality. Putative immaterial or incorporeal things—whether they be God, angels, human souls, or whatever—simply do not exist. Metaphysical materialism can also be found in various places. Ancient Epicurean philosophy was based on it; and the vast majority of contemporary analytic philosophers accept it as a matter of faith. But it seems clear that biblical religion is essentially committed to the reality of certain spiritual or nonphysical things, among them God, angels, demons, and the human soul. The last three items on that list—angels, demons, and souls—may be somewhat controversial among Christian thinkers. But the first item—God—is not. God, who is a spirit (John 4:24), alone suffices to show that biblical religion is essentially committed to the falsity of metaphysical materialism. At least one nonphysical thing exists; ergo, materialism is false.

3. *Time is linear.* I take the main alternative to the view that time is linear to be the view that time and history are circular, that history endlessly repeats itself, that there is no novelty or progress, and accordingly that no historical event can have eternal significance. Such views are found in virtually every prebiblical religious or mythological system and in many such systems existing today. But it seems clear that biblical religion is essentially based on the view that time is linear. That is, history is moving toward a certain goal or *telos*, that is, the kingdom of God. Novelty can and does appear from time to time; indeed, certain historical events can have eternal significance. Someday things will be different, and infinitely better, than they are now.

4. *Moral values are objective.* I take the claim that moral values are objective to mean that moral relativism is false. Moral relativism is the view that right and wrong, as well as related notions like duty, obligation, moral goodness, moral evil, etc. depend on individuals or groups. There are no transpersonal or transsocietal truths in morality. What actions are right or wrong depends on who you are or what you believe or what the culture to which you belong holds is right or wrong. Moral objectivism is simply the claim that statements about moral right or wrong are true or false quite apart from what any human individual or group happens to hold. And it seems clear that biblical religion is essentially committed to moral objectivism. Certain moral claims are true (ultimately coming, as they do, from God) quite apart from what any human being might think about them.

5. *Human beings are morally responsible for what they do.* I take the claim, "Jones is morally responsible for X," to mean that Jones can legitimately be praised or blamed, punished or rewarded, for X. The refrigerator is not morally responsible for keeping the food cold or even (when it malfunctions) for letting it spoil. A person who acts out of legitimate self-defense (so we normally think) is not morally responsible for injuring or maybe even killing someone. Or, better, the person *is* responsible but is excused. Generally, Jones is morally responsible for X if and only if (1) Jones did X or caused X to occur, (2) X is an event or action with moral connotations (like causing pain or pleasure to someone), and (3) there were no legitimate excuses. Now some philosophers have held that nobody is ever morally responsible; everything we do is brought about by unavoidable causal forces; we are victims of forces beyond our control.[8] But it seems clear that biblical religion is essentially committed to the notion that human beings are morally responsible for (at least much of) what they do. Accordingly, God can legitimately hold us morally responsible for our failure to obey God's commands.

6. *Epistemological skepticism is false.* I take epistemological skepticism to be the view that no knowledge claim can ever be justified, that nothing can ever be known for sure. There are, of course, crudely self-contradictory versions of skepticism (like the view of the person who claims to know that nothing whatever can be known); but there are also much more sophisticated versions. But it seems clear that biblical religion is essentially committed to the view that knowledge is possible, that God created us human beings with the ability to learn certain things on our own, that is, with our own cognitive equipment, and that we know certain other things because God has revealed them to us. Human reason is uniquely designed by God for the acquisition of knowledge and sometimes succeeds in attaining it.

7. *Linguistic realism is true.* Linguistic realism is a term that I am using technically. I take it as the negation of those extreme postmodern or deconstructionist views that: deny the possibility of secure communication between one person and another, claim that texts have no stable meanings, and insist that all thinkers are trapped within the confines of their own perspectives. But I take it that biblical religion is essentially committed to the view that texts can have stable meanings, that genuine communication between one mind and another is possible,[9] and indeed that it is possible for a divine mind to communicate truth to human minds.

V

Let me return to the quotation from Bultmann with which we began: "Every exegesis that is guided by dogmatic prejudices does not hear what the text says, but only lets the latter say what it wants to hear." I see myself in the present chapter as agreeing with Bultmann, although one suspects he would not agree with the spin I have placed on his words. We should not approach the texts with prejudices—that is, with preconceptions that cannot rationally be justified. But we cannot approach the text of the Bible without any presuppositions at all (and Bultmann would agree with that), and so we had best approach the Bible with that set of presuppositions that allows the text to speak what it wants to say.

I have been describing a method of exegesis for Christians, both philosophers and nonphilosophers. I am aware that not every exegete shares Christian assumptions. As noted above, I do not want to be interpreted as ruling out the methods practiced by many members of the Society of Biblical Literature, for example, where exegesis is a purely academic discipline and Christian assumptions are not allowed to intrude. I wish such folk well. But I do want to claim explicitly what I think my overall argument in this chapter entails, viz., that interpreting the Bible Christianly (as the Word of God, as a unity, in conjunction with Christian history) is the correct method of exegesis. It aligns us better with the character the Bible actually has. This does not mean, in specific cases, that Christian exegetes always interpret the Bible better than non-Christian exegetes do. I do mean that, everything else being equal, a Christian "take" on the Bible is epistemologically superior to all others.

My argument, then, is that it is not only allowable but in some sense essential for Christian philosophers to approach the reading of the Bible with these controversial philosophical theses intact. But it is also essential for Christian philosophers to allow the teachings of Scripture to influence their philosophical views. Indeed, as noted, I think Christian philosophers are to be encouraged not to fear doing that. It is part of the official view of philosophy's methodology that philosophers accept nothing "on authority," for example, just because the Bible says so or just because Plato or Quine said so. (Whether philosophers actually follow this rule is another question.) Still, in my opinion, philosophers ought not to imitate the procedure that was apparently followed by a biology professor at a Christian college whom I once met and who told me: "I keep my faith in one pocket and my science in another."

We are instead required to do our best to integrate all that we know, our faith and our learning, the teachings of Scripture and the results of our research. One of the things that this means concretely is (as Alvin Plantinga has also argued in recent years): don't give up too quickly on a given teaching from the Bible or theology just because it seems to conflict with current academic orthodoxy.[10]

Part II

Theological Issues

7

Should Evangelicals Be Pluralists?

I

I was raised in a Christian culture. Although it seems strange to our ears now, in the late 1940s and 1950s virtually everybody in the United States was considered Christian unless they were Jewish. And my family certainly saw itself as a Christian family. But I began to take Christianity seriously as a result of a conversion experience that occurred when I was a teenager. I was, of course, aware that there were other religions besides Christianity in the world, and I remember thinking about that fact. The high school that I attended had a high percentage of Jewish students. On Jewish holidays the school had a strange empty feel. There were also several Jewish families in the neighborhood in which we lived. I remember wondering how Christians ought to think about Judaism. In college I took a fascinating course on the religions of the world, and that experience very much raised my awareness of Asian religions, especially Hinduism and Buddhism.

But it was not until years later, when I was a young assistant professor at the then-called Claremont Men's College, that I began to think not just about religious diversity as a sociological fact about the world but as a problem in the philosophy of religion. This awareness coincided with and was surely caused by the arrival of John Hick as Danforth Professor of the Philosophy of Religion at Claremont Graduate University. I had studied under Hick a few years earlier at Princeton Theological Seminary, but that was the prepluralism Hick. By the time he arrived at Claremont, religious pluralism was his major project.

This chapter appears here for the first time.

I had always identified myself as an evangelical or at least orthodox Christian (there are some theological points that probably place me at the leftward end of the evangelical spectrum). And I quickly noticed that most of the scholars who were deeply interested in the problem of religious diversity, Hick included, identified themselves as being at the far left end of the Christian spectrum. Most evangelical scholars did not seem to be thinking or writing about religious pluralism.[1] So I began to do so. The present chapter represents my current thoughts about the subject.[2]

II

The broadest way of looking at this problem is to ask how members of the various religions of the world ought to understand the other religions and deal with their adherents. But most (not quite all) of the impetus for the academic discussion of the problem of religious diversity has come from within the Christian camp, broadly construed. Here the problem is: how should *Christians* understand the other religions (other religions beside Christianity, that is) and deal with their adherents, especially since (1) there are impressively saintly people in other religions and (2) the beliefs of those people seem to be held with sincerity and intellectual honesty? That is the way that I will approach the issue.

We cannot just say, with maximum generosity, that all the religions are true. This is because of the obvious fact that truth claims are made in all the religions (some of the claims are historical, some metaphysical, some moral), and frequently the truth claims made in one religion are logically inconsistent with truth claims made in other religions. For example:

- Christians claim that there is one and only one God; many Hindus claim that there are many Gods; many Buddhists claim that there is no God.
- Buddhists and Hindus believe in reincarnation, while most Christians believe in resurrection.
- Christians believe that ultimate reality (which we call God) is personal, while Advaita Vedanta Hindus affirm that ultimate reality (which they call Brahman) is impersonal.

Which claims are true? Of course religions do not consist merely of truth claims—there are different practices, liturgies, moral commands, dietary regulations, sacred texts, polities, etc. as well. But we cannot sensibly gainsay the fact that the crucial claims of the various religions cannot all be true. And maybe the most important question we can ask about any religion is whether its crucial truth claims are true.

Let us say that a "true religion" is one all of whose crucial truth claims are true. And let us say that a false religion is one in which at least many of its crucial truth claims are false. Is there, then, a true religion? Should Christians simply hold that their religion, Christianity, is true and that all the others are false? Or just what should Christians say?

There are three main theological options available on this point; they are called exclusivism, inclusivism, and pluralism. Exclusivists in effect say, "My religion is the one and only true way and those who disagree with it are mistaken." Christian exclusivists typically add that salvation can only come through baptism or through a conscious decision for Jesus Christ. All who die as non-Christians must suffer eternal hell. Christianity is true because it has been revealed by God; the other religions amount to human wisdom on religious matters. Christians accordingly have an obligation to evangelize adherents of other religions. (I should point out that so far as I can tell, the vast majority of adherents of the various religions of the world are exclusivist in some such sense as this.)

Inclusivists also affirm that their religion is the one true way, or at least the best way, but they also argue that other religions are partly true and are somehow included in their own religion. Christian inclusivists, for example, typically affirm that salvation is through Jesus Christ but suggest that people of other religions can be saved without ever having heard of Christ or the church. An underlying unity of all religions, especially on ethical matters, is recognized and emphasized. For example, the great twentieth-century German Jesuit theologian Karl Rahner argued that Christianity recognizes itself as the "absolute religion" that is intended for all human beings. But at least some non-Christian religions are "lawful religions" that contain truth and spiritual wisdom. There are, Rahner famously said, "anonymous Christians" who have "implicit faith." They show that faith by their moral actions and by their adherence to the truth as they best know it.[3] Inclusivists thus see great value in other religions but argue that those religions are completed or fulfilled in Christianity. Christianity makes the religious truth explicit and clear.

Pluralists say that my own religion is my way, or my community's way, but insist that other religions are equally valid and valuable roads to salvation. No religion (not even mine) can claim absolute superiority. You can certainly be deeply committed to your own religion—so pluralists say—but no one religion is intrinsically superior to others. There must be tolerance and honest dialogue between the religions. The aforementioned

John Hick has undoubtedly offered the most sophisticated and well-worked-out version of religious pluralism.[4] So let me move next to an examination of Hick's position.

III

John Hick started his academic career as a liberal but clearly Christian thinker of a broadly Reformed or Presbyterian persuasion. He became deeply interested in religious pluralism after his move to the University of Birmingham in the 1970s. The city of Birmingham, England, was at the time undergoing a painful transition to the multicultural, multiracial, and multireligious community that most British cities are today. He found himself working for justice and equal opportunity alongside people of various religions—especially Hindus, Buddhists, Moslems, and Sikhs—and respecting them as sincere religious folk. Hick is known for saying that no sensible person can encounter genuine and saintly members of another religion and hold that such folks are totally mistaken on religious matters and are destined for hell. Hick's experiences in Birmingham began a long process of thinking and writing about religious pluralism that culminated in his magnum opus, *An Interpretation of Religion* (1989), in which his pluralist theory is thoroughly spelled out.

Most religious people probably do regard their own religion as true and all others false. But Hick points out that the vast majority of religious people in the world follow the religion of the nation, locale, or family in which they were raised. This point—which is undoubtedly true—is, I suppose, designed to relativize peoples' exclusivistic commitment to their own religions. What is called for—so Hick insists—is a new Copernican revolution in peoples' opinions, not in this case about astronomy but about the religions. That revolution is what he aims to provide.[5]

It is important to note that what Hick proposes is a pluralistic theory that is realist on religion. Hick is no atheist or naturalist; he wants to respect the various religions as valid ways of apprehending and responding to reality. He does not want to say that all the religions are wrong, let alone a waste of time. But he can hardly say that they are all true. As noted, there are too many logically incompatible truth claims made. As also noted, one such truly fundamental distinction is that some religions think of ultimate reality or the religious absolute as personal in nature (e.g., the Gods of Judaism, Christianity, and Islam are "persons"), while others hold that ultimate reality or the religious absolute is impersonal (e.g., Brahman, Emptiness, the Dharma, the Tao). Hick sees his theory as a way of avoiding both naturalism (all religions are wrong) and exclusivism (all religions except mine are wrong).

The core of Hick's theory is based on a distinction that he borrows from Immanuel Kant and applies (as Kant never did) to religion. To pick a simple example, suppose that there is an apple on my desk that I intend to eat today for lunch. What I know of the apple is what Kant called the *phenomenon*; this is the apple as it appears to me. It has a certain look, smell, and taste; it is through them that I experience the apple. But there is also the *noumenon*; this is the apple as it is in itself, quite apart from how it appears to me or to anyone. Hick's point is that we never experience the noumenon and can know virtually nothing about it. All that we know is the phenomenal apple.

How does this distinction apply to religion? There is one ultimate reality (Hick calls it "the Real") that is the largely unknown and unknowable religious noumenon, and the different religions of the world are different phenomenal ways of apprehending the Real. Hick says:

> The great world faiths embody different perceptions and conceptions of, and correspondingly different responses to, the Real from within the major variant ways of being human; and that within each of them the transformation of human existence from self-centeredness to reality-centeredness, is taking place. . . . I want to say that the noumenal Real is experienced and thought by different human mentalities . . . as the range of gods and absolutes which the phenomenology of religions reports.[6]

These reports are not illusory; they are authentic manifestations of the Real. All are different but authentic ways of experiencing the Real under the influence of different human histories and cultures.

So far as the Real itself is concerned, Hick insists that we can know virtually nothing about it. We can know that it is the ground of reality and of human religious experiences. But the Real

> cannot be said to be one or many, person or thing, substance or process, good or bad, purposive or non-purposive. None of the concrete descriptions that apply within the realm of human experience can apply literally to the unexperienceable ground of that realm. . . . We cannot even speak of this as a thing or an entity.[7]

So we know very little about the religious noumenon. Beyond what has already been said, Hick will only allow that certain purely formal concepts, generated purely logically, apply to the Real. Concepts with actual substantive content apply only to the various religious phenomena.[8] But the central point is that the various religions are different and equally valid ways of experiencing the transcendent Real. None of the truth claims made in those religions is strictly true of the religious noumenon; all are phenomenally valid apprehensions of it. Indeed, Hick holds that none of the metaphysical beliefs associated with the various religions are essential to salvation.[9]

Hick also argues that the various religions have a common core: the attempt to move people toward salvation, liberation, *moksha*, or whatever term is preferred. Hick believes that the soteriological aim of all religions can be understood as the attempt to move people from ego centeredness to reality centeredness. And Hick claims that all the great religions of the world are equally good, so far as we can see, at achieving this end.

Of course not all religions are acceptable to Hick. Religions that produce immorality or cruelty (e.g., child sacrifice) are not valid phenomenological manifestations of the Real. So the way Hick suggests that we go about grading religions is a pragmatic or ethical way: we consider the point just made, viz., how good they are at producing saints or reality-centered people. Some religions probably produce more saints than others, but Hick's judgment is that all of the world's great religions are about equal on this point.[10]

Hick concludes that tolerance, cooperation, mutual understanding, and honest dialogue between people of different religions are badly needed in today's world. And that is surely true. Whether his pluralism will tend to promote those results is a good question. But that is clearly what Hick hopes for.

IV

Is Hick's theory acceptable? Should it be acceptable to Christians? Should it be acceptable to evangelical Christians? Despite Hick's best intentions, I think the answer to all three questions is no. Let me raise five criticisms of Hick's theory.[11]

1. *Religious people will fail to recognize their own religion here.* In some ways this is a strange and (some will say) unfair criticism. For Hick aims not to propose a new religion but to offer a theory in the philosophy of religion. Still, it is clear that adoption of Hick's theory will have religious implications. It does not quite leave the religions untouched. I am not thinking so much of the fact that most people in most religions are in some sense exclusivists and so will reject any version of pluralism, including Hick's. My point is more like this: suppose that as a Christian I want to affirm that God created the heavens and the earth. Hick's theory allows and perhaps even encourages me as a Christian to make that statement;

still, it is undeniable that Hick's pluralism entails that the statement is false. Indeed, virtually any truth claim made in any religion will have to be considered false, on Hick's theory. And, as I say, most religious people will want to resist that conclusion. So Hick's theory will not be greeted warmly by most religious people. What his theory must say about the vast majority of religious beliefs—that they are strictly false—is just what the atheists and naturalists have been saying.

Hick's pluralism comes to us in the guise of a purely descriptive theory about the phenomenon of religion, but it is clearly prescriptive as well. It, in effect, calls for a liberal theological revolution in the religions. On troublesome beliefs like the Christian belief that Jesus is the incarnate Son of God, Hick's theory is reductive. It does not allow Christians to hold that this is true; it is only true of the Real as apprehended by Christians; it is only (as Hick explicitly says) mythologically or metaphorically true.[12] I suspect most Christians will judge this result to be an evisceration of their religion rather than a way of respecting it. This is obviously because Christians, like virtually all religious people, are trying to make true statements about reality.

2. *Do the religions all have a common soteriological aim?* It is true that all the religions in one way or another try to address the fact that human beings are not in the optimal moral or spiritual state; and all propose some sort of recipe for moving people toward that state. But Hick goes much further—he holds that the soteriological aim of all the religions is the same: they are trying to move people from a state of ego centeredness to a state of reality centeredness, which Hick calls salvation/liberation. And this claim seems to me to be simply false. It amounts to what might be called "least common denominator religion." The Zen view of satori and the Advaita Vedanta notion of moksha seem to me quite unlike the Christian notion of the justification of human beings and their reconciliation with God. And that last theory can only be adequate if the fact is that human beings are sinners who are alienated from God and from one another. That they are in such a condition will be disputed by adherents of other religions, especially by those who hold that the deepest human problem is not sin and guilt but ignorance and the need for enlightenment.

3. *Hick's use of Kant's distinction.* Hick insists that we can know almost nothing substantive about the Real beyond the fact that it is the ground of our religious experiences. It is, as Hick says, ineffable. As noted, he says that the Real "cannot be said to be one or many, person or thing, substance or process, good or bad, purposive or non-purposive." Such a view would seem to lead to a rather robust religious skepticism or at

least agnosticism. But, interestingly, this is not where Hick goes. Indeed, there are several things that Hick confidently asserts about the religious noumenon. He affirms the following:

- it exists;
- it is the ground of valid religious experiences;
- it is the ground of all the religions that excel at producing saints;
- morally good people respond to it correctly;
- it explains religious diversity; and
- it is one.

But it is extremely difficult to see how all of this can be known about the Real, given Hick's epistemology.[13]

On the last point listed, Hick has an argument in favor of his claim that there is but one religious noumenon. It is that saintly behavior in all the religions looks pretty much the same; so it is plausible, as well as simpler than affirming a plurality of religious noumena, to say that the Real is one. Still, if the Real is actually ineffable, one cannot help but wonder whether consistency should have dictated that Hick remain agnostic on this and other points. How can concepts like *ground*, *real*, *explain*, and *one* even apply to something that is ineffable?

4. *Why should we believe Hick's theory?* Suppose that some overenthusiastic and sophomoric Kantian were to claim that (1) my desktop computer (located on my desk in my office in Pitzer Hall, Claremont) and (2) a certain panda (located at the Panda Research Center, near Chengdu, China) were two different phenomenological apprehensions of the same one noumenal reality. I presume everyone will admit that this thesis has little to commend itself to us. The two items mentioned are far, far too different for any such thesis to make any sense. There is no reason to believe the thesis and many compelling reasons to reject it.

But it seems to me that the Christian God and the Taoist notion of the Tao are also far too different from each other for such a thesis to make any sense. Indeed, I suspect that they are far more different from each other than my computer and the relevant panda are different from each other. Of course, if someone were to claim that the God of Christianity and the God of Judaism are the same, that thesis might make sense despite some obvious differences (e.g., Christians hold and Jews deny that God is a Trinity). This is because there is a clear historical connection between the two; Christians have always held that their God is the same God as the God of the Hebrew Bible.

What, then, is the evidence that Hick's thesis is true? So far as I can see, the evidence against it is overwhelming. The only evidence in its favor (if evidence is the right word) is the strong desire on the part of Hick and his supporters that it be true in order to avoid atheism and exclusivism. In some sense I suppose it is trivially true that all the religions represent different responses to the transcendent. But admitting that much does not go very far in validating Hick's pluralist theory.

5. *Is Hick's theory triumphalist?* In some sense it surely is. Hick's theory insists: (1) that all the religions are wrong in their central truth claims; (2) that the beliefs of ordinary religious people are either false, superstitious, or unnecessary for achieving reality centeredness; (3) that religious people should give up trying to make truth claims about reality; (4) that the religions at core agree in their salvific goals; and (5) that religions can be graded by ethical means. (Can Hick rule out the possibility that some religion that requires child sacrifice is the true religion? I hope but very much doubt that he can do so.)

V

It is time for me to develop my own stance on these matters. I would describe my own views on this subject as located somewhere near the border of exclusivism and inclusivism; my theory is either a fairly liberal exclusivism or a fairly conservative inclusivism. I am not particularly concerned over which category I will be said to fit in.

Let me begin with the thought that Christians do not have a monopoly on God or on religious truth. Christians can admire the spiritual wisdom and insight that is found in other religions and especially saintly people from other religions; we can learn from other religions. I myself have greatly benefited from exposure to the religions, particularly from Jews whom I have known and Jewish books that I have read. I reject the idea that all the truth worth knowing is found in Christianity and that the other religions are not worth studying. In my opinion, Christians must repent of the imperialistic attitudes that many Christians have had. Christian triumphalism—allied, as it often has been, with a sense of American or Western superiority—has manifested itself in some extremely ugly ways in the past and probably continues to do so.

I believe that God loves all people, Christian and non-Christian alike, that God reaches out to all people, and that the Holy Spirit works in other contexts than the Christian church. (As Paul argued in Romans 1 and 2, no one is totally ignorant of God; some truths about God are "written in [our] hearts.") We must treat people of other religions with respect and dignity. I will speak of evangelism later; I will just say here that Christian methods of evangelism must never be coercive or manipulative or even discourteous. We must allow people to practice their own religions freely and without interference. And we must stand shoulder to shoulder with adherents of other religions in efforts to promote justice in the world.

I also believe that our current world badly needs tolerance and acceptance between the religions. So I would highlight the need for dialogue between members of the various religions. What dialogue requires, I believe, is honesty, intellectual curiosity, and willingness to learn. *Honesty* in religious dialogue means saying what you think is true in one's own position and false in your partner's position without subterfuge or evasion. It also means openly admitting difficulties in one's own position and strengths in your partner's position. *Intellectual curiosity* means a desire to learn what your partner sincerely believes in religion, especially when it differs from what you believe. *Willingness to learn* means wanting to learn about the other religions and allowing previously unrecognized truth to emerge in the process of dialogue itself.

There are two issues on the general topic of disagreement where Hick and I part company. First, I think he holds that the mere fact that some people disagree with you on religious topics ought to make you doubt your own beliefs or at least retreat from an exclusivistic stance. But I do not think that follows at all.[14] Of course I think religious people should avoid dogmatic narrow-mindedness, but that is another matter. Second, I think Hick and other pluralists must hold that religious disagreement is the deepest problem and that if a plausible pluralistic theory could be found, those disagreements could be made to go away and a harmonious world community might ensue. Well, I, too, desperately hope for global cooperation, mutual understanding, and trust among peoples. But why say such a result can only be achieved on the basis of agreement? I would have thought that something like the reverse is true. The only way in which people of various religions and cultures can come to understand and cooperate with one another is honestly to recognize their differences. Minimizing them or subsuming them under some unifying theory is not the way forward.

So as a Christian I believe both that the supreme revelation of God to human beings is Jesus Christ and that the way in which people are reconciled to God is through Jesus Christ. I further believe that anybody who disagrees with these claims is mistaken. But I insist that there is no necessary connection between holding that Christianity is true and other religions false, and treating people of other religions in disrespectful ways. It is possible to be a tolerant, nonimperialist exclusivist.

The *locus classicus* of Christian exclusivism is John 14:6, where Jesus is quoted as saying, "I am the way, and the truth, and the life. No one comes to the Father except through me." I agree with this statement. Salvation, I believe, is found only in Jesus. That is why I reject the pluralist idea that the other religions are equally good paths to salvation. Anyone who has ever been reconciled to God, or justified in God's eyes, or saved, is saved only through the life, death, and resurrection of Jesus Christ. I do not agree that all religions are equally valid and valuable paths to salvation, nor do I think that Jesus Christ is just one among many lords, saviors, prophets, and gurus in the religions of the world. Jesus Christ is the incarnate Son of God. He is, as the villagers of Sychar in John 4 said, "the Savior of the world."

So I do not accept the idea that Christianity and the other religions are on an epistemic or evidential par. Christians recognize many confirming signs of Jesus' status—his intimate relation to God, his authority to forgive sins, his call for belief in him. But the central sign for the church has always been Jesus' resurrection from the dead. In the history of the world, other people besides Jesus have apparently been raised from the dead—some of them even in the context of other religions. I think that is quite possible; I have no problem with the idea that God can work miraculously in contexts other than the Christian context. (Naturally, that does not mean that I accept all such claims.) But like Lazarus in the Bible, these people were resuscitated; they were restored to their old manner of life, only inevitably to die a second time—this time presumably for good—at some later point. Jesus Christ was not resuscitated but resurrected; he was raised to a new level of life; he was transformed into what Paul called a glorified body; he still lives today. The resurrection of Jesus from the dead was a graphic way for God to repeat what the Holy Spirit had said about Jesus at his baptism: "This is my beloved Son with whom I am well pleased."[15]

There are many views of Jesus Christ in the world today. Moslems honor Jesus as a great prophet, but the Koran denies the resurrection by insisting that Jesus did not really die on the cross. Some people in the Christian community see Jesus as essentially a great teacher, acutely conscious of the presence of God in his life, but not the incarnate Son of God. I respect the right of Moslems to have their own beliefs about Jesus or about anything else. And I do not question the integrity of people like John Hick who disagree with me on Christology. But I reserve the right to argue against views of Jesus that I consider wrong or unhelpful to the Christian community. Jesus Christ is Lord. Jesus Christ is the way to God.[16]

Must all non-Christians then go to hell? That is the question critics always ask at this point. And in truth it is both a good question and something of a red herring. Few Christians in the history of theology have insisted that all non-Christians must end up in hell. What about Abraham or Ruth or Jeremiah? Haven't we always thought that we would see them in the kingdom of God? And isn't it absurd to think that they were Christians? Or what about people who lived and died in the interior of Borneo five thousand years ago? Must they be condemned to hell because they never believed in Christ or were never baptized?

Of course not. I have never thought that idea made any sense, nor do most exclusivists. I believe that through the grace and mercy of God some way unbeknownst to us is provided for them. There is insufficient material in Scripture or in Christian tradition to provide us with clear direction here. We cannot dogmatize. We do not know how God reaches and judges such folk. Some suggest that they can be saved on the basis of the best they know about God and the moral life. Others suggest they can be saved by a sincere desire and intention to be righteous. Still others suggest they are given a chance after death to hear and respond to God's good news. (At this point I believe that C. S. Lewis' book *The Great Divorce* has been a helpful myth for many Christians.) I myself have argued for this third option,[17] but I do not push it as the only available alternative. All we know is that God loves all persons, wants all persons to be saved (1 Tim 2:4), and that God is a God of justice. That is enough for me. I trust that God will be fair.

On the topic of religious diversity and Christian attitudes toward it, how can we distinguish between theories that are or ought to be acceptable to the Christian community and those that are not? My criterion is a practical rather than a theoretical one—it is evangelism.[18] My claim then is this: any theory that in effect minimizes, belittles, discourages, or rules out evangelism is to be rejected. In my view, all versions of religious pluralism and many versions of inclusivism do just that. We sever the vital nerve of Christian faith when we feel no urgent need to share the good news with people and convert them, if possible, to Christ. As Jesus said in what we call the Great Commission (Matt 28:19): "Go therefore and make disciples of all nations." And as Bishop Stephen Neill says (a man who is familiar with non-Christian religions), "The church cannot compromise on its missionary task without ceasing to be the church. If it fails to see and accept this responsibility, it is changing the Gospel into something other than itself."[19]

Christian pluralists almost always espouse what I consider not only a deficient Christology but also an impoverished view of revelation.[20] Indeed, it should be pointed out that differences between various Christian thinkers on the question of religious diversity always reflect differences on at least some of the more foundational theological topics, topics like the nature of God, Christology, redemption, and revelation. The Bible for most pluralists seems to be an entirely human book, in some ways religiously valuable, but possessing little in the way of theological authority. Indeed, one could almost say that for them theology has been reduced to philosophy. Little or nothing is taken as having been revealed to human beings by God, and there is no authority for theology other than human reason. Thus the recent phenomenon of global theology. This is where theologians do their work syncretistically, that is, on the basis of the best insights that they can find in any religion or tradition. John Hick is one of the foremost global theologians.[21]

I am opposed to global theology for two reasons. The first is that Christianity is a religious system (the same is true, I assume, of the other great religious traditions); it is not a set of discrete gems of spiritual wisdom from among which we can pick and choose. Second, and more important, I believe that God has been decisively revealed in human history, preeminently in Jesus Christ and foundationally in the Scriptures. I certainly think Christian theologians ought to read great works like the Koran and the Bhagavad Gita, but they ought to do their theological work primarily on the basis of what the Christian church has always taken to be Scripture.

Of course I do not hold that theology is a set of rigid and airtight propositions that pass authoritatively from one Christian generation to the next. The church must rethink theology in every age, figuring how best to be the church and to speak to the world in changing circumstances. But my deepest worry about pluralism is a pragmatic one. When crucial Christian notions are denied—notions like the incarnation, the authority of Scripture, the need for evangelism—I wonder what the result would be if such denials became prevalent in the church. Could the Christian church survive another twenty centuries? Or even twenty years?

VI

Exclusivists are sometimes accused of being arbitrary in picking out their religion, among all the other equally well-founded ones, as the true religion. They are also sometimes said to be arrogant in doing so. But the arbitrariness objection can only stick if it be granted that all the religions are epistemologically and evidentially on a par. I am unwilling to grant that point. I believe that a decisive noncircular case can be made in favor of many crucial Christian claims. As for arrogance, it is hard to see why Christian exclusivists are any more arrogant than the pluralists themselves. Both hold that their theories are true and that all theories inconsistent with theirs are false. Moreover, if crucial Christian claims are true—for example, we are all sinners and need to ask God for forgiveness—the best thing that Christians can do for both religious skeptics and adherents of other religions is tell them the truth.

Let me close with something of a confession. It is this: I am not existentially interested in the religions of the world. I am of course intellectually and academically interested in them. I have always been personally curious about them. And I think the world badly needs understanding and tolerance among the religions. But I am not interested in them existentially, that is, relative to my own spiritual enlightenment and well-being. As a longtime teacher of ancient philosophy, I can use this analogy: I admire the religions of the world much as I admire, enjoy, and respect the dialogues of Plato. I look neither to Plato nor to the religions to solve life's deepest puzzles or to provide answers to our spiritual problems. Those answers, I believe, are to be found in Jesus Christ.

8

Holocaust Theology and *The Passion of the Christ*

I

I grew up in the 1940s and 1950s. Because my mother and father were divorced when I was an infant, in effect I had two families. The family with which I spent the most time (my mother, stepfather, five younger siblings, and myself) was nominally Protestant. The other was Catholic. I cannot remember ever being taught, in either family, to hate or disrespect Jews. I do not know when I first heard the canard that all Jews were "Christ killers," but it must have been when I was old enough to recognize the absurdity of the charge, because I have never believed it. People are culpable for what they themselves do wrong—not for what other people do.

Two events motivate the writing of the present chapter. The first was the appearance in the 1970s of a way of doing Christian thinking that can be called Holocaust theology. Some of its themes still resonate in theological circles today. The second is the appearance in 2004 of Mel Gibson's movie *The Passion of the Christ.* It raised again—in powerful and passionate ways—the question of Christianity's relationship with Jews and Judaism. I want to say something in this essay about both Holocaust theology and *The Passion of the Christ.*

The present chapter is based in part on three previous essays of mine: "Evangelical Christians and Holocaust Theology," American Journal of Philosophy and Theology *2, no. 3 (1981); "The Question of Miracles, Ascension, and Anti-Semitism," in* Jesus' Resurrection: Fact or Figment? *ed. Paul Copan and Ronald Tacelli (Downers Grove, Ill: InterVarsity, 2000); and "Crucifying Jesus: Antisemitism and the Passion Story," in* After the Passion Is Gone: American Religious Consequences, *ed. J. Shawn Landres and Michael Berenbaum (Walnut Creek, Calif.: AltaMira, 2004).*

Some thirty years ago, a small but influential group of Christian theologians in the United States began to do theology under the influence of Jewish thinking and the Holocaust. They were convinced—as I am—that Christians ought to think long and hard about the theological and religious implications of that event. Some such theologians proposed what can only be called radical revisions in Christian thought.

For example, some seemed to regard the Holocaust as a kind of theological absolute, almost as if it were on a par with divine revelation as a basic datum of Christian theology.[1] Others held that the traditional God of Christianity died in the Holocaust or at least, less metaphorically, that given Auschwitz, it is no longer rationally possible to believe that God is both all-powerful and perfectly good.[2] Some even suggested that in the light of anti-Semitism and the Holocaust, Christians must give up themes that are offensive to Jews, for example, the notion that Jesus is the Messiah or the notion that Christians ought to engage in evangelism.[3]

As a fairly orthodox Reformed Christian, I am frankly attracted to none of these proposals. But I do want, if possible, to think sensitively and clearly about Judaism and the Holocaust from the perspective of Christian evangelicalism. It is my aim to do so in the present chapter.

II

Many theologians who reflect on the Holocaust single out for criticism the traditional Christian notion that Christianity succeeds or supercedes or fulfills Judaism. Christian successionism comes in many forms, and I agree that some of them are unacceptable. However, I do hold and am not prepared to give up the notions that (1) Jews were once God's sole elect people and that Christians are now chosen too, and (2) all people should believe in Jesus.

Do these propositions entail that Judaism is a religious relic, that it has been nullified, that it had no *raison d'être*, that Jews no longer have any standing before God and should have disappeared? Apparently Franklin H. Littell thinks so. In *The Crucifixion of the Jews*, he argues that "the cornerstone of American Antisemitism is the superseding or displacement myth." This myth, he says, "already rings with a genocidal note," having "murderous implications which the murderers will in time spell out."[4]

Most evangelical Christians would find these remarks by Littell not only false but outrageous. In the first place, they do not accept that the notion that Christianity succeeded Judaism is a myth. In the second place, they will point out that there is no necessary connection whatsoever between believing in successionism and being an anti-Semite, let alone a condoner of genocide. Anti-Semitism and genocide are both about as contrary to Christian ethics as anything is. In the third place, it does not follow from successionism, as I have defined it, that there is no longer any justification for the existence of Judaism. St. Paul argues in Romans 9–11 that Israel has a continuing role to play in God's redemptive plan, and evangelical Christians follow Paul in affirming that it is so. Furthermore, as we all know, for understandable reasons most Jews find it psychologically impossible to believe in Jesus. This being so, I believe they should continue to practice Judaism. In the fourth place, we cannot hold Paul and other "successionist" biblical writers morally guilty of the later murder of Jews even if it is true (which can certainly be doubted) that theological successionism helped motivate the later murderers. The crucial point is that Paul and the others had no intention of supporting genocide, nor any reason to suspect that their words might later be used to support genocide.

Jews should not expect Christians, even given their desire for good relations with Jews, to surrender crucial Christian notions. Some revisionist Christians seem to be eager to do so, but orthodox Christians will not. What such folk must say to Jews, then, is, I imagine, something like this: "We love you as Jews and not just as candidates for baptism; we affirm your freedom to believe and practice Judaism without any sort of coercive interference from us; we will cooperate with you and stand shoulder to shoulder with you in areas of agreement (e.g., opposition to anti-Semitism), but we believe that Jesus is the Messiah and Son of God and that those who deny it are mistaken."

III

The Christian church has been guilty of many egregious faults throughout its history. One of the worst, if not the very worst, is its complicity in anti-Semitism. I understand the term "anti-Semitism" to mean prejudice against Jews that expresses itself in hateful attitudes, hateful words, and immoral actions. The Old Testament makes clear the fact that active hatred of Jews antedates Christianity. Nevertheless, it cannot be denied that the record of Christian attitudes toward and treatment of Jews is, at its best, mixed indeed. By our own admission and even insistence, Christians are fallible people, capable of evil. Sadly, one area where we have exercised that capacity for evil is in our relations with Jews.

Despite the arguments of certain Jewish thinkers and Christian Holocaust theologians, I reject the claim that the New Testament is anti-Semitic. Let me explain why.

Most of the New Testament was written when it was becoming clear that there would be an irrevocable split between Christianity and its disapproving parent or elder sibling, Judaism. Accordingly, there is a great deal of anti-Judaism in the New Testament. (I define "anti-Judaism" as theological or religious disagreement with Jews or Judaism.) There was less anti-Judaism in the earliest years of the Christian movement, before any decisive break had occurred between the early Christians and the Jewish theological establishment. As the Christian movement expanded, it attracted increasing numbers of non-Jews; simultaneously, antagonism between Jewish Christians and mainstream Judaism continued to grow. Eventually the Christian movement, suffering repudiation and even persecution, became an alternative (and a highly disapproving one) to the rabbinic Judaism that developed after A.D. 70. As such, much of the New Testament is highly critical of those forms of Judaism that reject Jesus.

But it would be a priori surprising if the New Testament contained much anti-Semitism (as opposed to anti-Judaism), since most of its authors were themselves Jews. I believe that it is often tacitly assumed that since the New Testament (along with the Hebrew Bible) is the church's Scripture, the New Testament is a Christian book. In one sense, that is certainly true: its writers all saw themselves as followers of Jesus of Nazareth. But the New Testament is also largely a Jewish book. Craig Evans rightly points this out:

> It is surprising how many fail to perceive the oddness of the assumption that the New Testament and early Christianity were anti-Semitic. Should it not strike us as hard to explain how a first-century Jewish sect, centered around a revered Jewish teacher thought to be Israel's Messiah, God's Son, and fulfillment of Israel's scriptures, within one generation of its founding could mutate into an anti-Jewish, perhaps even anti-Semitic, movement? Surely this is improbable. I suspect that scholars have unconsciously and uncritically read the New Testament through the eyes of the patristic church, which, sad to say, did give vent to anti-Semitic expressions.[5]

Certainly there is material in the New Testament that anti-Semites can twist in order to buttress their anti-Semitism. For example, Jesus' attack on "the scribes and Pharisees" in the Synoptic Gospels is scathing indeed (Matthew 23), but it does not necessarily constitute an attack on Pharisaism per se, let alone on Jews or Judaism. Indeed, it has all the earmarks of a conflict within Judaism rather than an exercise in anti-

Semitism. It is similar in tone to criticisms that we find, for example, in the oracles of the prophets Amos or Jeremiah, criticizing the Judaism of their day. Jesus himself was, of course, a Jew, and he never appears to have doubted the covenant with the patriarchs, the election of Israel as God's chosen people, the divine authority of the Hebrew Bible, or the appropriateness of temple worship.[6] He saw himself as fulfilling, rather than negating, the law and the prophets (Matt 5:17).

Much as the apostle Paul criticized the Jews who rejected Jesus and (as he saw it) misinterpreted the Mosaic law, he remained until his death a Jew, proud of his heritage, training, and status as a Jew (2 Cor 11:22; Phil 3:4-6; also Acts 25:8; 26:5; 28:17). He regarded as irrevocable both Israel's privileges (the covenants, the law, adoption as God's people, the promises, etc.) and Israel's responsibilities, such as being a light to the Gentiles (see especially Rom 9:4-5; 11:2-29).

One passage is often singled out by those who hold that Paul was anti-Semitic. Speaking of the suffering Judean Christians, Paul says:

> You suffered the same things from your own compatriots as they did from the Jews, who killed both the Lord Jesus and the prophets, and drove us out; they displease God and oppose everyone by hindering us from speaking to the Gentiles so that they may be saved. Thus they have constantly been filling up the measure of their sins; but God's wrath has overtaken them at last. (1 Thess 2:14-16)

The language here is polemical and even reveals a degree of anger. But it amounts to a theological argument, and an intramural one at that. There is no national, ethnic, or racial hatred here. Paul never turned against the Jewish people or his own Jewish heritage.

The Fourth Gospel uses the term "the Jews" in different ways. At times it refers to the entire Jewish nation or to a specific group of Jews, especially where Jewish customs are being explained (John 2:6, 13; 3:1, 25; 4:9, 22; 5:1; 6:4; 7:2; 12:9, 11, etc.). Elsewhere, it refers to Jesus' enemies, those who plotted against him (John 5:15-18; 7:1, 13; 9:18, 22; 10:31-33; 18:14, 36, 38; 19:7, 12, 14, 38; 20:19, etc.).[7] So it is possible to develop a mistaken interpretation of the evangelist to the effect that the entire Jewish nation was somehow responsible for the death of Jesus, which was not his intent at all. Notice also Jesus' affirmation in his conversation with the Samaritan woman that "we [Jews] worship what we know" and that "salvation is from the Jews" (John 4:22).

The content and limits of Christian Scripture were set long ago. Obviously, there is no way that I have, or would ever want to have, the authority to change anything in them. But I confess that one text has always troubled me. This is the "blood curse" of Matthew 27:25, where the crowd shouts to Pontius Pilate, "His blood be on us and on our children." I myself believe that Matthew included that statement in his account of the trial because he believed that it had actually occurred.[8] I make no judgment at this point on that. But in the light of the horrible implications that this statement has had in Jewish-Christian relations, I have often wondered whether history might have been less harsh for the Jews had Matthew not included that statement in his account.

However, we hardly can blame the New Testament writers for later anti-Semitism or even genocide, since they did not intend to support either, nor had they any idea how their words might later be twisted. In the end, the charge that the New Testament is anti-Semitic is anachronistic and unhistorical. It is based on the erroneous practice of subjecting first-century writings to categories and ideologies that developed later, some of them much later. It is also based on the practice of holding earlier writers culpable for the ways in which their words (whether innocently or not) were later misinterpreted and misused to help produce unfortunate events.

IV

But quite apart from the Bible, what about Christian anti-Semitism? Let's begin with this question: are all Jews, including Jews today, responsible for Jesus' crucifixion? Of course not.[9] Certain Jews of Jesus' day must apparently bear considerable responsibility for that crime, but so must certain Romans. Crucifixion was, after all, a Roman punishment determined and carried out by Romans. In the New Testament passion accounts themselves, the responsibility for Jesus' death seems to be spread far and wide. One of Jesus' own disciples betrayed him; certain Jewish leaders plotted against him; most of his followers either denied him or abandoned him; the crowd mocked him; Pontius Pilate sentenced him to death; and Roman soldiers brutalized and crucified him. I think the Gospel writers (as well as Paul, writing before them) want us to understand that we—all of us, Jew or Gentile, Greek or barbarian—are responsible for his death. Their view is that he was dying for us.

Thus, to claim that the whole Jewish nation was responsible is ridiculous; to claim that all Jews, even those who were born afterward, were responsible is perfectly absurd. The claim would not even be worth commenting on except for the sad fact that there have been people who have accepted it. Perhaps there are occasional events where the shadowy notion of "collective moral responsibility" for a crime makes some sense, but certainly not here.

Much has been made by Holocaust theologians of the *Adversus Judaeos* tradition in Christian theology, especially the anti-Jewish polemic of some of the church fathers. Certainly there are statements made by the Fathers that are wrongheaded and mistaken—not to mention ill-advised in the light of later events. Here again we find points where the church must plead guilty of anti-Semitism. But while we cannot condone the excesses of the Adversus Judaeos tradition, perhaps we can understand its existence. The earliest Christians were Jews and wanted to make no break with Judaism. When they were later forced by events to see the Christian movement as quite separate from Judaism, it was natural that they and their spiritual descendents tried to work out the meaning of Christianity in terms of its opposition to Judaism. A crucial factor here was Jewish persecution of the earliest Christians (1 Thess 2:14-16), who like European Jews during the Holocaust, were largely powerless. And although Christianity's early competition with and persecution by Judaism led certain Christians to regrettable excesses in polemics and theological mistakes, it is also perhaps understandable that the early Christians felt a strong need to establish the superiority of Christianity over its disapproving parent, Judaism.

But we can hardly blame the New Testament writers and church fathers for failing to foresee the future. Unfortunately, their words can be used by later anti-Semites; we (knowing what we know) would rather in places that they had expressed themselves differently. There are things said by some of the Fathers and later theologians (Luther particularly) that can be considered anti-Semitic. But we can hardly blame them for later acts of genocide.

Is Christianity *necessarily* anti-Semitic? Certainly not—or not, at least, if it can be agreed that it is not necessarily anti-Semitic just to disagree with Jews. Few Jews will agree that Jesus is the Messiah and Son of God and that it is God's will that all people believe in him. But belief in these claims hardly commits one to anti-Semitism. However, in her book *Faith and Fratricide* (New York: Seabury, 1974) Rosemary Ruether pointedly asks, "Is it possible to say 'Jesus is Messiah' without, implicitly or explicitly, saying at the same time 'and the Jews be damned'?" She goes on to argue that the real root of Christian anti-Semitism is Christology; the higher the view of Christ, she says, the more the anti-Semitism. "The anti-Judaic root of Christianity cannot be torn out until the church's Christology is rid of its negation of the ongoing validity of the Jewish faith."[10] "Anti-Judaism," Ruether says, "developed theologically in Christianity as the left hand of Christology. That is to say, anti-Judaism was the negative side of the Christian claim that Jesus was the Christ."[11]

But surely Ruether's point is not to be taken seriously—not, at least, at face value. There just is no necessary connection between holding a high Christology and being an anti-Semite, that is, someone who is actively prejudiced against Jews because they are Jews. Surely there are far too many counterexamples to that notion for it to be at all believable. American fundamentalists—christologically orthodox to a fault—are among the strongest supporters of the nation of Israel. Strong American Christian supporters of the Palestinian cause—at least the ones whom I know—all seem to be members of mainstream denominations where christological orthodoxy seems less prevalent.

Moreover, if the connection that Ruether detects did exist, we would be entitled to ask why an even worse Holocaust than the 1939–1945 event did not occur during the medieval period or some other period of virtually universal christological orthodoxy. What is true, probably, is that some anti-Semites used Christology as an ideological support for anti-Semitism. But there appears to be no good reason to believe that Christians can only avoid anti-Semitism by abandoning their orthodox view of Christ.

In general, it is difficult to show that historical forces and events have hidden theological causes. Despite this point, I am far from denying that Christian anti-Semitism helped make the Holocaust possible. I am sure that it did. Nevertheless, let me propose a hypothesis that, like Ruether's, is extremely difficult to prove but which seems to me more plausible. I shall state the point radically: I have often wondered whether the genocide of the Holocaust was not merely the partial result of Christian anti-Semitism but also of nineteenth-century liberal criticism of the Old Testament.[12] That is, the Christian church was severed from its Jewish roots, and the door was opened to the extermination of the Jews because biblical criticism convinced people that it was no longer possible to believe in (1) the divine authority of the Hebrew Bible, (2) the absolute nature of the Old Testament law, and (3) the uniqueness of Jews as God's chosen people. Jews became merely a dispensable residue. Once these three points are rejected, perhaps anti-Semitism and even genocide can become more thinkable than they might otherwise have been.[13]

It is sometimes suggested that, in a curious way, Christianity depends on the existence of Judaism and even anti-Semitism, as if Christianity somehow cannot survive without Jews around as enemies or at least as "existing others." What an absurd idea! Anti-Semitism is not only not essential to proper Christian belief and practice, it is contrary to them. There are doubtless many Christians who have no idea who Jews are or even that there is any connection between the people of the Bible and the

Jews of today. Notice, too, that Christianity thrives in many parts of the world, for example, Africa and Korea, where there are few if any Jews. Perhaps the argument that Christians need anti-Semitism is more subtle than this, but it is not clear to me how the argument could be presented in such a way as to turn out at all plausible.

In one sense, it is surprising that there has existed such a sorry history of Christian anti-Semitism, since that ideology is so obviously contrary to Christian teachings. It is an essential part of the Christian ethic that we are to love all people, even our enemies, and forgive those who sin against us. Thus Jesus said:

> You have heard that it was said, "You shall love your neighbor and hate your enemy." But I say to you, Love your enemies and pray for those who persecute you, so that you may be children of your Father in heaven. (Matt 5:43-45)

> Peter came and said to [Jesus]: "Lord, if another member of the church sins against me, how often should I forgive? As many as seven times?" Jesus said to him, "Not seven times, but, I tell you, seventy-seven times." (Matt 18:21-22)

> I say to you that listen, Love your enemies, do good to those who hate you, bless those who curse you, pray for those who abuse you. If anyone strikes you on the cheek, offer the other also: and from anyone who takes away your coat do not withhold even your shirt. Give to everyone who begs from you; and if anyone takes away your goods, do not ask for them again. Do to others as you would have them do to you. (Luke 6:27-31)

Moreover, even the apostle Paul, who, as we have seen, was capable of speaking strongly against his fellow Jews who rejected Christ, firmly believed that God's covenants with Israel still stand, that Christians are like a branch grafted on to the vine of the Jewish people, and that Jews have a continuing role to play in the redemptive purposes of God (Romans 9–11).

Since anti-Semitism is not the same thing as disagreeing with Jews (I take it that, at important points, all Christians do that), I will make a bold statement: anyone who practices anti-Semitism is not practicing Christianity.[14]

V

Were Christians responsible for the horrors of the Holocaust? Well, the question is ill-formed and cannot be answered precisely until a distinction is made. The word *Christian* can mean many things, as we all know. I believe that Jews often use the term quite broadly, that is, as a synonym or near-synonym for the term *Gentile* or, better, *Western* (i.e., non-African and non-Asian) *Gentile*. Here virtually any non-Jewish and non-Muslim Caucasian citizen of Europe or the Americas is a "Christian." But in this sense of the word, to speak paradoxically, not all Christians are Christian. A second way of using the word *Christian*, then, is: "an active and serious follower of Jesus Christ," or something of the sort.

Were Christians responsible for the Holocaust? In the first sense of the word *Christian*—what we might call a "cultural Christian" as opposed to a "committed Christian"—the answer is obviously yes. Does Christianity have anything to do with the fact that certain cultural Christians committed acts of murder and genocide? This is a complex question. The Hitler regime, as we all know, was a pagan regime, strongly opposed to Christianity, and its leaders were not committed Christians. Many Christians died in the Holocaust. The Nazis, in fact, seemed bent on destroying all who confessed an absolute moral alternative to Hitler—God for Jews, Christians, and Jehovah's Witnesses; history for Marxists.

Nevertheless, the main victims of the Holocaust were Jews, and it is fair to conclude that historic attitudes toward Jews fostered in the church did play a role in the success of the Nazis in achieving their ends. Here, I believe, the church must plead guilty. These attitudes distort true Christian teachings, to be sure, but they existed, nonetheless. The culturally Christian anti-Semites who did Hitler's work were able to do so with relative ease and impunity in part because of (1) anti-Semitic attitudes sanctioned by the church; (2) idolatrous nationalism approved of by virtually all Western Christians, cultural and committed; and (3) the silence of many committed Christians in the face of genocide.

Were committed Christians responsible for the Holocaust? For the anti-Semitic attitudes that many of them had, yes. For their silence in the face of mass murder, yes. But were any active and serious followers of Jesus Christ murderers? Here I must say no (although, as I will admit, my argument for this conclusion is somewhat circular). It is impossible for any sane person to reconcile Christianity with genocide. Here I recall a statement sometimes made by postwar Germans—that there were no intelligent and moral Nazis. There were intelligent Nazis, it is said, but they were not moral. There were moral Nazis, but they were not intelligent. People who had both a strong sense of right and wrong and who were intelligent enough to grasp the implications of Nazism did not become Nazis.

I have no idea whether this statement is true. Perhaps it is merely an exercise in self-justification by postwar Germans. But I do not believe that any intelligent committed Christians were murderers. Naturally, a great many people bear some responsibility for the Holocaust, including some committed Christians. And I confess that it will take me a very long time to understand how a committed Christian can be an anti-Semite. It is depressing indeed for a Christian to contemplate the case of Poland, the most Christian nation in Europe. By all accounts, it was also the most anti-Semitic. Again, there are points where Christians must plead guilty of sins against Jews.

In *A Jew Today*, Elie Wiesel says, "In Auschwitz all the Jews were victims, all the killers were Christian." He goes on to say, "As surely as the victims are a problem for the Jews, the killers are a problem for the Christians."[15] There is a sense in which Wiesel is profoundly correct here. But again there is a problem with the word *Christian*. Wiesel's statement and the sensitive and pointed questions that he addresses to "Christians" in many of his works, could much better be made on the basis of some clear thinking about the meaning of the word *Christian*.

In the First Epistle of John we find the following words: "Those who say, 'I love God,' and hate their brothers or sisters, are liars; for those who do not love a brother or sister whom they have seen, cannot love God whom they have not seen" (4:20). And: "All who hate a brother or sister are murderers, and you know that murderers do not have eternal life abiding in them" (3:15). My own view, then, is that anybody who claims to be a committed Christian and commits murder has shown that he or she is not a committed Christian. I recognize that there is a certain circularity in my argument—"Were any committed Christians murderers? No, because no committed Christian can be a murderer"—but nevertheless I stand by it.

VI

One undoubted area of tension between Jews and Christians is evangelism. Throughout much of its existence, Christianity has been a missionary faith; its adherents believed strongly in trying to convince others to become Christians. Recently, at least in the mainline denominations in the United States and Europe, Christianity seems to have lost its missionary fervor. But that would not be true of evangelical Christians. Such folk—along with many nonevangelicals, of course—still believe in and practice evangelism.

It is easy for Christians to understand Jewish sensitivities at this point. In the first place, many Jews are for understandable reasons quite hostile to Christianity. In the second place, evangelism directed at Jews represents a threat to the continuing existence of the Jewish people. Naturally, many Jews are suspicious of and strongly opposed to anything—genocide, mixed marriages, secularization, or evangelism—that tends to reduce the number of Jews in the world. Accordingly, some theologians, including Reinhold Niebuhr, have proposed that Christians abandon any further attempts to convert Jews.

But such a proposal will not be acceptable to evangelicals, who consider themselves still under the biblical mandate to "Go and make disciples of *all* nations, baptizing them in the name of the Father and of the Son and of the Holy Spirit" (Matt 28:19, emphasis added). We should not favor singling out Jews as a special target group more important than other non-Christians, nor should we favor any deceptive or coercive or discourteous methods of evangelism. But evangelicals will insist that they be free to preach the gospel to Jews as well as other people and will doubtless continue to do so. Christianity, they believe, loses its essence and vital force when Christians cease to feel the need to evangelize.

VII

Christian hatred of Jews has often centered on the Passion Narrative in the four canonical gospels. Accordingly, that story is painful for Jews to hear, and a film about it—especially a movie by a talented and famous filmmaker—inevitably will raise Jewish concerns.

Let me briefly return to those revisionist Christian theologians mentioned above who seem prepared to edit, revise, or even jettison important Christian claims if somebody alleges that they promote evil. The evils usually mentioned are: slavery, patriarchy, imperialism, militarism, and anti-Semitism. Some of the usual suspects for the cause of such evils in the world—especially anti-Semitism—are Christian practices like evangelism and Christian beliefs like "Jesus is the Messiah," "Jesus is the Son of God," or "Jesus' death paid the penalty for our sins."

My only point here is that the vast majority of Christians—Catholic, Protestant, and Eastern Orthodox—are not prepared to follow the revisionist path. All Christians recognize that the passion story raises Jewish suspicions and fears, and for understandable reasons. But most Christians are quite unwilling to jettison the passion and death of Jesus as crucial cornerstones of our religion. Moreover, Christians certainly are entitled to give their version—even in a movie—of what happened during Passion Week.

One aspect of the theological revisionism of which I speak is this: certain Christian theologians, clergy, and laypersons no longer seem to accept the theological necessity for any kind of atonement for sin, and especially not any kind of atonement that involves sacrifice, substitution, or suffering. In their understanding of Christianity, they tend to place much greater emphasis on the teachings of Jesus and the example of his life than on his death. So it is no surprise that many of these more liberal Christians today place little theological emphasis on the passion story. Accordingly, many of them were shocked and horrified by Mel Gibson's movie. To them, what they saw was just meaningless violence. So it is hard for me to imagine that many liberal Protestants, for example, approved of the film.

Evangelical and other theologically orthodox Christians—the people for whom I am trying to speak in this essay—are not at all inclined to deemphasize the life and teachings of Jesus. But most of them are convinced with the church fathers that the passion, death, and resurrection of Jesus give meaning to what precedes those events in the Gospels, rather than vice versa. The very idea of atonement seems gory and premodern to many of our contemporaries. However, most Christians see the atonement accomplished by Christ as much in line with teachings in the Hebrew Bible. (See, for example, the institution of the sin offering in Leviticus 5 and of Yom Kippur in Leviticus 16—both of which involved sacrifice.) Whether it accords with our modern tastes or not, it appears to most Christians that God has chosen to associate atonement with sacrifice and the shedding of blood. Indeed, the writer to the Hebrews can say: "Without the shedding of blood, there is no forgiveness of sins" (Heb 9:22). Thus the Christian tradition that Jesus was "the Lamb of God who takes away the sin of the world!" (John 1:29). Jesus was not just a guru but a savior.

VIII

Is Mel Gibson anti-Semitic? Is his movie anti-Semitic? In the runup to *The Passion of the Christ*, I saw in print many questions about it:

- Is the film anti-Semitic?
- Is the filmmaker anti-Semitic?
- Is the film capable of causing Jews pain?
- Is the film capable of reinforcing or legitimating anti-Semitism?

Having seen the movie and having seen an interview with the filmmaker, I am inclined to believe that he is not anti-Semitic, and I hold that the movie is not anti-Semitic. Still, other people—people whom I respect—reacted otherwise. It is almost as if we saw two different movies. Perhaps the essential problem is, as noted, that the symbol of the cross means very different things to Jews and Christians, as well as to orthodox and revisionist Christians.

But with regard to *The Passion of the Christ,* I am quite sure that the answer to my third and fourth questions is yes. That is, I am sure that the film caused Jews pain. And I suspect that the film was capable of reinforcing already-existing anti-Semitism in those who already hate Jews. If that happened, it was unfortunate indeed. As we all know, though, almost anything can reinforce stereotypes and hatreds of that kind. This is not to deny the fact that as human beings, we must sometimes be responsible not only for what we say but for how what we say is likely to be heard. I suspect that rational people will disagree about whether Mel Gibson satisfied that duty.

Unless signs mislead, anti-Semitism has been increasing in the world in the past few years. But I do not think the passion story in the Christian Bible is behind this new anti-Semitism. Indeed, I suspect that little of it is driven by Christianity. Far more of it, in my opinion, is driven by the far-reaching implications of the Arab-Israeli conflict and by political and religious extremism in the Islamic world. Still, I do not deny for a moment the duty of Jews—and all morally sensitive people—to be constantly on the watch for anti-Semitism. As I write this essay, we are only sixty-two years past the Holocaust, and it had nothing to do with Arabs or Islam.

When I saw *The Passion of the Christ,* my criterion for testing it was this question: was the basic message of the film political or spiritual? Judging by his public statements, Gibson himself seemed to hope that his movie would cause people to examine themselves and ask to what extent they are guilty, because of their sins, of making the crucifixion of the Son of God necessary. On the other hand, if you think the film explicitly or implicitly urges viewers to take up sides against those evil people the Jews—and I do not think that it does—then you are justified in regarding it as an anti-Semitic movie.

Like many viewers, I found the unremitting violence of the movie numbing. Gibson, I believe, was trying to depict the sufferings of Jesus as fully and graphically as the medium of cinema allows. One can disagree with various decisions Gibson made about what to include and what to exclude in the film, and how to interpret what he included, but my own view is that most of his choices can be defended. I did not especially resonate with the devilish children who taunted Judas, with the hideous baby carried by Satan, or with the raven that pecked out the eye of one of the thieves on the cross. But I found the portrait of Mary and of her sufferings moving. In the "pieta" scene at the end, when she stares into the camera, that is, at those of us who are viewing the movie, in my heart I heard her saying, "Look at what you have done." I also appreciated the incisive picture of Simon of Cyrene, who moves from outrage at being forced to carry the cross to determination to bear it and profound sympathy for the one who was to die on it. The flashbacks to the institution of the Eucharist at the Last Supper were also highly meaningful to me, since, as an ordained Presbyterian minister, I often have repeated Jesus' words. And there is no denying—well, *I* cannot deny—that the movie constitutes a spiritually gripping portrayal of the agonies that Jesus endured for our sake. In sum, I cannot say that I enjoyed the film, but I learned from it and am glad I saw it.

That all human beings—Jews and Gentiles alike—are complicit in the death of Christ is Christian teaching. But the idea that the Jews as a people ought to be hated or singled out for punishment is contrary to Christian teaching.

IX

The picture that emerges thus far is quite clearly that there are points where evangelical and other orthodox Christians are less willing than most Holocaust theologians to accommodate Jews. Will the position that I have outlined here be acceptable to Jews? I do not know. Very possibly it will not. While most evangelicals are sensitive to the evils of anti-Semitism and are determined to do their part in preventing future holocausts, they are unwilling to make theological decisions on the basis of Jewish approval or disapproval. Most of them will continue to believe in some form of successionism and in the messiahship of Jesus whether Jews like it or not. Jews ought to recognize that fact—indeed, I think most of them do (better than Holocaust theologians do).

But let me close on what I take to be a note of agreement between Jews and Christians, viz., their opposition to a common enemy. Following Jacob Bronowski, let us call this enemy "push-button philosophy." In a chapter near the end of *The Ascent of Man*, Bronowski introduces a discussion of Auschwitz and the Holocaust in the following way:

> There are two parts to the human dilemma. One is the belief that the end justifies the means. That push-button philosophy, that deliberate deafness to suffering, has become the monster in the war machine. The other is the betrayal of the human spirit: the assertion of dogma that closes the mind, and turns a nation, a civilization, into a regiment of ghosts—obedient ghosts, or tortured ghosts.[16]

Standing beside a pond at Auschwitz into which the ashes of its victims were flushed, Bronowski says:

> I owe it as a scientist to my friend Leo Szilard, I owe it as a human being to the many members of my family who died at Auschwitz, to stand here by the pond as a survivor and witness. We have to cure ourselves of the itch for absolute knowledge and power. We have to close the distance between the push-button order and the human act. We have to touch people.

I am not sure that I understand everything Bronowski was saying here, nor do I wish to suggest that he would agree with the interpretation that I shall place on "push-button philosophy." Nevertheless, I believe he saw something that is utterly crucial in a discussion of the Holocaust and of relations between Jews and Christians. Let us define push-button philosophy as the point of view that holds: (1) the end always justifies the means, and (2) decisions about human affairs are to be made solely on the basis of considerations of power and cost efficiency. Concepts like human rights, justice, the will of God, or morality are excluded as irrelevant.

Unless all signs mislead, push-button philosophy, like an insidious cancer, is growing in influence. It has grown by leaps and bounds since the 1940s, when the Holocaust occurred, and even since the 1970s, when Bronowski wrote. I believe it was pushbutton philosophy, and not Christian values, that led to the Holocaust. Whether or not Jews will agree with me on that point, two things are clear. First, both religious traditions oppose push-button philosophy. Second, members of both traditions are potential victims of it. Here Jews and Christians alike are outsiders. On this issue, which is perhaps the most important moral issue of our time, we ought to stand together.

9

Is the God of Process Theology a Valid Option?

I

I came to Claremont as a graduate student in philosophy in 1966 and started teaching full time at (what was then called) Claremont Men's College in 1970. I soon learned that Claremont was the world center of Process Theology (PT), a way of doing Christian theology that is based on the thought of Alfred North Whitehead. Charles Hartshorne, a disciple of Whitehead, is also an important source. John Cobb and David Griffin were longtime colleagues of mine. I have been widely (and correctly) perceived here in Claremont as an opponent of PT. Despite that fact, I have always felt that Whitehead's philosophical system is one of the most brilliant intellectual accomplishments of the twentieth century. And one thing that I have always appreciated about Process theologians is their emphasis on rationality, rigor of argumentation, and logic. In a time when many other theologians seem not to espouse such ideals, the Process emphasis is badly needed.

There have been several occasions over the years in which I have interacted with Process thinkers, usually in conferences or at presentations here in Claremont. I have always enjoyed such events, and it has been stimulating to think about the rebuttals to my arguments against Process thought that have been offered by Cobb, Griffin, and others. I do not claim to be able to refute Whitehead's philosophical system (although I disagree with it), but I think

Much of the present chapter is taken from my "Why God Must Be Unlimited," in Concepts of the Ultimate: Philosophical Perspectives on the Nature of the Divine, *ed. Linda J. Tessier (London: Macmillan, 1989) and from my contributions to Davis, ed.,* Encountering Evil, *2nd ed.*

I can make cogent points against PT, that is, against the application of Process philosophy to Christian thought. So far as the concept of God is concerned (there are other points as well where I would part company with PT), I will try to do so in the present chapter. I will argue that the Process God is not a valid option for Christians.

My argument will go as follows: first, I will ague, contrary to PT, that Christian theology and practice need an unlimited God. Second, at the level of pure metaphysics, I will explain why I prefer what I call the Aristotelian ontology to the Process ontology. Third, I will defend the notion of creation out of nothing from criticisms offered by Process theologians. Finally, I will raise criticisms of PT on the problem of evil.

II

For people who believe in God, the question of what God is like is obviously crucial. What are God's attributes? How should we describe God? One of the most important such questions is whether God should be described as limited or unlimited.

One way to begin a discussion of this point is to note that there seems to exist a fairly broad consensus on what we might call criteria of divinity, that is, conditions that a being must satisfy if it is to be divine or worthy of worship. It seems that in order to be God, a given being must be: (1) very powerful (far more powerful than human beings); (2) the creator of the heavens and the earth (although there are various notions of what is meant by "create"); (3) everlasting (this term, too, is interpreted in various ways); and (4) loving, compassionate, gracious, and morally good. Beyond these points, however, Christians differ on many other questions about the nature of God. One of them is the question whether we ought to speak of God as *unlimited.*

Let us define this term in a relatively simple way. That is, let us say that an unlimited being is one that is not bound by causal constraints. Such a being might still be bound by logical constraints and so will be unable to do things like create a married bachelor or bring it about that the sum of 6 and 5 is 13. But such a being will be quite unrestrained by the causal or natural laws that prevent human beings from doing things like parting the waters of the sea or raising the dead. One difficulty with this way of understanding the term *unlimited*, however, is that only power is taken to be relevant. Possibly what makes a being unlimited is more than just omnipotence—perhaps maximal degrees of knowledge, wisdom, goodness, and so forth must be required too. But thinking of unlimitedness in terms of unlimited power will suffice for our purposes on this occasion.

I want to argue, in three ways, that the concept of an unlimited God is much preferable, both philosophically and theologically, to that of a limited God. My first way of doing so is to argue that it has been revealed by God that God is unlimited. It surely seems to me that there is ample scriptural material that would naturally lead those who hold to any even fairly robust view of scriptural authority toward a theory that God is unlimited, at least in power. For example, Job says of God, "I know that you can do all things, and that no purpose of yours can be thwarted" (Job 42:2). And the psalmist says, "Our God is in the heavens; he does whatever he pleases" (Ps 115:3). Jeremiah says to God, "Nothing is too hard for you" (Jer 32:17). Jesus says, "For God all things are possible" (Matt 19:26). And Paul speaks of "the immeasurable greatness of [God's] power" (Eph 1:19).

But in the current theological context, there are severe difficulties that such an argument would face. For one thing, the Bible is not a work of philosophy of religion or even of systematic theology; few and perhaps none of the biblical writers faced the precise question we are here exploring ("Is God limited or unlimited?"). Thus their writings—so it might be said—are not particularly helpful in the present context. For another, the Bible notoriously can be and is interpreted in a great variety of ways. Texts that might be quoted on one side or the other of the debate can always be interpreted in other ways. Finally, at least some of those who would argue on behalf of a limited God do not particularly care *what* the Bible says; accordingly, an appeal to revelation will not impress them. Thus David Griffin says, "The results of the historical-critical approach to the Bible that have been carried out in the past two centuries make it very difficult to consider it (the Bible) an external guarantee for any particular doctrines.[1]

III

A second way of arguing on behalf of the idea that God is unlimited is to offer criticisms of "limited God" notions, such as those that are found in PT. For example, there is a nagging problem that is faced by limited-God theologians that in my view has never been solved.[2] The difficulty appears most clearly (but not only) in discussions of the problem of evil. On the one hand, the theodicy project of limited-God theologians will only succeed if God is sufficiently impotent to make God (in Griffin's words) "not indictable" for the evil that exists; God must be weak enough to be incapable of unilaterally preventing evil from existing. On the other hand, the question then emerges whether a being who is this impotent is

God or is worthy of our worship. Such a being can surely be pitied for the fact that things have turned out so badly in the world. God is working very hard to bring about a better world but does not seem to be getting anywhere. Evil runs rampant.

Power, of course, is not the only criterion for worthiness of worship. An omnipotent moral monster (like Descartes' "Evil Genius") would not merit our worship. But power surely is one of the relevant criteria—we would also be disinclined to worship a morally perfect being who was about as powerful as a typical human being. As a matter of horseback sociology, it seems to me that limited Gods work best and appeal most in time of high-flying optimism. The idea is that "we will all work together with God to make a better world." But in times of pessimism and even despair like ours, where the vast majority of us feel able to do precisely nothing to prevent the world's destruction, limited views of God seem to me to produce only a kind of melancholy desperation.

Those who defend limited views of God will doubtless want to reply to this criticism. The first move they typically make is to ridicule the idea of omnipotence or the worship of power per se.[3] But of course, as noted, the worship of power per se is not what I am recommending. They also stress that their God is worthy of worship in virtue of both God's moral goodness and the persuasive power God in fact has (power, for example, to lure the universe toward greater value). But it is still true that their God is quite unable to do things like part the waters of the sea or bodily raise the dead.

Finally, they argue that the sort of persuasive power their God has is the highest degree of power that any being can possibly have. But this argument turns out to depend on a questionable assumption, viz., that all power must be shared, that all actual beings have power of their own over against God. But why is it logically impossible for God to have all the power? And even if we grant (as I am unwilling to do) that it is metaphysically necessary that every actual being must have power of its own over against God, the much stronger claim that God cannot directly deflect speeding bullets or moving automobiles does not follow from it. In Whiteheadian thought, this is said to follow because God's power is persuasive only, and in "aggregational societies" like bullets and automobiles there is no dominant member (like the mind or brain in humans) for God to persuade. But why say that God's power is only persuasive? It may be true both that every being has power of its own over against God and that God can, whenever God wants, overcome that power.

The notion that God possesses all the power and voluntarily shares it with the creatures seems to me perfectly conceivable. Indeed, I believe it is true. But even the much stronger picture entailed by a rigid and all-encompassing predestinarianism seems a possible picture. Perhaps, contrary to appearances, God has all the power and shares none of it; perhaps every action apparently taken or decision apparently made by X is really taken or made by God. There are theologies that come close to saying something like this. I do not myself hold that this picture is a true picture, but it is surely a possible picture. And if so, the traditional concept of omnipotence is coherent, and a limited God still seems unworthy of worship.

Omnipotence is essential to Christianity. The God of traditional Christianity can create the stars, part the waters of the sea, heal people of diseases, and even raise people from the dead. But the God of PT cannot heal people of cancer or deflect moving rocks, bullets, or automobiles from their paths. David Griffin admits that God cannot influence inanimate objects at all. Again, while I do not recommend the worship of power per se (an omnipotent scoundrel would not be worthy of worship), I believe the God of PT to be nowhere near powerful enough to merit worship. Could a sick person rationally pray to such a being for healing?

IV

My third way of arguing on behalf of the notion that God is unlimited hits some of the same notes; it is to argue for that point on pragmatic or practical grounds. To be "religiously adequate," it could be said, God must be unlimited as opposed to limited. Perhaps such arguments are of limited value because of the obvious fact that people differ in their notions of "religious adequacy." Nevertheless, I will suggest one such pragmatic argument here; we can call it the "petitionary-prayer argument."

To be religiously adequate, I claim, God must be the sort of being to whom it makes sense to address petitions. Surely that will be granted by all Christians. And I will argue further that God is not God and is not religiously adequate unless God is in a position to hear and grant our petitions. That, too, will perhaps be allowed. But what sorts of petitions? Here is where I will make a claim that limited-God theologians will not allow. I want to suggest that no God is worthy of worship and is religiously adequate unless granting the following sorts of petitions is within God's power:

- petitions for healing from disease (not just psychosomatic disease);
- petitions for forgiveness of sins (even heinous sins);

- petitions for deliverance from death, that is, for eternal life;
- petitions for prevention of the world's destruction.

Naturally, I do not say that a religiously adequate God is under obligation to *grant* all such petitions; my point is just that such a God must be able to do so. Otherwise, God is not God or at least is not worthy of the worship, love, and obedience that Christians believe we owe God. As noted above, this sort of argument is subject to severe limitations. One such limitation is that it will convince few of those who defend conceptions of limited Gods. Such people can always deny that these sorts of petitionary prayers make sense anyway. Asking God to heal your father of his apparently terminal cancer makes about as much sense as asking God in 2007 to bring it about that nuclear weapons were never invented, or so it could be said. Nevertheless, I find the petitionary-prayer argument convincing and am prepared to defend it. It is, I think, a strong argument against limited-God theologies—their Gods are just not able to do all the things asked for.

Must God be unlimited (as defined earlier) in order to be able to grant such requests? Surely so; God has to be free of the causal constraints that prevent human beings themselves from bringing about the things that they pray for. Moreover, I am willing merely to stipulate that in my view any God who can grant the sorts of petitions mentioned above is unlimited (in its power, in any case) in the religiously relevant sense of that term. Such a God will be acceptable to me, as long as this being also possesses the other properties mentioned in the fifth paragraph of this chapter.

A much larger point—one that is not limited to petitionary prayer—is involved here. To be religiously adequate, it would surely seem that God must be able to accomplish God's purposes. But if God is limited in power, then quite possibly there are not only prayers that God will not be able to answer but creatures that God will not be able to control and divine aims that God will not be able to achieve. If God is limited in power, then neither God nor we who worship God know whether God's purposes, aims, and hopes for the world will be fulfilled. To put the point bluntly: there is no good news in the news that God is trying hard and might just succeed. Of course, this argument (like the petitionary-prayer argument) does not show that it is logically impossible for a limited God to exist. What it shows, I claim, is that limited Gods are religiously inadequate and provide little good news for those who worship them.

As I have noted, there are difficulties with each of the arguments against a limited God that I have presented. The argument that God's unlimited nature has been revealed by God faces the problems that the Bible can be variously interpreted and that at least some of those who believe in a limited God do not particularly care what the Bible says. The objections that I raised against the notion of a limited God may be subject to cogent replies. And the petitionary-prayer argument will only be impressive to those who agree with me that the sorts of petitions that I listed make sense, and few believers in a limited God will so agree.

Nevertheless, I am prepared to defend each of these three ways of arguing that God must be unlimited in power. The notion of an unlimited God is, I believe, the best way of capturing what Christians find out about God both in Scripture and in the tradition. Such a notion is indirectly supported by the difficulties that plague limited-God theologies. And it, unlike them, seems religiously adequate.

V

Next I will offer a purely metaphysical criticism of Process ontology. I do not see this point as a refutation of Process thought, but it certainly constitutes one central reason why—again, at the level of pure philosophy and not theology—I reject it. Whitehead's view entails that the ultimate units of reality are not enduring substances but momentary events. Let's call this theory the *Process ontology*. An event, let us say, is a real change in a thing or a relational change between things. The alternative to this view I will call the *Aristotelian ontology*. It claims that reality ultimately consists of substances or things.[4] A thing, let us say, is an enduring object that has properties, relations, and an identity apart from other things.[5]

Now a question: which metaphysical viewpoint is intellectually superior as the basis of a worldview? Perhaps it is impossible to say whether reality ultimately consists of events or things. Or maybe the question itself is incoherent or ill-formed or in some way intellectually untoward. Or maybe in some contexts one perspective is more heuristically promising than another; which we opt for may well depend on which context we are in.[6] Still, I want to press the question: which ontology is true overall or in the long run has more explanatory power or is more intellectually promising as the foundation of a worldview?

For three reasons, I find the Aristotelian theory superior. Let me explain why.

First reason: do the events that Process philosophers consider metaphysically ultimate endure for certain finite amounts of time? If they do not, then they are merely limits or boundaries, like Euclidian points, and it is difficult to see how any sort of reality can be made of them. A set of boundaries of reality does not create or consist in any sort of reality. But if events do endure (and Whitehead did hold that actual occasions have duration), they can have attributes and relations just like substances, and indeed are substances, just in virtue of being enduring property bearers. So we have not avoided substances as ultimate after all.

Second reason: on the assumption that Aristotle was correct in his belief that substances persist through time (have more than just momentary existence), it is possible to explain what a thing is without mentioning or presupposing events. But it is not possible to explain what an event is without mentioning or presupposing things. That is, we can identify and individuate things by means of their properties and relations; we can only identify and individuate events by means of the things to or about which the events occur. More simply, things can exist without events (there are possible worlds in which only immutable things exist); events cannot exist without things. Ergo, things are more ontologically ultimate than events.[7]

Third reason: unlike the first two, it is more theological than purely metaphysical. As I understand Christian theology, God must be basic, and the world, with its events, secondary. I illustrate (but do not argue for) this point by means of the words of Genesis 1:1: "In the beginning God created the heavens and the earth." (This is an illustration rather than an argument, because I am not here discussing the thorny question of whether creation out of nothing is implicit in these words; I will briefly consider that point in the next section.) My simple point here is that the first *thing* is God and the first *event* is God's creating the heavens and the earth. God, the thing, existed (metaphysically if not temporally) prior to the act of creation. Ergo, things are more ontologically basic than events.

VI

PT importantly denies the traditional Christian notion of creation out of nothing. This is for two reasons. First, in Whiteheadian metaphysics, the notion that God once existed all alone makes no sense. God has always existed in company with the other two Whiteheadian ultimates that he calls "Creativity" and "Eternal Objects." (I will not pause to explain these terms or how they are said to work together with God to bring about the world.) Second, in Process solutions to the problem of evil (which I will discuss more fully in the next section), it is important that creation out of nothing be denied. For the Process theodicy requires that God's power be limited both by the uncreated, preexistent material out of which God fashioned the world and by the built-in power over against God that every actual thing has. So whenever the subject comes up, Process theologians attack the idea of creation out of nothing.

But I want to affirm the notion. So in this section, I will mount a brief defense of the doctrine against the kinds of criticisms that Process theologians typically raise.[8] Let me make five points.

First, I agree that the words "creation out of nothing" do not appear in Genesis[9] or anywhere in the Bible and that the doctrine is not explicitly taught in the Bible. That fact ought not be particularly surprising; the biblical writers were not metaphysicians or even systematic theologians. But the doctrine does seem to be presupposed, implied, or strongly suggested in several biblical texts, for example, Psalm 90:2 (God alone is everlasting); Isaiah 44:24 (God needed no help in creating); 45:18 (God created the heavens and the earth); John 1:3 (all things came into being through God); Romans 4:17 (God calls into existence things that do not exist); 11:36 (all things are from God); Colossians 1:16 (in him all things in heaven and on earth were created); Hebrews 11:3 (what is seen was not made out of visible things). Process theologians will deny that these texts imply creation out of nothing, and many non-Process theologians agree with them. Regrettably, I have no space to prove this point, but the plain sense of these and other biblical texts indicates that this is so.[10]

Second, the doctrine of creation out of nothing is implied both in the biblical notion of the power of God (for whom "all things are possible" and "nothing is impossible") and in the biblical notion of the absolute lordship and sovereignty of God over the world, that is, the absolute dependence of the world on God. The world was created in time and exists only because of the freely exercised will of God; God alone is everlasting.

Third, the doctrine is a virtually unanimous aspect of the Christian tradition from early theologians (e.g., Hermas, Theophilus of Antioch, Irenaeus, Origen) until today.

Fourth, there is no suggestion in Genesis 1:1 (however the verb *bara* is to be interpreted) of any preexistent "stuff" that was not created by God and that God depends on in creation. The argument that I am inclined to give from Genesis 1 does not concern lexical issues but rather the fact that God creates with a kind of effortless ease, that is, by merely speaking the word (cf. also Ps 33:6-9).[11] This point puts Genesis 1 in strong contrast with most of the other creation stories from the ancient Near East. There is no hint of any long and laborious struggle to construct the world out of resisting preexistent stuff.

Fifth, it is possible, pace Griffin, rationally to believe in creation out of nothing without holding that God is the source or cause of literally everything. God was not the cause of the last sin that I committed, for example (although I could not have committed it without God's permission).

VII

David Griffin solves the theodicy problem by making God weaker than classic Christianity does. But such a move will suffice only if God is so weak as to be unable to destroy truly wayward worlds, or at least quietly put them out of their misery. Otherwise, obviously, God would be indictable for not so dealing with wayward worlds. But if God does not possess the ability to do so, then God is hardly worthy of worship.

Griffin makes a distinction between apparent evil and genuine evil. He stipulates that "genuine evils" are "occurrences that make the universe worse than it might have been, all things considered."[12] This definition does indeed imply, as Griffin argues, that those theists who hold that all evil helps lead to a greater good deny that "genuine evil" exists. They implicitly affirm that all evil is only apparent. But it is important to notice something here. It may well be true to say, of some heinous event, both that it makes the universe worse than it might otherwise have been (i.e., that God will not use it causally to produce a greater good) and that God in the end will nevertheless produce a greater good. This, indeed, is my own view: genuine evil (as Griffin defines it) exists, but God's policy of creating a world where such events can and do occur will turn out best.

But my deepest reservation about PT's theodicy is that it is not strongly eschatological. I do not believe that the problem of evil can be solved without crucial reference to the future. Thus in response to Griffin's view that God aims, intends, seeks, works, and tries to overcome evil, we must ask: does God have the power, influence, or persuasive ability to make the divine intentions succeed? If God might not succeed (and this is what Process thinkers must say; they cannot be sure but can only hope that God will emerge victorious), then, again, God is not worthy of worship. God is a good being who works hard; we can sympathize with and perhaps even pity God. Some of us will choose to fight on God's side in the battle against evil, and we can all hope that God will win. But I see no reason to worship such a being.

In a sense, God ran a risk in creating this sort of world. But was the risk worth taking? Most Christians believe it was. They believe God foresees the future of the world, that is, the coming kingdom of God, and they believe God has revealed that the risk was worth taking. But in Process thought we do not know whether the risk was worth taking, for we do not know how the world turns out, and neither does God.

Griffin hints that he believes in eternal life, but clearly eschatological concerns play little role in his theodicy. He says he cannot imagine that present and future evil is so bad as to make it better that human life had never been created. Is Griffin saying that the intrinsic goods that now exist are so great that they outweigh any evil events that might occur in the future? It would seem an exercise in Pollyanna optimism if so. What if ten years from now all human beings die, cursing God, after years of horrible physical and mental suffering? Will God's great adventure have turned out worthwhile? I hardly think so. At this point orthodox Christianity seems far more realistic. Good events do indeed occur—so it declares—but the power of evil is pervasive. The world is not worthwhile as it stands: it needs to be redeemed.

So even if we grant PT its view of the power of God (which I am unwilling to do), it still follows that God is indictable for creating the world if in the end evil outweighs good. The God of PT reminds me of a mad scientist who fashions a monster whom the scientist hopes will behave but whom he cannot control. If the monster runs amok, the scientist's decision to make the monster will turn out to have been terribly wrong. The scientist will be indictable.

VIII

My conclusion is that the God of PT is not a valid theological option for Christians. The church should continue to affirm that only God is everlasting; that the world was created in time; and that God created it out of nothing.

10

Is Theological Nonrealism Dangerous?

I

Most of us who believe in the existence of God made our peace long ago with the fact that there are intelligent and moral people who do not believe in God. We also know that some of these same people wish to retain certain aspects of the religious life. If Don Cupitt belongs in this last category (and I believe he does), there is nothing here so far that is particularly threatening to believers in God. But what does seem grotesque is Cupitt's implicit suggestion that his views are superior to belief in God for purely religious reasons.

The stakes here are high. Cupitt's thesis is not a matter of abstruse technicalities at the theological margins. This is an issue about which Christians—scholars and laypersons alike—will care deeply.

Let me offer three criticisms of Cupitt's paper.

II

The first concerns what we might call rhetorical method. Cupitt has an objectionable tendency to offer what I can only call absurd parodies of positions he opposes. It is almost as if being an orthodox Christian, or a religious realist of

The present essay is a response to an essay of Dan Cupitt's called, "Anti-Realist Faith," in Is God Real? *ed. Joseph Runzo (London: Macmillan, 1993). My response, in the same volume, was titled, "Against 'Anti-Realist Faith.'" Since Cupitt has written many books and essays since 1993, I should note that the present chapter (a slightly revised version of my essay for the book) constitutes a critique of Cupitt's thinking as expressed in "Anti-Realist Faith" and* His Taking Leave of God *(London: SCM Press, 1980).*

any sort, is an exercise in sheer buffoonery. I take the term "realism vis-à-vis X" to be the view that X exists (or does not exist) independently of beliefs about X. "Realism vis-à-vis God," then, is the view that God either exists or does not exist quite independently of what anyone believes about God. But as Cupitt depicts realism, it entails all sorts of bizarre intellectual baggage—most of which would only startle most realists.

For example, according to Cupitt, realism entails that (a) there are unchanging and invisible essences; (b) there is an invisible higher world beyond this world, which our language describes; (c) meaning is a spirit being that inhabits a word; (d) mind is a spirit being that inhabits a body; (e) a law of nature is a spirit principle that controls events by pulling them with invisible wires; and (f) there are three (rather than the standard two) modalities of truth—"true," "necessarily true," and "absolutely true."

Now perhaps there are realists who hold such views, but not all realists do or logically must. In fact (a) some realists believe in invisible essences, and some do not (not all realists are Platonists); (b) some realists posit an invisible higher world and some do not; (c) I cannot think of anyone—realist or nonrealist—who reifies meaning (a spirit being that inhabits a word) in the way Cupitt describes; (d) some realists are Cartesian dualists, but some tend toward physicalism; (e) most philosophically inclined folk these days realize that natural laws are descriptive rather than coercive. The law of gravity, for example, does not pull apples toward the center of the earth—it describes the fact that in our experience, when left unsupported near the earth, apples always fall toward the center of the earth. Lastly, (f) I do not know what Cupitt's term "absolutely true" means. I think I have a fairly good grip on what it is for a statement to be "true"; I also think I know what it is for a statement to be "necessarily true." But the modality that Cupitt repeatedly criticizes throughout his paper ("absolutely true") is mysterious to me. At the very least, Cupitt needs to tell us what it means and how it differs from the other two modalities.

Religious realism, Cupitt says, includes or entails that (a) Christianity is a timeless, coherent, and pragmatically immutable system of thought; (b) the oldest version of the faith is the purest; (c) biblical and Christian language has timeless, transcultural meaning; and (d) God's language isn't real human language. As a result of religious realism, Cupitt says, Christianity has become barbarous ("locked into truly frightful excesses of power and guilt, cruelty and sentimentality").

But it surely seems possible to produce versions of religious realism that contain none of these items. Aquinas, Schleiermacher, Barth, and Tillich all seem to me to be religious realists who would embrace few or none of them. I count myself a religious realist, and I would embrace precisely none of them (although I do of course hold that Christianity is coherent).

The point is that religious realism is not nearly so ridiculous a specimen as Cupitt implies. In order to demonstrate its implausibility, one must refute realism's most plausible versions, not just the absurd ones. A person can be a Christian realist without being committed to any of the picturesque caricatures that Cupitt dismisses.

III

My second criticism is that I believe Cupitt's position is self-stultifying, that is, it refutes itself. Suppose I were to make the statement, "I am unable to produce a sentence of English." That statement would be self-stultifying. So would be the position of someone who claims to know that "Nothing whatever can be known."

Cupitt describes sympathetically a position that he calls perspectivism; this is apparently the theory that we cannot know how things are but only how they seem to us. But does he think perspectivism is *true*? If it is true, then in one important respect we *can* say how things are, namely that we cannot know how things are but only how they seem to us. Thus, perspectivism is self-stultifying. But if perspectivism is not supposed to be true but rather is itself only one among the available perspectives—it is merely somebody's point of view—then why should nonperspectivists take perspectivism seriously? What Cupitt must do, in this case, is provide a reason why they should do so, an argument that involves no truth claims about perspectivism.

Similarly, Cupitt says, "There is no single grant overarching dogmatic truth any longer." I do not claim to know precisely what this statement means, but I do wonder whether Cupitt considers it true. Does he think this very statement is itself the grand overarching truth that we must now respect? His paper certainly gives that impression. "There cannot be any absolute descriptions of what is going on," Cupitt also says. Again, I am not sure what the word *absolute* means here—perhaps it just means "true." But the position that there cannot be any true description of anything (involving, as it does, a purported true description of something) refutes itself.

Later in the paper Cupitt allows that antirealism is not "the metaphysical truth of the human condition." "No one vision of things," he admits, "can any longer be compulsory." But then we naturally wonder what epistemological status antirealism is supposed to have. If it is just one among many perspectives, why should realists take it seriously? In another passage, however, Cupitt seems to argue that religious realism is not only false but necessarily false. "Religion," he says, "is historical and cultural all the way through." And then he adds, "it could not have been otherwise." The point is that Cupitt's position is either self-stultifying, that is, cannot consistently be held, or else is open to objections along these same lines to which he owes readers an answer.

IV

My third criticism concerns the question of the essence of religion. One of the most intriguing aspects of Cupitt's position (and one that I suspect puzzles many laypersons) is that, despite his views, he goes right on practicing religion. The answer, I think, is to be found in that line of Cupitt's paper where he says, "the goal of the religious life is a spiritual state that is beyond all the symbols." So if spirituality (understood as a certain sort of psychological state) is the goal and heart of religion, then, obviously, one can be a nonrealist or even an atheist and still be religious. Indeed, one of my friends—a practicing Zen Buddhist—is an atheist, and his level of spirituality is, I believe, higher than mine.

I cannot disprove Cupitt's contention that spirituality precedes doctrine and is what really matters in religion. I can, however, lay on the table my own view. The essence of Christian faith is not a kind of spirituality to which God is logically and causally and (so to speak) teleologically dispensable. It rather concerns a call from God that we respond appropriately to the love of God as it is revealed preeminently in Christ. "Man's chief end," as the Westminster Shorter Catechism of 1647 beautifully says, "is to glorify God, and to enjoy him forever."[1] So God—by which I mean a being whose existence is independent of anybody's views about God—is essential to Christian faith.

The point is that the basic issue is belief in God. So anyone who wants to evaluate the turn Cupitt's theology has taken in recent years must begin by asking: did God create us or did we create God? Those who believe we created God and that, accordingly, there is little point in being religious will be atheists. Those who believe we created God but that there is still value in being religious will follow a path like the one Cupitt has marked out. Those who believe that God created us and that our highest duty as human beings is to glorify God will be religious realists who will strive to live lives of worship and service.

This chapter is titled "Is Theological Nonrealism Dangerous?" My own view is that it certainly is dangerous. The danger is that people who read the writings of its defenders might come to hold that God is dispensable to Christian faith. That outcome would be tragic indeed.

11

Resurrection and Eschatology

How Are They Related?

I

Christian eschatology presupposes a linear view of time. On circular views of time, as are found in many ancient and tribal cosmologies, history endlessly repeats itself, no one event or person has eternal significance, and history is mythology. Following its parent, Judaism, Christianity holds instead that human history and the creation itself are moving in a certain direction. As St. Paul says, in a crucial but often overlooked line, "Salvation is nearer to us now than when we became believers" (Rom 13:11). We are moving toward a goal or *telos*, in which history will come to a dramatic end, a final apocalyptic battle between good and evil will be fought, God will emerge triumphant, and a limitlessly good end state will exist. We can refer to this end state as the kingdom of God or the eschaton.

A distinction should be made between two sorts of eschatological theories: An individual eschatological theory holds that there is life after death for human beings, and it describes our postmortem fate. A cosmic eschatological theory holds, like Christianity, that all of creation and history are moving toward a goal and typically describes what will occur at the end of history. It is important to note that it is possible to have one sort of eschatological theory without the other. Plato, for example, argued strongly in several of his dialogues that human souls survive death, but he offered little or nothing in

The present chapter is a slight revision of an essay of mine titled "Eschatology and Resurrection" that appeared in The Oxford Handbook of Eschatology, *ed. Jerry L. Walls, 384–98 (Oxford: Oxford University Press, 2007).*

the way of a cosmic eschatology. Karl Marx, on the other hand, did not believe in individual survival after death, but offered a cosmic eschatology that involved inevitable historical progress toward the overthrow of capitalism and the advent of the classless society. Christianity, like many religions, offers both an individual and a cosmic eschatology.

The focus of the present chapter is resurrection. This concept is firmly embedded in Christian teaching and is crucial to the entire Christian plan of salvation, including eschatology (1 Cor 15:12-19). In this chapter, we will discuss four afterlife theories and their relationship to eschatology. Then we will examine Christian teachings about resurrection, both the resurrection of Jesus and the resurrection of everybody else (the "general resurrection"). Four quite different ways of understanding the general resurrection in classical and current Christian thought will be contrasted. We will then emphasize the fact that the Christian notion of resurrection has virtually always been bodily resurrection. This point is important because recently several theologians have argued for a notion of resurrection that is nonbodily or "spiritual." Then we will discuss two important objections that have been raised against Christian teachings about resurrection. Next we will consider the negative eschatological views of those cosmologists who hold that the universe, in its distant future, will pass out of existence from heat death or freezing. We will ask whether Christian eschatological theories are viable in the light of such predictions. Finally, we will discuss the relationship between resurrection and what has been called "the beatific vision."

II

Is there life after death? If so, what happens to us after we die? These sorts of questions have always been of vital interest to human beings. There appear to be four main answers.

(1) Death ends all. Death is the complete and final end of our existence as human beings. The atoms of which our bodies consist may continue to exist after we die; our lives may be remembered by people of the future; our descendents may carry our genes to the future; we may even be able in our lifetimes to contribute to the overall progress of the human race. But there is no life after death in the sense of continuing, conscious existence as individuals. "Death ends all" theories obviously deny any individual eschatology but may (as with Karl Marx) or may not (as with the ancient Greek philosopher Epicurus) offer a cosmic eschatology. Obviously, people who accept such theories spend little time talking about the next life; their efforts are normally directed toward arguing that

the prospects for life after death are dim and toward drawing implications from that point for how we ought to live our lives here and now.

(2) Reincarnation. At death our bodies die and permanently disintegrate, but some essential and immaterial aspect of us (a soul or mind or "jiva") continues to exist. At some point, it is reborn into and animates a new human (or, on some theories, nonhuman) body. The process continues for a very long time or even (on some theories) eternally. The status and station in life of each incarnation is a karmic function of its moral and religious behavior in previous lives. Reincarnational theories obviously offer an individual eschatology, involving continued incarnations until (at least in some religions) salvation or enlightenment is achieved. This escape from the cycle of life, death, and rebirth can be conceived in various ways; in Advita Vedanta Hinduism, for example, the goal is oneness with Brahmin. Apart from the idea of the undifferentiated unity of all things, reincarnational theories typically offer little in the way of cosmic eschatology.

(3) Immortality. At death our bodies die and permanently disintegrate, but an immaterial aspect of us called the soul or mind lives on forever (with no further bodily incarnations in this world) in an immaterial world. The idea is that souls quite naturally survive death; no divine miracle is required. It is important to note that the theory posits not just that the soul is indestructible but that it is the essence of the person; the real Jones is Jones' soul, not Jones' body. Otherwise, what survives death will be only one aspect or vestige of Jones, but not Jones. This theory, which is usually called "immortality of the soul," was strongly defended by Plato and Kant, as well as by other philosophers and thinkers, especially in the nineteenth and early twentieth centuries. Such a theory obviously offers an individual eschatology (our souls will go on living after death) but not necessarily (and not usually) a cosmic eschatology.

(4) Resurrection. The last theory to be mentioned, and the one with which we will be centrally concerned, is bodily resurrection. On this theory, at death our bodies disintegrate, but on some future day God will miraculously raise them from the ground, constitute us again as living persons (the same individuals whom we were on earth), and bring about the eschaton. In Christian thought, the idea is not (as immortality says about souls) that human bodies naturally (so to speak) resurrect after death. The claim is rather that bodily death would mean permanent annihilation for human beings apart from God's miraculous intervention.[1] But resurrection and immortality of the soul have a complex relationship in Christian thought, which we will discuss in more detail below.

III

Christianity has always envisioned resurrection as coming in two stages: first there is the resurrection of Jesus, which occurred on Easter morning in (most probably) A.D. 29 or 30; then, in the eschaton, the general resurrection occurs. Indeed, the New Testament is clear that Jesus' resurrection is the promise or guarantee or "first fruits" of our resurrection (Rom 8:11; 1 Cor 15:20, 23; Phil 3:20-21; 1 Thess 4:14; 1 John 3:2). So the ability of Christians to defend the plausibility of the general resurrection in the eschaton depends in part on their ability to defend the plausibility of the resurrection of Jesus. Such an effort would require, among other things, dealing with two crucial issues that will not be discussed here, viz., Hume-like arguments to the effect that belief in miracles is never rational; and the concerns of biblical scholars about the New Testament evidence in favor of the resurrection of Jesus, especially the reliability of the empty-tomb tradition and the appearance traditions.[2]

As noted, in Christian thought resurrection and immortality have a complicated relationship. Most Christian theologians from the second century onward in effect combined the two in a theory that we can call *temporary disembodiment.* Its basic claim is that when I die, my body disintegrates, but my soul continues to exist; for an interim period of time I exist in the presence of God as a mere disembodied soul; then on one future day, God will raise my body, reunite it with my soul, and constitute me a whole and complete person again. During the interim period, my soul is conscious and can engage in such mental activities as thinking, believing, remembering, intending, hoping, etc., but cannot engage in bodily activities like eating, talking, or taking a walk. This is, then, taken to be a highly attenuated and limited type of existence. Aquinas accordingly argued that no person in such a state can attain complete happiness. That must await the resurrection.[3]

Temporary disembodiment was seen by Christian thinkers as being consistent with biblical teachings and especially Pauline thought. It also provides a neat way of reconciling Paul's notion that the general resurrection will not occur until the eschaton (1 Cor 15:20-26, 52; 2 Thess 2:1-15) with Jesus' promise to the good thief who was crucified with him, "*Today* you will be with me in paradise" (Luke 23:43). The solution is that the thief's soul would be present with Jesus in paradise immediately after his death but that his body would not be raised and reunited with his soul until the eschaton.

A second theory of the general resurrection (and very much a "minority report" of Christian theologians), is called *soul sleep.* This theory agrees with temporary disembodiment in that there is an interim period between one's death and the general resurrection and that during that period one exists as a mere soul. But its distinctive feature is that during the interim the soul is said to be in an unconscious state ("asleep"). It is difficult, however, to make a convincing scriptural case for soul sleep (Heb 12:23; Rev 6:9-11), and the possibility of disembodied, conscious existence is already necessarily accepted by Christians because God is a conscious spirit (John 4:24) (in whose image human beings were made). Moreover, many Christians hold that soul sleep is inconsistent with the spirit of Jesus' aforementioned words to the good thief on the cross, as well as with such texts as Philippians 1:23 and 2 Corinthians 5:8.

A third theory of the general resurrection is one that has yet to be fully spelled out by theologians but seems to be a possible implication of the views of those contemporary Christian thinkers who are committed to some version of materialism or physicalism vis-à-vis human beings. We can call this theory *temporary nonexistence.* The essential idea is that during the interim period between my death and the general resurrection I do not exist at all. In the eschaton, when God raises my body, I will come back into existence.

The metaphysical theory known as *materialism* entails that the only thing that exists is physical matter in its various permutations; few Christians are attracted to this theory, since, as noted, God is held to be a nonphysical being. But some contemporary Christians are attracted to materialism vis-à-vis human beings, which theory holds that we are essentially identical to our bodies. There is no immaterial soul or mind.[4] This theory, too, is a minority opinion, even among contemporary Christian philosophers, and needs further exploration before its value (or disvalue) for Christian thought can be fully assessed.

A fourth theory is also available to Christian materialists; we can call it *immediate resurrection.* On this theory, there is no interim period, because at the moment of death, God raises the body and reconstitutes the person. Since there is no temporal gap, the problem of personal identity seems at first glance less intractable than on other theories. However, there are two serious difficulties for immediate resurrection. First, although there are biblical texts that can be interpreted as supporting this theory (e.g., Luke 23:43; 2 Cor 5:1-10), the preponderance of New Testament testimony is that the general resurrection will occur in the eschaton. Second, the continuing presence of the corpse or remains (in the grave or in the form of ashes) presents a problem. If materialism is true, it seems that Jones is identical to or is essentially constituted by Jones' body; but when Jones dies, it then seems that Jones is simply Jones' corpse. If so, any new Jones-like body that God might create will apparently be (not Jones but) a duplicate of Jones.[5]

Let us return to temporary disembodiment. This basic picture—which has definitely been the view of most Christian theologians who write about the topic—was strongly challenged in 1956 by influential New Testament scholar Oscar Cullmann.[6] He radically separated the two theories and argued that only resurrection is a genuinely Christian notion. Immortality of the soul, he claimed, is an alien concept. It was imported from Greek philosophy by certain church fathers, played no role in biblical or primitive Christian conceptions of the afterlife, and ought not to be part of Christian thinking about the afterlife today.

There is something profoundly correct and something wrong here. Cullmann is surely right to distinguish between the two theories. As noted, defenders of immortality hold that surviving death is a natural property of souls, while defenders of resurrection usually hold that human persons quite naturally live no longer after death but only do so if God miraculously intervenes. Immortality holds (at least in its Platonic versions) that the body is the intrinsically evil prisonhouse of the soul; resurrection holds that both body and soul were created by God and so are intrinsically good until corrupted by sin, and that accordingly both need to be redeemed. Immortality recognizes death as a good thing (at least, as Plato says, for the philosopher) because it means escape from the body; resurrection sees death as a frightening enemy that must be defeated. Immortality must be based on the philosophical theory known as *mind-body dualism*, while resurrection, although it is normally based on the same theory (and temporary disembodiment must be) need not be. As we have seen, resurrection based on an entirely physicalist notion of human beings is quite possible.

But perhaps Cullmann was too hasty in rejecting any notion of immortality as unchristian. Surely the traditional and Thomistic notion of the bodiless interim state can easily be purged of the problematic aspects that Cullmann correctly sees in Platonic and other versions of immortality. The life after death of even the soul can be attributed to a gracious and miraculous act of God. Moreover, it can be affirmed that souls as well as bodies are corrupted by sin and need to be redeemed. And death can still be seen as an enemy. Finally, if the idea of the interim period populated by conscious souls be rejected, it suddenly becomes much more difficult for those who hold that the general resurrection will occur in the eschaton to understand Jesus' promise to the good thief.

IV

It is important to establish the point that Christian theories of resurrection—both God's raising of Jesus some twenty centuries ago and of all others in the eschaton—are *bodily* theories of resurrection. That resurrection is "of the flesh" has been a virtually unanimous aspect of Christian teaching from the first century onward. But in recent years several theologians have found attractive the idea of "spiritual resurrection."[7] Their basic claim seems to be that Jesus' *body* was not raised (it might still be decomposing in the tomb) but rather his person or self. The theory is almost never spelled out philosophically; no proposals are made in the area of what philosophers call the mind-body problem or the problem of personal identity. One naturally thinks of immortality here; perhaps the implicit idea is that Jesus' mind or soul was raised, quite apart from his body. But the trouble with that idea is that few scholars want to argue that Platonic or Cartesian dualism is the Bible's implicit theory of human nature. So the notion of "spiritual resurrection" remains at the level of a vague suggestion. However, those who push the concept of the spiritual resurrection of Jesus also usually turn the idea into a theory of the general resurrection. We, too, will be raised in this way: our persons, our selves will be resurrected, but not our bodies.

The motivation for such a theory seems to be twofold. First, some theologians who endorse this idea have grave doubts about the tradition in the four gospels that Jesus' tomb was found empty on Easter morning (bodily theories of Jesus' resurrection virtually require an empty tomb), as well as grave doubts about "physical" motifs in the resurrection-appearance stories (e.g., that Jesus walked, ate, was touched, etc.). Second, these same theologians argue that Paul's notion of a "spiritual body" (1 Cor 15:44) constitutes a denial of bodily resurrection. They always cite Paul's claim: "Flesh and blood cannot inherit the kingdom of God" (1 Cor 15:50). (One also wonders whether a desire to deemphasize the miraculous aspects of the Easter story in the New Testament, or a desire to render it immune to the acids of historical-critical scholarships, plays a role in the development of this theory.)

It is important to note that Jesus' resurrection was not a mere resuscitation. Let us define *resuscitation* as the restoration of a clinically dead human being to her former life. As thus defined, resuscitations not infrequently occur in hospitals these days, and there are apparent cases of resuscitation in the Bible too, for example, Jesus' raising of Lazarus (John 11:1-44). The crucial distinction is this: when a person is resuscitated, that person must inevitably die a second time at some later point, and on that occasion, death would presumably be final. But the Christian claim is not that Jesus was resuscitated, but rather that he was resurrected. He was transformed into a new and exalted mode or condition of life fit for the kingdom of God. He still lives today and will never die.

As for the arguments in favor of spiritual resurrection, doubts about the dating, consistency, and reliability of the New Testament accounts of the empty tomb and the resurrection appearances can be answered.[8] And Paul's notion of a "spiritual body" means a transformed body or perhaps a supernatural body, not a nonphysical body. The preresurrection body, he says, is dishonorable, weak, and subject to decay and death, while the transformed body is honorable, powerful, and immune to decay and death (1 Cor 15:42-44). When Paul says, "flesh and blood cannot inherit the kingdom of God," he is not saying that a body (the very term Paul uses, *soma,* implies physicality[9]) cannot enter the kingdom of God, but that a body that has not yet been transformed by God via resurrection cannot do so. Paul is not denying that resurrected bodies are physical but that they are frail and corruptible like natural bodies. So Paul's notion is that when God raises us, God will change our bodies into spiritual bodies, bodies controlled by the Holy Spirit, bodies fit for the kingdom of God. But they will still be bodies, and will be continuous with (because they are the result of changes in) our old natural bodies.

V

Many objections have been raised against the Christian notion of the general resurrection. Here we will consider two of them, one ancient and the other largely modern.

The venerable objection—it was the first philosophical objection that was ever raised against resurrection—begins in this way: What if a Christian dies at sea and various parts of his body are eaten by various sea creatures that then scatter to the seven seas? How can God possibly resurrect him? What the church fathers typically did in response to these questions was appeal to divine omniscience and omnipotence. No human being would be able to locate and reconstitute the many particles (atoms, let's say) of the Christian's body—certainly not after years have passed—but an all-knowing and all-powerful God could do so. And as long as the basic atomic building blocks of matter endure through time (as, of course, atoms normally do) and God's only problem is to locate, collect, and reassemble them, the church fathers were certainly correct: God could do that very thing.

But there is an equally venerable and far more serious version of this first objection to resurrection; we can call it the "cannibalism case." What if another Christian dies and her body is eaten by cannibals, so that some of the material of her body becomes some of the material of their bodies? And suppose that God later wants to resurrect all of them from the dead, cannibals and Christian alike. In the eschaton, who gets which bodily particles? How does God decide?

In the light of the cannibal case, is resurrection still viable? It seems minimally that God must have some sort of criterion or policy for deciding which constituent parts of bodies go where in the kingdom of God. Augustine made the interesting suggestion that atoms will be raised in that human body in which they *first* appeared.[10] Or perhaps it could be argued that some constituent parts of human bodies are essential to those bodies and some are not. So if God wants to raise Jones after Jones' death, God only need locate those atoms that were essential to Jones, having already ensured that they have never appeared (or have never appeared as essential atoms) in anybody else's body. Perhaps then God can use them as building blocks around which to reconstruct the rest of Jones' new body out of entirely new atoms.

The second and more contemporary objection is related to the first. Both revolve around the issue of how God can raise someone from the dead and ensure that the raised person is the same person as the person who died.

Note that the objection just considered is based upon an important assumption; it is one that the church fathers (unlike most contemporary advocates of resurrection) were willing to make. It is that in resurrecting Jones from the dead, God must use the very same matter, the same atoms or "stuff," of which Jones' premortem body consisted. The fathers assumed, that is, that if God wants to resurrect Jones after Jones' death, God must find and reassemble the same matter of which Jones' body previously consisted. Otherwise, it will not be Jones but a mere replica of Jones. (We can call this the *patristic theory of resurrection.*) But many contemporary defenders of resurrection reject this assumption. Most of them hold that God could use entirely new atoms; as long as they are structured and configured in precisely the old Jones-like way, it will still be Jones.[11] (We can call this notion the *modern theory of resurrection.*)

We are, in effect, discussing what philosophers call the problem of personal identity. Some philosophers insist that because Jones has died, a resurrected "Jones" in the eschaton cannot be Jones. It will be at best—so they say—a replica of Jones. (A replica of Jones is a person who is indistinguishable from Jones but does not have Jones' history and is not

Jones.) The problem of personal identity is the problem of establishing the criteria that can or must be used for identifying and especially reidentifying persons. On what basis can someone in the afterlife be said to be the same person as someone who lived before?

This is a complex problem, and we will only be able to deal with it briefly here. There are three main approaches to it.

(1) Those who accept what is called the *memory criterion* (which includes not just memory but other mental characteristics such as personality and dispositions) argue that a given Jones-like person in the afterlife *is* Jones just in case the two Joneses have the same set of mental characteristics. And we do of course sometimes safely reidentify people on the basis of this criterion alone. For example, when you receive an e-mail message or a typed letter, you normally assume that it was written by the person who claims to have written it if the message shows that its author has the appropriate memories and personality traits.

(2) Those who accept the *bodily criterion* hold that the Jones-like person in the afterlife *is* Jones just in case the two Joneses have the same body (at two different times). We do frequently identify and reidentify people on this basis. Thus I might recognize somebody walking down the hall as the dean of the college by his voice, attire, and physiognomy. The deepest issues here concern questions such as: Is either criterion a necessary or sufficient criterion (or both) of personal identity? Does one criterion take priority over the other?

(3) A third position has emerged in recent years. For two main reasons, some philosophers have given up on the task of trying to establish necessary and sufficient conditions of personal identity. First, they argue that there are certain objections to all theories of personal identity that cannot be overcome, for example, the so-called "duplication objection." (There are many variants of this argument; one way of stating the core idea is this—the mere possibility that God could create multiple qualitatively identical "Joneses" in the afterlife entails that no Jones-like survivor of Jones' death really is Jones.[12]) Second, they argue that in certain imagined but logically possible test cases, personal identity seems either indeterminate or undecidable apart from arbitrary stipulation.[13] These philosophers no longer talk about personal identity in cases of survival of death. Instead of asking whether some Jones in the eschaton is the same person as the Jones who lived before, they instead ask whether the Jones-like person in the afterlife is Jones' "closest continuer" or has "psychological continuity" with Jones.[14]

This last theory will not be satisfactory to believers in resurrection (or to most believers in reincarnation or immortality, for that matter), since resurrection is embedded in a theology that requires that *we*—the very persons whom we are—will survive death. Otherwise, such theories would face the specter of people's being punished or rewarded in the afterlife for things that some other person did or did not do in this life. The biggest "personal identity" difference among our three life-after-death theories is that reincarnation and immortality must bank on the ability of the memory criterion alone to establish personal identity (since, obviously, on those theories there is no bodily continuity between the premortem and postmortem person), while resurrection allows the use of both criteria.

And it does seem that if a certain Jones-like person in the afterlife appears to have both Jones' body (even if that body has been dead for a time) and Jones' personality, memories, character traits, etc., then the denizens of the eschaton will be well within their intellectual rights if they accept that the Jones-like person before them *is* (i.e., is the same person as, is a continuation of the life of) Jones. And it seems that this will be true whether God resurrects Jones' body in the patristic way or the modern way. That is, defenders of the modern theory seem to be correct—even if God uses entirely new atoms, it would be Jones and not just a replica of Jones. But that does not rule out the possibility of God's resurrecting people in the patristic way too, if that is the route God chooses to follow.

VI

In recent years certain theologians have begun to look at Christian eschatological claims in the light of science and especially in the light of what current science says about the universe's long-term future.[15] And as a methodological point, it certainly does seem appropriate to compare Christian theological claims about resurrection (embedded, as they are, in Christian eschatological considerations) with current scientific theories. Creative dialogue between science and theology is to be encouraged.

Some such theologians worry that Christian eschatological hopes for a supremely good future seem to be inconsistent with current cosmological theories about how the world will end. Whether the cosmos "freezes" in eternal expansion or "fries" in a recollapse into heat death, neither result seems particularly hopeful. Both seem gloomy and pessimistic, hardly suggesting a limitlessly good end state.

The first possibility is raised by Big Bang cosmology plus entropy. If the universe is a closed system, and if accordingly energy in it always flows from heat to cold, and if the Big Bang was the hottest moment in the history of the universe, then its future involves only further and further expansion and cooling. Entropy will increase to a point where the temperature of the cosmos asymptotically approaches absolute zero. The second possibility is raised by the specter of the total amount of matter in the universe, including dark matter, being great enough to overcome the initial explosive force of the Big Bang. If this is indeed the case, then gravity will eventually cause the cosmos to stop expanding and start to collapse; its fate is the death of an incredibly high density and temperature (the "big crunch"). The point, then, is that in either case the cosmos and all life in it will come to an end. As theologian Ted Peters puts it, "The freeze or fry scenarios for the far future do not fit with the Easter promise of a coming new creation."[16]

Of course, Christian eschatological hopes are already somewhat counterintuitive before end-of-the-cosmos theories are even introduced. Those who read the newspaper every morning can testify to the impression that things in general are hardly on an economic or political or moral upswing.

But at one level, the profound worry of the theologians who write about this issue is puzzling.[17] Their concern would be entirely appropriate if God did not exist at all or existed but never intervened in the world's affairs. But resurrection points the way for us here. No Christian holds that the resurrection of Jesus occurred, or that the general resurrection will occur, as natural consequences of the laws of physics. The idea is rather that at a certain point God miraculously intervenes and brings about an event that, absent divine intervention, would not have occurred. The universe is not a closed system.

So Christians should not envision the end of all things as the natural and predictable result of the operations of the present laws of nature. We should see the eschaton as the result of a mighty act of God. At a decisive point in history, God will seize the initiative and give those who love and obey him a new "heart of flesh." At that point, "they shall be my people, and I will be their God" (Ezek 11:19-20). In that act, God will "[make] all things new" (Rev 21:5).

VII

Christian tradition unites in seeing the proper end or goal of human life as our eternal presence with God in paradise. One concrete way of conceptualizing the kingdom of God is in terms of the "beatific vision." That is, in paradise, the redeemed will see God's face.

But is it possible to see God? It might seem that the answer must be no. Part of the problem is that Scripture seems to suggest that no one can see God. Also, apart from the incarnation of the Second Person of the Trinity, God is not an embodied being (John 4:24) and accordingly—or so it seems—cannot be seen. So let us briefly explore this problem.

The Scriptures take us on a long journey on this issue of seeing God. Three points are noteworthy. First, several texts insist that seeing God, or at least seeing God's face, is forbidden. There is, for example, the curious passage in Exodus 33 where Moses asks to see the glory of God. Eventually, God does pass by, during which time Moses is hidden in the cleft of a rock, and (speaking anthropomorphically) he only gets to view God's back. But the key phrase of the text is surely Exodus 33:20: "You cannot see my face; for no one shall see me and live."

Second, many biblical texts stress that it is because of human sinfulness that we are forbidden to see God's face. People who are upright, holy, and pure do get to see God. Psalm 11:7 says that "the upright shall behold [the Lord's] face." The sixth beatitude says, "Blessed are the pure in heart, for they will see God" (Matt 5:8). In Matthew 18:10, speaking about children, Jesus declares, "in heaven their angels continually see the face of my Father." And Hebrews 12:14 says, "Pursue peace with everyone, and the holiness without which no one will see the Lord." These are uplifting thoughts, but if our hope is to see God, to achieve the beatific vision, these words sound like bad news. Which of us can truthfully claim to be upright, pure, or holy?

Still, the hope of seeing God persists in Scripture. Notice how the psalmist pleads for the sight of God (Ps 27:7-9):

> Hear, O Lord, when I cry aloud,
> Be gracious to me and answer me!
> "Come," my heart says, "seek his face!"
> Your face, O Lord, do I seek,
> Do not hide your face from me.

And although there are thorny textual and lexical problems connected with this text, the NRSV translates Job 19:25-27 as follows:

> I know that my Redeemer lives,
> and that at the last he will stand upon the earth;
> and after my skin has been thus destroyed,
> then in my flesh I shall see God,
> whom I shall see on my side,
> and my eyes shall behold, and not another.

Third, the hope that we will see God is surely eschatological. In 1 John 3:2, it says, "Beloved, we are God's children now; what we will be has not yet been revealed. What we do know is this: when he is revealed, we will be like him, for we will see him as he is." And Revelation 22:3-4, in the passage about the New Jerusalem, says, "The throne of God and of the Lamb will be in it [i.e., in the city], and his servants will worship him; they will see his face."

The expression, "seeing God," can be used in two senses. The first is the sense in which believers do and nonbelievers do not, here and now, see God. This is clearly to use the word *see* in a nonliteral way. It means roughly that believers cannot avoid interpreting their experience, and indeed all of life and reality, in terms of the presence of God. And nonbelievers do not do so. The second is the sense in which no one can now see God, at least not God's face, and that one day the blessed *will* see God. This is doubtless a literal sense of the word *see.*

How is this possible? Once again, resurrection points the way for us. If you believe both in a general resurrection that is essentially bodily and in the continuing incarnation of the Second Person of the Trinity, you will have no trouble accepting the idea that the blessed, in the eschaton, can literally see God.[18] But will the blessed also see the Father and the Holy Spirit? Here Christian theology comes to the end of its tether. The only answer we can give is perhaps. In Psalm 36:9, the psalmist, speaking to God, makes the puzzling statement, "in your light we see light." We normally see physical objects like trees and embodied persons in ordinary light, the kind provided by the sun. But perhaps there is a sort of supernatural light (Rev 21:23) that both makes ordinary vision possible here and now and, in the eschaton, will make possible vision of the Blessed Trinity itself.

VIII

Christian eschatology entails that in the end God will win over all the forces that oppose him—sin, death, suffering, injustice, poverty, disease—and everything will be transformed. In the kingdom of God, our earthly bodies will be changed into new resurrection bodies (1 Cor 15:35-57), and we will experience the beatific vision (Rev 22:1-4). We will know a love, joy, and peace that will be incommensurate with anything we have ever experienced. Thus Paul can say: "I consider that the sufferings of this present age are not worth comparing with the glory about to be revealed to us" (Rom 8:18).

Part III

Issues in the Philosophy of Religion

12

Despair over Genocide—Can There Be Hope?

I

Occasionally we have experiences that make us proud to be members of the human race. When we watch a Shakespeare play or listen to a Mozart symphony or look at a Rembrandt painting or admire an Ansel Adams photograph or benefit from a medical discovery—in those moments we can feel thrilled and uplifted. We sense that this sort of thing is the work of Homo sapiens at its best.

But our feelings are not quite the same when we think of the Holocaust of 1939–1945, in which some six million Jews and five million others were murdered by the Nazis. As with all acts of genocide, when we think about the Holocaust, we feel profoundly ashamed to be a member of the human race. We ask: How could it have happened? How could the hatred of the perpetrators, as well as the indifference of the bystanders, have reached such a shocking level? We sense that this sort of thing is the work of Homo sapiens at its worst.

Here we see, par excellence, the dual and indeed polar nature of human beings. We can create and discover things that are breathtaking in their beauty, goodness, and utility. We can do things that are outrageously evil and that will stain the pages of history for millennia. We are capable of the loftiest heights and the most hellish depths. This seems an inexplicable mystery. Virtually all

The present chapter is a slightly revised version of an essay that appeared in Genocide and Human Rights: A Philosophical Guide, *ed. John K. Roth (New York: Palgrave Macmillan, 2005).*

religions, and many philosophies, try to explain this tendency toward evil in the hearts of human beings.

Let's perform a *gedankenexperiment.* A term from physics, a "thought experiment" is simply a situation where we do not have the money or the technology actually to perform the test, so what we do is try to imagine, as best we can, what the likely result would be if we were able to perform it. The ancient Greek Archimedes was conducting a thought experiment when he said, "Give me a long enough lever, a fulcrum, and a place to stand and I will move the earth."

My thought experiment is not from the realm of geometry or physics but morality. It concerns a crime that has been called omnicide. Suppose human beings possessed the technology to destroy the entire universe. Is there any doubt that there are people who, if they could lay their hands on that technology, would use it? There is no such doubt in my mind. I believe that such people exist. Just as there are people who would kill another human being in a given situation if the technology (a handgun, let's say) were readily available, so there are people (doubtless a much smaller number) who would destroy the universe, including themselves, if they could.

Genocide appears to be a crime that is situated somewhere between the crime of murder and the crime of omnicide. Genocide is the crime of intentionally destroying or attempting to destroy an entire group of people, usually a racial, ethnic, linguistic, or religious group.[1] Just as there are people who would commit murder if they could, and just as there are people who would commit omnicide if they could, so there are people who would commit genocide if they could.

The moral of this depressing scenario is this: genocide should not surprise us. (I am not saying that it should not horrify us.) Occasionally there will be people who hate another group enough to kill all its members and are able to seize control of the technology and social organization necessary to achieve that end. Most fortunately, not all humans are guilty or even potentially guilty of genocide. Most of us are not. But it is troubling that most genocides appear to be carried out mainly by ordinary people who have adopted an ideology of hatred for the persecuted group or else see themselves as simply obeying the orders of their superiors.

So far as we know, mass slaughter and perhaps even genocide have been part of history ever since human beings first organized themselves into social groups. But something changed in the twentieth century. It was during that period that human hatred began to be allied to governmental bureaucracies, propaganda machines, transportation services, and technologies for mass killing. But I doubt that the fairly late appearance of that sort of systematic genocide on the human scene is because people before (roughly) 1900 were morally superior to those who came after that date. Surely it is because genocide in the fullest sense was not then technically possible.

But, alas, the mechanisms and technologies of genocide are now available. So we can almost say this: human beings and human progress are such that genocide or at least attempted genocide is now something that is to be expected (as well as, of course, resisted with all the power at humanity's command).

Another way of making the point, one that relates more to human communities rather than individuals, is this: If human-group A has complete control over human-group B, it is very possible that the members of A will oppress the members of B and perhaps even engage in genocide against the members of B. (Notice that the victims of genocide are almost always politically and militarily powerless.) It will probably be the first if the B people are economically useful to the A people, probably the second if the A people hate the B people sufficiently.

II

Why are human beings capable of moral evil and indeed of gross moral outrages like genocide? In order to try to answer that perplexing question, I am going to appeal to two of the foundational myths of Western culture: the story of Cain and Abel and the story of the Tower of Babel. Both stories are found in the book of Genesis in the Bible. They are terse, and each raises important questions that the text does not attempt to answer. But as Albert Camus said, "Myths are made for the imagination to breathe life into them."[2] I will supply my own interpretation of the stories, doing something like what Jewish tradition calls *midrash*. Taken together, I believe the two texts illuminate the phenomenon of genocide.

In Genesis 4, the Bible tells us that Adam and Eve, the first human beings, had two sons whom they named Cain and Abel. Abel, the younger, was a keeper of sheep, and Cain, the firstborn, was a farmer.

> In the course of time Cain brought to the Lord an offering of the fruit of the ground, and Abel for his part brought of the firstlings of his flock, their fat portions. And the Lord had regard for Abel and his offering, but for Cain and his offering he had no regard. So Cain was very angry, and his countenance fell. The Lord said to Cain, "Why are you angry, and why has your countenance fallen? If you do well, will you not be accepted? And if you do not do well, sin is lurking at the door; its desire is for you, but you must master it." Cain said to his

> brother Abel, "Let us go out to the field." And when they were in the field, Cain rose up against his brother Abel, and killed him. Then the Lord said to Cain, "Where is your brother Abel?" He said, "I do not know; am I my brother's keeper?" And the Lord said, "What have you done? Listen; your brother's blood is crying out to me from the ground! And now you are cursed from the ground, which has opened its mouth to receive your brother's blood from your hand. When you till the ground, it will no longer yield to you its strength; you will be a fugitive and a wanderer on the earth. (Genesis 4:3-12)

When Cain complained that his punishment was too great for him to bear and that anyone who met him might kill him, God placed a mark on him so that no one would kill him. The story concludes with Cain leaving the presence of the Lord and settling in the land of Nod, east of Eden.

This is the story of the first murder. It is a crime of fratricide. The text presupposes, but does not attempt to explain, the tendency toward pride, arrogance, envy, and oppression of the weak (what the rabbis called *yetzer ha-ra*) that seems to reside in the human heart. Murder is different from, and far more serious than, most other crimes and offenses. There are two related reasons for this: first, since no human being has the power to bring the dead back to life, a crime of murder can never be made good again in the sense of reversing its effect; second, since no human being has the power to create life, it follows that life and death belong to God alone. Murder, then, is a crime both against the victim and his family and friends but also (and most importantly) against God.

We do not know why God preferred Abel's sacrifice to Cain's. Perhaps there was no reason other than God's sovereign choice. After all, we read in Exodus 33:19 that God said to Moses: "I will be gracious to whom I will be gracious, and will show mercy on whom I will show mercy." But the story contains hints of prior religious or even moral culpability on the part of Cain: Cain, it says, brought only "an offering of the fruit of the ground," while Abel brought "the firstlings [the choicest] of his flock" Perhaps Abel took the ritual more seriously than his brother did. Maybe Cain's sacrifice was a mere outward act while Abel's was sincere, heartfelt. Moreover, when Cain's countenance fell because God dishonored his sacrifice, God asked him, "If you do well, will you not be accepted?" as if he had failed to do well. What he had failed to do, it turns out, was prevent sin from lurking at his door.

The story is clear that Cain, even in his fury at Abel, had freedom of choice. Sin was lurking at his door—so God advised him—but "you must master it." Here we see the Lord appealing to Cain's better motives: God gave him a chance to amend his ways. The myth is apparently saying that we human beings are able to resist our murderous impulses; it is up to us to decide whether we will do good or evil. But sin in the Bible seems to have a kind of active power, a way of gaining control over human beings. This explains the human tendency to kill, or at least to want to kill, our enemies. Cain did not master his murderous impulse.

We do not know how Cain did the deed. Since the killing involved spilling his brother's blood, we naturally think of a stone or club. Whatever the implement, a technology of death was available to him. He lured Abel out into the field where he thought the act would not be observed and struck him down.

In the end, we learn from the Cain and Abel story that murder, and all crimes greater than murder (like genocide), are morally wrong. They are evil for three reasons. First, murder is wrong because no human being has the right, out of self-centered motives like anger or jealousy, to take the life of another. Second, murder is wrong because even nature itself, in receiving Abel's blood, cried out in protest to God over what Abel had done. Human life is sacred. Third, murder is wrong because once that crime is introduced into human history, it is liable, like an infectious disease, to spread. Even Cain recognized as much. In protesting his punishment, he said to God: "I shall be hidden from your face; I shall be a fugitive and a wanderer on the earth, and anyone who meets me may kill me."

The implications of Cain's act are still with us today. In the year 2001, there were 13,653 persons arrested for murder (in its various degrees) in the United States.[3] In that same year, there were 15,980 victims of murder (in its various degrees) in the United States.[4] In the year 2000, 8600 people were convicted of murder in the United States.[5] Since 1976 (when the Supreme Court reinstated the death penalty), 885 people have been executed by the various states (71 in 2002; 65 in 2003), the vast majority for murder.[6] As of July 1, 2003, there were 3,517 prisoners under sentence of death in the United States.[7] Murder has been with us ever since Cain and shows no sign of going away.

Murder also seems to corrupt the murderer even further. After his deed, Cain's heart was hardened to such an extent that he lied to God. When God asked him the whereabouts of his brother, Cain replied, "I do not know." This was also the point where Cain posed his famous sarcastic question, "Am I my brother's keeper?" I think Cain was trying—as most criminals do—to find somebody else to blame. I think he was saying to God, "It's not my job to protect Abel from all the dangers that might prove fatal to him in this world that you created: that's your job." So murder and lying about it were now parts of human experience and would remain so. Cain was condemned to the life of a wanderer, or nomad, in the land of Nod ("restlessness").

In Genesis 11, we read a story about a great tower:

> Now the whole earth had one language and the same words. And as they migrated from the east, they came upon a plain in the land of Shinar and settled there. And they said to one another, "Come, let us make bricks, and burn them thoroughly." And they had brick for stone, and bitumen for mortar. Then they said, "Come, let us build ourselves a city, and a tower with its top in the heavens, and let us make a name for ourselves; otherwise we shall be scattered abroad upon the face of the whole earth." The Lord came down to see the city and the tower, which mortals had built. And the Lord said, "Look, they are one people, and they have all one language; and this is only the beginning of what they will do; nothing that they propose to do will now be impossible for them. Come, let us go down, and confuse their language there, so that they will not understand one another's speech." So the Lord scattered them abroad from there over the face of all the earth, and they left off building the city. (Genesis 11:1-8)

The story concludes that the city was called Babel, because that is where the Lord confused the language of all the earth.

This deep and puzzling myth also presupposes the human tendency toward self-aggrandizement and rebellion against God, although it interprets that tendency in a more corporate or social way than the Cain and Abel story does. Here technology is an explicit part of the story, and technology becomes an aid to the evil tendency in human beings. The human race had developed to the point of living in cities, using bricks to build with, and erecting great towers. Genesis wants us to understand that the attempt to build the great tower at Babel was an act of pride on the part of the people who lived there. They wanted to "make a name" for themselves and even to reach "the heavens." That is, they wanted no longer to have to serve God. They wanted to equal God or even *be* God. They reached too high.

God saw that human beings were now capable of great evil. God grasped immediately that "this is only the beginning of what they will do." Those are prophetic words indeed. In our own age, a time not only of genocide but of nuclear weapons, worldwide terrorism, genetic engineering, and global degradation of the environment, we see the truth of God's words, "Nothing that they propose to do will now be impossible for them." Humans now have powers that people once sensibly thought only God had. It is depressing to contemplate how those powers have been used thus far and sobering to wonder how they will be used in the future.

At Babel, God intervened. God confused the language of the people and thus their ability to continue building. Unable to understand each other, they could no longer organize themselves to complete the project or even stay together in one place. The crisis—at least at that moment—was averted. But now it seems to us that the God of the Bible, after the great flood in Genesis 6–9 and the confusion of the languages in Genesis 11, no longer intervenes to prevent gross evils. Evil runs rampant. What the Bible calls sin has become a landslide. After the murder of Abel and the episode at Babel, genocide is not only possible but actual.

III

Before turning to the problem of genocide and hope, I must discuss further a point about genocide that I just claimed we can learn from our two biblical texts. It is the claim that murder, in all its forms (one of which is genocide), is wrong. In one sense, this claim seems perfectly obvious. But I need to point out that moral relativism has a long history in the discipline of philosophy and has made a strong comeback in recent decades.

What exactly is moral relativism? Let us define it as the philosophical position that says that nothing is morally right (or wrong) per se. There are no transpersonal normative truths in morality. If I say, "Murder is morally wrong," I am only reporting my own opinion that murder is morally wrong. And of course murder *is* morally wrong if I believe it is morally wrong, but that means only that it is morally wrong "for me." Other people might think that murder is morally right, and of course that view is correct too—for them. The theory is called moral relativism because it crucially claims that the truth or falsity of normative moral claims is relative to the person or group making them.[8]

It seems to me that genocide is the *reductio ad absurdum* of moral relativism. Indeed, I believe we all know that murder in all its forms is morally wrong. When we read Genesis 4, we recognize, in our revulsion at Cain's behavior, as much. We *are* our brothers' keepers. Abel's blood does cry out from the ground. Here is the strongest thing that a moral relativist can say against genocide: I hold that genocide is morally wrong. Or perhaps: I hold, and my community holds, that genocide is morally wrong. But the problem is that that allows the perpetrator of genocide (a Nazi, perhaps) to reply: Sorry, but my community holds that genocide is morally right.

It is painful even to ponder such an exchange. We want to cry out: "It isn't a matter of what people *think* is right or wrong; genocide is just plain morally wrong." That is, it is morally wrong per se, morally wrong no matter what any person or community may think. I would be so bold as to claim that anyone who holds that genocide is morally wrong only for those who believe it is morally wrong is either badly confused, malicious, or insane.

IV

Does God exist? Well, theists say yes; atheists say no; and agnostics say neither yes nor no. But let me now try to argue, on the basis of what I have said thus far, that God exists. My proof, which we might call "the Genocide Argument for the Existence of God," can only be convincing to those who agree with me that moral relativism is false and that genocide is morally wrong. This argument I will give is related to the traditional "moral argument" for the existence of God,[9] but is also different at crucial points.

Suppose it is true that genocide is morally wrong. Now those things that we consider to be morally wrong constitute departures from the way (so we believe) things ought to be. And those things that, in fact, *are* wrong are departures from the way things ought to be. That is at least part of what we mean by "morally wrong." It follows, then, that genocide is a departure from the way things ought to be. And if that much is true, then it follows that there *is* "a way that things ought to be." In other words, certain things are morally right, and certain things are morally wrong quite apart from what anybody believes. And if that much is true, it then follows that there exists what we might call a "design plan" for human life and experience. A full design plan would simply be a list of all those things that constitute the ways that things ought to be (presumably it would include items like compassion, truth telling, promise keeping, etc.) and a list of all those things that should not be (presumably it would include items like cruelty, lying, murder, and, of course, genocide).

Now if there is a design plan for things, then there must be an author of the design plan, a designer, a sentient agent of some sort. I can make no sense of the notion of an authorless design plan or a design plan that emerged merely from nature or the cosmos. The cosmos is the way that things are; it has nothing whatever to do with the way that things ought to be. If then there is a designer, we can call it "God." Of course the Genocide Argument does not prove that the designer possesses all the properties that the God of theism is traditionally said to have—oneness, omnipotence, omniscience, benevolence, etc. Certainly the moral designer that we have just proved to exist might well have all those properties; the point is just that the Genocide Argument by itself does not prove that it must. Still, if the genocide argument is sound, then God, the moral designer of the universe, exists.

Here, then, is the way the argument can be summarized:

1. Genocide is a departure from the way things ought to be.
2. If genocide is a departure from the way things ought to be, then there is a way things ought to be.
3. If there is a way things ought to be, then there is a design plan for things.
4. If there is a design plan for things, then there is a designer.
5. This designer we call "God."

What can we say about the Genocide Argument? Is it a convincing argument? And where does it lead, so far as genocide and hope are concerned?

V

Nothing in human experience is more disgusting and profoundly depressing than genocide. To return to the question that I have postponed until now, let me ask: is there any sense in which genocide can be a springboard for hope? Or even: is there any room for hope in a world in which genocide occurs?

My central answer is this: unless God exists, our grounds for hope, in the light of genocide, are limited indeed. I recognize that this bold claim will meet with disapproval in many circles. But it seems that if no creator or higher power like the God of theism exists, the only hope we can sensibly have, in the light of genocide, is tenuous. It might be the hope that some day we can so design our educational, social, political, and diplomatic systems that no more genocide occurs.

I have no doubt whatsoever that that is a goal all right-thinking human beings, believers in God or not, must pursue. My wife and I instructed our own children that they were to hate no one and that they were never to be a party to, or in any sense support, any acts of genocide. Much, much more is required than that, of course, but it is at least a place to start. We know there are places in the world where children are apparently not taught along those lines.

But if God does not exist, a genocide-free world is the best for which we can hope. Those who believe in inevitable human progress will find it a possible hope. Those, like me, who do not share that belief will reply that we can certainly *hope* for such a world, but it will be something like a hope that continental drift will cease. Certainly, if God does not exist, there is no hope whatsoever for any experience of reparation or even joy by the victims of genocide. They are gone forever. That sort of hope only makes sense if God exists. If one holds that God does not exist, and if one's assessment of human nature is such that the possibility of genocide can never be excluded . . . well, that reasoning seems to me to lead to despair.

Notice that there are hints of grace even in our two dark biblical stories. God does not kill Cain, much as Cain had killed his bother, and when Cain protests that his punishment is too severe, God acts to protect him. He places a mark on Cain, perhaps a tattoo on his forehead (the rabbis thought it was one letter of the divine name), in order to protect him. The fact that he continues to live gives him the time and opportunity to repent of his crime. I think God was saying to Cain: "There is still time, Cain; it is not too late; you can still master the evil that you have allowed to lurk at your door." God is merciful. And the denizens of Babel, despite their arrogance and desire to worship themselves instead of God, are not killed. Nor are they so afflicted that they all speak different languages. They can continue to live in communities based on language groups, and they, too, are given time and opportunity to amend their ways and learn again to worship only God. God is merciful.

Is it possible for evil to be redeemed? Is it possible that all the acts of genocide ever committed can be redeemed? That of course will depend in part on how we define words like *evil* and *redeem*.

Let us simply define *evil* as undeserved human suffering. I actually believe that the category of evil is broader than that (it is sometimes evil when animals suffer, for example, and it is possible to do an evil deed that does not cause any suffering), but I will ignore those sorts of complications. The notion of undeserved human suffering will suffice to cover all that I will want to say about genocide. Undeserved suffering might be caused by another human being or other human beings, or by natural, nonhuman causes such as earthquakes, diseases, famines, etc. We can call the first "moral evil" and the second "natural evil." Both sorts of evils can equally cause pain and death, but moral evil is more troubling because human beings are culpable in bringing it about. Genocide is clearly an instance of moral evil; it is about as bad as moral evil gets. Natural evils can wipe out entire populations of people, but such events do not constitute genocide.

If "redeeming genocide" means making it such that an act of genocide like the Holocaust never occurred, then obviously genocide cannot be redeemed. This follows from the metaphysical principle that the past is fixed and unchangeable. It is too late for anyone, even God, to do anything about the fact that the event occurred. Nor can the Holocaust be redeemed, in my opinion, in the sense that we will one day understand that it was really good. Some evils can surely be redeemed in that sense. Probably all human beings have experienced undeserved suffering where they later came to understand that it was for the best that it occurred.

But this hardly applies to the Holocaust. Good did come out of it, one could suppose. It is sometimes said that the nation of Israel would never have been reestablished in 1948 had the Holocaust not occurred. That may be true. And I regard the existence of Israel as a good thing (this does not mean that I always support that nation's policies). Perhaps the Holocaust also strengthened the resolve of Jews, and of many non-Jews, that there shall be no more Holocausts. If so, that is, in my opinion, a good thing. But do those goods produced or caused by the Holocaust outweigh the evil of the Holocaust? Of course not. The very suggestion seems absurd, almost obscene.

Well then, is there any sense in which genocide can be redeemed? The answer is yes, but only if God exists. If no God exists, genocide cannot be redeemed at all. But if a perfectly good and all-powerful supreme being exists (as Jews and Christians claim), a sort of redemption is possible. Suppose that such a being provides a limitlessly good afterlife for murder and genocide victims (as well as others, of course) in which their horrific earthly experiences fade further and further away in memory and eventually pale into insignificance in the light of the goodness then revealed and experienced. If that occurs, it will, I think, amount to something like redemption of genocide.[10]

Religious skeptics will dismiss talk like this as sheer silliness. And certainly they are allowed to declare with bravado their credo—that this life is all there is, that death is the final and complete end for human beings, and that we had best just get used to the idea that we live in a radically unjust world. There simply is no redemption of genocide—so they will insist—or compensation for its victims.

But there is no denying that most human beings have a deep longing for justice and a hope that our world will turn out just. I believe that for most people the reality of genocide in our world increases, rather than decreases, that longing. For those of us who wish to avoid despair, that hope is appealing. For those of us who believe in God, it is not just a hope but a conviction.

13

Is "Survival of Death" Coherent?

I

In a famous and influential essay written over fifty years ago, "Can a Man Witness His Own Funeral?"[1] Antony Flew argued that the notion of life after death is incoherent. He offered three related arguments for this conclusion. Although Flew's argument has been around for some time and has been discussed in the journals, I am not sure that it has ever been decisively refuted. In this brief essay, I will attempt to do that very thing.

II

First, Flew argues that one statement typically made by those who affirm life after death—"We all of us survive death"—is self-contradictory. In an airplane crash, there are two mutually exclusive and exhaustive categories: the dead and the survivors. So the question, "Did Jones (one of the passengers) survive the crash?" makes perfect sense, but the question, "Did Jones survive Jones' death?" does not. Accordingly, the sentence "We all of us survive death" has no clear meaning.

Second, according to Flew another statement typically made by those who accept life after death—"We all of us live forever"—is simply empirically false. Notice, Flew says, that *the* paradigmatic true statement throughout the

The present brief essay is an excerpt from a chapter titled "Philosophy and Life After Death: The Question and the Options," in Philosophy of Religion: A Guide and Anthology, *ed. Brian Davies (Oxford: Oxford University Press, 2000). I had, however, been thinking along these lines against Flew for many years.*

history of logic is this: "All men are mortal." This generalization is as massively confirmed as any generalization can possibly be, and it is, as Flew argues, the "flat contrary" of "We all of us live forever."

Flew was aware of a possible objection to his first two arguments. One way to decide whether a given state of affairs is logically possible is to ask whether it is coherently imaginable. And a defender of life after death might claim that "survival of death" is coherent after all because it is possible to imagine one's own funeral.

But here Flew makes a distinction among three situations. (1) What it would be like to witness my own funeral. Of course this situation is imaginable, Flew says. It is quite possible for me to close my eyes and imagine people witnessing my funeral—I am in the casket, my mother is crying, a priest is offering prayers, etc. But imagining this picture does nothing to support the claim that life after death is imaginable. (2) What *would* support the claim would be imagining what it would be like to witness me witnessing my own funeral. But the problem is that this picture is not imaginable; if it is really me who is witnessing the funeral, then it is not my funeral; and if it is really my funeral, then I cannot witness it because I am dead in the coffin.

But, (3) Flew (speaking for his imagined critic) asks, why can't I imagine what it would be like to witness myself as an invisible, incorporeal spirit witnessing my own funeral, that is, the funeral of my body? But, replies Flew (speaking now in his own voice), this does not differ in any significant or empirically relevant way from (1), that is, from simply imagining my own funeral without being there at all (except as a corpse in the coffin). All talk about an "invisible, incorporeal spirit" and of its "being there" is devoid of any empirical sense. So life-after-death theories either presuppose the absence of genuine death or else violate the normal use of such terms as *I* or *me*. Flew's conclusion is that his first two arguments still stand.

Third, Flew introduces his dictum, "People are what you meet." Person words (by which Flew means words like *I, me, you, father, mother, butcher*, etc.) refer not to mysterious elusive things like souls but to real human persons, that is, bodies plus behavior. We know this because children who have no idea what a soul or immaterial essence might be can use person words perfectly well. Persons are publicly locatable and observable things. You don't ever take a walk or have a conversation with an immaterial essence. You engage in such activities with other human beings—not just with their bodies, of course (the term *father's body* would normally mean *father's corpse*), but with their bodies plus behaviors. Since the bodies and behaviors of human beings do not survive death, Flew's overall conclusion is that human beings do not and cannot live after death.

III

Flew no longer develops his critique of life after death in precisely this way, but his argument has had a lasting impact on the discussion and is still occasionally cited. In one sense, this is surprising, since the argument is hardly convincing.

For one thing, Flew's ex cathedra claims about the incoherence of "surviving death" will only be convincing to those whom we might call lexical fundamentalists. These are people who stubbornly insist that the meaning of a word is indelibly established by its original usage; thus Flew's dogged insistence that you might "survive a plane crash" but never "survive your own death." But it is obvious that as new human situations arise, words sometimes get stretched in meaning in order to make valid, and quite communicable, points. If talk of "surviving death" communicates with people, as opposed to systematically misleading them, that way of talking is fine.

Similarly, it would be surprising indeed if anybody who said, "We all of us live forever," meant that sentence to deny that "All men are mortal." I would have thought that the reverse is true—those who speak in this way would want to be interpreted as insisting on the mortality of human beings. This, in fact, is precisely the point—we all die, and after we die, we go on living forever in another form or world. I have never heard of a believer in life after death who wanted to deny that people must die.

Finally, Flew's dictum, "People are what you meet," has clearly overlooked something, viz., the first-person perspective. If the range of the term *people* is other people, that is, people other than me, then Flew's dictum is beyond reproach. But it is obvious that by introspection human beings know themselves as something different from and other than "body plus behavior." It is perfectly possible for me to know many things about myself (e.g., my present mood, my first impression of Kant, my sense that a certain person whom I know is pompous) that may never have been evident in my body or my behavior.

Whatever this missing something is, and it has been called by many names in philosophy (the self, the mind, the soul, the realm of the mental, consciousness), those who believe in life after death hold that it is the thing that survives death. This would be true of all those who believe in reincarnation, all those who believe in the immortality of the soul, and all those who believe in Christian resurrection. Flew has not refuted such theories.

14

Wittgensteinian Philosophy of Religion—A Valid Option?

I

Are religious belief and unbelief metaphysical choices? I am to answer that question in this chapter. So I must obviously first define terms like *metaphysics*, *belief*, and *unbelief*. These words are defined variously, and debate about the proper definitions of these and related terms can be vigorous. I will try to avoid such debates by simply stipulating how I will use them on this occasion.

I understand the term *metaphysics* in a broad way.[1] It is, as a first approximation, simply the attempt to say how things are. But that definition is too inclusive. On this understanding, I would be practicing metaphysics if I were to say things like:

1. There is a Toyota in my driveway.
2. San Francisco is north of Los Angeles.
3. Water at sea level boils at 212 degrees.

And such statements do not seem to be, in any ordinary sense, metaphysical statements. Now it seems that what is normally called metaphysics is motivated in part by the conviction that reality is sometimes hard to detect or get clear on; sometimes how things are hidden, so to speak, behind how things appear to be. The hallmark of both ordinary empirical statements and scientific statements is

The present paper is a revision of my 2006 conference paper, "Belief and Unbelief: A Metaphysical Choice?" Since D. Z. Phillips came to Claremont as Danforth Professor of the Philosophy of Religion in 1993, I have had to think about Wittgensteinian philosophy of religion much more than I had previously. The present version includes material from two or three of my writings since 1993.

that there are established and agreed-upon criteria for verifying or falsifying them. But statements that are typically classified as metaphysical are extremely difficult, maybe impossible, to verify (if they are true) or falsify (if they are false). In that way, they are quite unlike 1–3, which seem fairly easy to verify or falsify.

So perhaps we should say that metaphysics is the attempt to say how things are in nonordinary empirical and nonscientific situations, or metaphysics is the attempt to say how things are in cases where reality is difficult to discern. Or maybe we should say even that metaphysics is the attempt to say how things are in cases where the statements that we make are extremely difficult or impossible to verify or falsify. But one problem here is that some statements that everybody recognizes as scientific are exceedingly difficult to verify or falsify, for example, "There is enough matter in the known universe eventually to cause a Big Crunch" or "The Neanderthals did not pass on their genes to modern humans." Still, definitions like the ones cited above do have the strong point that they allow as metaphysical such universally accepted metaphysical statements as the following:

4. Human beings consist of material bodies and immaterial souls.
5. Human beings are sometimes libertarianly free.
6. The A Theory of time is true.

So for the purposes of this chapter I will stipulate that metaphysics is the attempt to say how things are where reality is difficult to discern in nonempirical and nonscientific situations. If that definition includes too little or too much, it will not particularly matter for our purposes.

II

What, then, are *belief* and *unbelief*? Since in the present chapter I want to discuss religious belief and unbelief, I will say that a believer is someone who has beliefs like the following:

7. God exists.[2]
8. We will live on after death.[3]
9. There will be a last judgment.

And a nonbeliever is someone who does not have such beliefs. Obviously, there are religions that do not require or even allow belief in (7), (8), and (9), so there are plenty of religious people who reject them. But I will intentionally confine myself here to Christian religious belief, because this is the religion that I know best. In Christian religious contexts, beliefs like these seem typical. (I believe, however, that virtually all of what I will say in this chapter also applies to other theistic traditions such as Judaism and Islam.)

The question that I want to address, then, is whether a choice between believing or disbelieving items like (7), (8), and (9)—disbelieving them either by denying them or simply by not affirming them—is a metaphysical choice. In other words, does religious belief (or unbelief) inevitably commit one to metaphysics?

It certainly seems natural to hold that (7), (8), and (9), if they are believed by someone, constitute or at least entail metaphysical beliefs for that person. Indeed, they seem to be paradigm cases of the sorts of beliefs that most philosophers would classify as metaphysical. Anyone who wants to deny that these are or entail metaphysical beliefs is someone who at least appears to be under the sway of some sort of theory. (Of course that does not mean that the controlling theory must be false.) So I will assume throughout this chapter that theological statements like (7), (8), and (9) are metaphysical statements. Not all religious or theological statements are metaphysical, but ones like these are. They do seem to constitute attempts to say how things are where reality is difficult to discern in nonempirical and nonscientific situations.

Since the Enlightenment, as we all know, there have been many attacks on metaphysics. Hume, Kant, the logical positivists, and Wittgenstein have all argued, in quite different ways and for different reasons, that metaphysics as traditionally understood, is impossible, meaningless, or confused. Contemporary antirealists in philosophy and in science seem also to hold low views of metaphysics. Peter van Inwagen and Dean Zimmerman helpfully distinguish between strong versions and weak versions of antimetaphysical theories. Strong versions claim that metaphysics is impossible because there is no reality there to be described or discovered; accordingly, all metaphysical statements are either false or meaningless. Weak versions admit that reality is there all right but hold that we human beings are unable to reach it; it is beyond our intellectual powers to know which metaphysical statements are true and which are false.[4]

III

Let me next develop a theory or argument to the effect that the choice between religious belief and unbelief is *not* a metaphysical choice. The argument that I will put forward is roughly Wittgensteinian, but probably neither Wittgenstein nor any of his followers in the philosophy of religion hold it precisely.

The theory, which I will call "Theory T," consists of three theses:

A. Metaphysical assertions often look like factual assertions, but in fact they are grammatical or conceptual.[5] It is never possible to step outside our language and compare metaphysical statements and beliefs with some reality independent of language in order to see which ones are true and which false.[6] To think that we can do so is confused; it is to treat metaphysical statements as if they were ordinary empirical statements or scientific hypotheses. It is to misconstrue our language. Our network of concepts, our grammar, cannot agree with or conflict with facts; rather, our grammar determines for us what it makes sense to say; our concepts have meaning only within our language.
B. In order to see what a statement means, we must look at the attitudes and practices within which its usage is embedded. In order to see what a religious statement means, we must look to religious attitudes and practices.
C. Religion plays an important role in the lives of (certain) people. But those who try to prove the statement "God exists" mistakenly hold that "God" is some sort of object like other objects. Those who try to prove that they will live in another world after death are unwilling properly to say farewell to life and recognize it as a gift.[7] To be religious and to have religious beliefs is to have certain attitudes toward life and to follow certain practices.[8] This is what religious statements like (7), (8), and (9) mean. Accordingly, it is ludicrous to imagine that religious statements can be proved or disproved and attempts to do so are irrelevant to religious belief.[9]

It seems to me that there are two ways in which Theory T can be interpreted. Indeed, I suspect that both interpretations can find support in the writings of Wittgenstein and his followers. I will call them "the weaker interpretation" and "the stronger interpretation."

The weaker interpretation. Perhaps Theory T should be interpreted as emphasizing the point that understanding a metaphysical or religious belief (or any belief) means understanding what the people who hold it do and say. Their attitudes and practices show us what their statements mean. Of course there are people who have beliefs like (7), (8), and (9); they are allowed to have those beliefs, and the beliefs are not merely attitudes and practices. The beliefs say what they say, and no reductionism is being suggested. But attempts to prove statements like (7), (8), and (9) are confused precisely because the attitudes and practices tell us what those statements mean. Religious beliefs are not like scientific hypotheses.[10]

Is Theory T convincing when interpreted in this way? For the most part (i.e., except for the bit about its being confused to try to prove statements like (7), (8), and (9), I think it is. For example, religious beliefs are indeed unlike scientific hypotheses in striking and important ways. Moreover, attitudes and practices are indeed constitutive of what we call religion and are crucial in determining the meaning of religious statements. Finally, religious beliefs are indeed expressions of certain attitudes (whether that is *all* they are is another question).[11]

Accordingly, what I am calling the weaker interpretation of Theory T is largely sensible. I will not subject it to criticism.

The stronger interpretation. However, there is another way that Theory T can be interpreted. This interpretation also insists that trying to prove a metaphysical claim stems from confusion; the attempt treats a conceptual problem as if it were a factual or scientific one. But the stronger interpretation also importantly denies that religious beliefs like (7), (8), and (9) are metaphysical beliefs. The claim is that when someone says something like (7), (8), and (9), that person is not expressing a metaphysical belief. She is, in fact, expressing a certain attitude and living in a certain way. The language is being used figuratively. For example, those who say we will live on after death are expressing a certain attitude toward life and death.[12] A kind of reductionism is surely in view here. Being religious, so it seems, *just is* having certain attitudes and engaging in certain practices.[13]

Theory T, interpreted in the stronger way, can be criticized.[14] Let me mention at this point three sources of difficulty. I will add a fourth later.

First, suppose we admit for the sake of argument that it is impossible (because it is nonsensical) to get outside our language and see how thought and reality are related, or at least to see how they are related in metaphysical situations. That is, suppose it is impossible to verify or falsify metaphysical claims. But the point to be noticed is that it does not follow from this admission that having a metaphysical belief like (7), (8), and (9) is nothing but the having of a certain attitude or the following of certain practices. Perhaps the people who affirm life after death really do believe in a literal future life after death and are not merely expressing a certain attitude. They may or may not accept the idea that it is impossible to verify or falsify metaphysical claims. They may still accept (8) as literally true. In other words, Theory T may be right about the unverifiability of metaphysical statements, but wrong about what people mean when they make statements like (8).

Second, Theory T appears to be mistaken in claiming that those who try to argue for the truth of statements like (7), (8), and (9) are treating those statements like scientific hypotheses. There are in fact many obviously nonscientific statements that we regularly and confidently argue for and against, for example, moral statements like "Abortion is morally permissible if the woman decides to abort" or "Torture is never morally allowable."

Third, suppose somebody expresses belief in (8). How do we go about deciding whether this person actually believes that she and others will live on after death or whether the belief is rather the figurative expression of a certain attitude toward life and death and of a determination to follow certain practices in life? Well, I suppose nothing prevents us from simply asking the person which is the case. And if for some reason that strategy is considered insufficient (maybe she is confused about the meaning of her own words or is even lying to us), we might check to see whether she defends the literal truth of the statement in appropriate circumstances. Will she, for example, in the relevant situations, express disagreement with those who hold that "death ends all" or give arguments in favor of her statement? We might even check to see whether her practices are appropriate to the belief, that is, see whether she acts as if the belief were true. If the belief in question is

7. God exists,

we might try to find out whether she ever prays or attends religious services. If the belief in question is

8. We will live on after death,

we might ask whether she has ever sincerely said anything like "We will see each other again" to a dying friend, or (if she is Roman Catholic) whether she ever prays for the dead.

But, of course, the defender of Theory T might reply that all these tests are inconclusive. All they show—so it might be said—is that the person does indeed have the attitude toward life and death that Theory T attributes to her. And if having a certain belief entails having a certain dispositional property (as I admit), it is clear that all beliefs, once held, carry with them or essentially involve certain attitudes.

Yet even if all this is granted, we can ask this question: Is it possible to have the attitude toward life and death that Theory T has in mind (an attitude that stresses, perhaps, the grace of life and the necessity of saying farewell to it) and not believe in the literal truth of (8)? And the answer to that is surely yes. We have all known people who see value in religious attitudes and practices but are unwilling to affirm the literal truth of statements like (7), (8), and (9). Such folk are sometimes called religious nonrealists.[15] People like Richard Braithwaite and Don Cupitt certainly come to mind. I myself have known others.

Suppose religious realists and religious nonrealists always share the same attitude in connection with statements like (7), (8), and (9). (I doubt that this is, in fact, true, but let's suppose it is.) How then can we distinguish between the realists and the nonrealists? I would again reply that even if the attitude is the same (which, again, I doubt), we can fairly easily distinguish between them by their practices. Someone who does not believe that God is real may meditate but will hardly pray. Such a person may regret her shortcomings but will hardly ask God to forgive her. Such a person may rejoice in the blessings and graces of life but will hardly thank God for them. Someone who does not believe in an afterlife may appropriately say farewell to life but will hardly expect to see a dying friend again.

What follows from this piece of reasoning? What follows is that anybody who says that believing statements like (7), (8), and (9) is *just* a matter of having a certain attitude or following a certain practice is mistaken. The stronger interpretation of Theory T may or may not be a correct interpretation of Theory T, let alone of the intentions of Wittgensteinian philosophers of religion, but so far as I can see, its central claims are false.

IV

I will now try to establish the further point that metaphysical beliefs have consequences for life and practice.

It certainly seems that metaphysical choices can be crucial in determining behavior. That is, in many cases, it looks as if the metaphysical beliefs that people hold seem to constitute the reasons they have the attitudes they do and follow the practices they follow. But that point is possibly too strong, so the considered position that I want to argue for is this: for most people, their attitudes, practices, and metaphysical beliefs hold together in a mutually supporting web.[16]

The adherents of Theory T, if asked the meaning of apparently metaphysical statements like (7), (8), and (9), will emphasize the need to look at the practice within which such statements are embedded. In this case, the practice is religious practice. To try to establish the truth of such statements (so they will say) simply betrays confusion; the sense or grammar of (7), (8), and (9) is not that which enables or produces the practice; rather, the practice shows what the sense or grammar is.

But problems seem to me to emerge in the T theorist's further claim that religious worship is *the* practice within which statements like (7), (8), and (9) are typically embedded.[17] Praising God—so they will say—has nothing to do with trying to prove the truth of religious statements. That is certainly correct, but what is often overlooked here is the fact that religious instruction is another typical home base for statements like (7), (8), and (9). In such a setting, questions of truth and even criteria of truth do emerge. When my parents and others taught me, as a child, that God exists, I am persuaded that they wanted me to believe that statements like "God exists" are *true*. When I got a bit older, I even heard reasons given and objections answered. Moreover, I was taught and knew how to use the word *God* well before I ever experienced Christian worship.

Defenders of Theory T oppose any picture that claims that religious belief is the cause or foundation of religious practice. They claim that this places religious belief in a kind of grammatical vacuum: there is no context of human behavior that might give it meaning. But, as noted, my own view is that the beliefs and practices work together as a kind of mutually intertwined and mutually supporting web. Understood in this way, quests for religious, and thus metaphysical, truth, even apologetically motivated ones, do not have to be uprooted from the contexts in human practice that give sense to religious statements. It is quite true that in the midst of praising God, we don't troop out the cosmological argument. But some of the same folk who praise God on some occasions might well try to prove the truth of statement (7) on others. And it is a commonplace that some people quit the practice of religion when they no longer hold the relevant metaphysical beliefs.

It also seems clear to me that metaphysics does make a difference in the attitudes we have and the things we do. Of course, there are abstruse and highly technical metaphysical issues that seem unrelated to human practices—except perhaps practices like philosophers writing their academic papers in support of one theory as opposed to another. But not all metaphysics is like arguing (to pick a stock example) about how many angels can dance on the head of a pin or (to pick a more up-to-date example) whether a functionalist analysis of qualia can succeed.

For example, if I am committed to the metaphysical/moral position known as Hard Determinism,[18] certain attitudes will naturally follow. I will not, for instance, hold you morally responsible if you rob a bank (although for utilitarian reasons I could support locking you up in prison). If you are committed to the metaphysical position known as Logical Fatalism (every event happens under conditions given which it is not logically possible for anything else to happen), certain attitudes will naturally follow. You will not, for example, regret something bad that has happened on the grounds that it could have been avoided, for example, your contracting lung cancer due to your smoking habit. It seems that the attitudes just mentioned would almost certainly be changed if the associated metaphysical position changed. If I renounced hard determinist in favor of libertarianism, I might well hold you morally responsible for robbing the bank. If you renounced logical fatalism, you might well regret your smoking.

But what about religion? Well, among the people whom I know (admittedly a small sample of the world's population), there seems to be a strong correlation between those who believe statements like (7), (8), and (9) and those who engage in practices like praying and going to religious services. There seems to be an equally strong correlation between those who disbelieve statements like (7), (8), and (9) and those who do not engage in practices like praying and going to religious services. That correlation, even if I am right about it, does not prove that the beliefs *cause* the attitudes and practices. But I believe it does at least show, as mentioned above, that all three—beliefs, attitudes, and practices—at least exist in a mutually supportive web.

V

Theory T, when interpreted in the strong way, says that believing religious statements *just is* having religious attitudes and following religious practices. There is more to be said about that point. And there is more to be said about the different but related claim that the attitudes and practices are what religious statements like (7), (8), and (9) *mean*. (The following argument amounts to the fourth criticism of the stronger interpretation of Theory T mentioned earlier.)

It is obvious that I cannot refute these two claims, at least not the second. Assertions to the effect that when someone says X, what she really means is Y are notoriously difficult to disprove. I can only express my disagreement with these claims. And although truth is not decided by majority vote, I suspect that the vast majority of Christians and other theists would agree with the following alternative claims: yes, of course, attitudes and practices are deeply involved in and are inseparable from religion, but something utterly crucial is being omitted if we claim that that is all that religion essentially involves. What is missing, in my opinion, are beliefs in religious statements like (7), (8), and (9), which statements the typical religious person takes to be true and might want to argue for. That is, what is missing is the metaphysical element (making claims about how things really are where reality is difficult to discern in nonempirical and nonscientific situations) in all theistic religions.

Theory T comes to us in the guise of a theologically neutral philosophical analysis of religious talk. And in one sense that is just what it is. But we can now see that in its stronger or reductionist version it is more than that: it is also a recommendation—originally based I suspect on certain religious sensibilities of Wittgenstein—about what religion properly is or ought to be. That is, it is a proposed revolution in the religions; it amounts to a new theology—a theology without metaphysics—that is designed to replace much of the old theology. Its central claims (e.g., those of Phillips noted in n. 13) certainly do not follow merely from an examination of how religious people use terms like *God* or *eternal life*. And it is at that point that I think it is important to note how repugnant this new theology would be to most Christians and other theists.

Perhaps at this point Phillips might agree that religious people typically do have metaphysical commitments in my sense of the term (they try to say how things are where reality is difficult to discern). All that means—so he might say—is that they hold their religious beliefs to be true, to express how things really are. But he might go on to insist that concepts like truth and reality are internal to language games. Accordingly, the kind of "truth" and the kind of "reality" that religion is said to disclose is not like what we find in science or ordinary experience.[19] I do not accept the claim that truth and reality are internal to practices and have no application outside of them,[20] but I will not argue for that point in the present chapter. If Phillips will agree that religious people do typically make metaphysical commitments, that will satisfy my present purposes.

VI

Another question must be raised: Is metaphysics, so to speak, essential to religion (or at least to Christianity), or is it external to it? This is a troublesome question. To be a theist, do you have to have a metaphysic—do you have to believe, for example, in the truth of statements like (7), (8), and (9)?

One obvious difficulty here is that there are scores of metaphysical claims and theories existing out there in intellectual space, and they are variously related to religion, theistic religion, and Christianity. Some metaphysical theories are clearly excluded for theists, for example, metaphysical monism (about which I will say more momentarily).

Other metaphysical theories are, as we might say, available to Christians but not (or at least arguably not) essential to Christianity. Think of Augustine's use of Plato's "Great Chain of Being," Aquinas' use of Aristotle's theory of potentiality and actuality, or Swinburne's use of Cartesian mind-body dualism. So far as I can see, Christians are allowed to make use of metaphysical theories that fit in this second category, but they are not required to do so.

Even so, some metaphysical theories or statements are mandatory for Christian theism; some are even, as I would prefer to say, internal to theism. Statements (7), (8), and (9) seem to me to fit in that category. I would hold that they are internal to Christian theism because they are taught in Scripture and the creeds. Others (to speak somewhat paradoxically) are essential to Christianity but external to it. They are external because they are not part of the teachings of Scripture or the creeds, but they are essential because careful philosophical and theological thought can show that Christianity needs them. Let me mention four metaphysical theories or statements that seem to me to fit in this category.

1. *Metaphysical monism is false.* This is the theory that says all differentiation is illusory—I am the same thing as you, and we are the same thing as this book. Theism cannot follow this path, in my view, because it is at the very least committed to one real distinction. If X creates Y, then X and Y are different things; since God created the world, the distinction between God and the world is a real distinction. The world is different from God.

2. *Metaphysical materialism is false.* Some Christian philosophers argue that materialism vis-à-vis human beings is true,[21] although mind-body dualism seems the dominant position. But since Christians believe that God is real and that God is a spirit (John 4:24), they conclude that metaphysical materialism must be false; it cannot be the case that only matter is real. Angels, demons, and the human soul are also considered by most Christians to be nonphysical things, but these items can be somewhat controversial. But to Christians, the existence of God is not controversial, and God alone is sufficient to show that biblical religion is essentially committed to the falsity of metaphysical materialism.

3. *Time is linear.* The main alternative to the claim that time is linear is the theory that time and history are circular, that there is never novelty or progress because history endlessly repeats itself.[22] Accordingly, no one historical event can have eternal significance. The circular view is found in virtually all prebiblical religious and mythological systems and in some religions existing today, especially in tribal societies. But Christians are

convinced that biblical religion is essentially based on the notion that time is linear; that is, history is moving toward a goal or *telos*, viz., the kingdom of God. Novelty can and does occasionally appear, and certain historical events (e.g., the Exodus and the resurrection of Jesus) have eternal significance. Some day in the future things will be different from the way they are now, and infinitely better. Some day, indeed, history will come to a end.

4. *Human beings are morally responsible for what they do.* If Jones is morally responsible for act A, I believe that Jones can legitimately be blamed or praised, punished or rewarded, for A. My Toyota is not morally responsible for getting me to work every morning or even (when it malfunctions) for failing to get me there. In most cases, Jones is morally responsible for A if, and only if, (1) Jones did A or caused A to occur, (2) A is an event or action that has moral connotations (like causing pain or pleasure to someone), and (3) there were no legitimate excuses. Now Hard Determinists hold that nobody is ever morally responsible; everything we do is brought about by unavoidable causes; we are the victims of forces beyond our control. Yet it is clear that biblical religion is committed to the notion that human beings, at least much of the time, are morally responsible for what they do. Accordingly, God can legitimately punish or reward us.

VII

If my arguments in the previous section of the chapter are correct, then metaphysics is essential to Christian theism. There are certain metaphysical claims that Christians must affirm and others that they must deny. One that they must accept, of course, is "God exists." And this leads me naturally to consider briefly some of what D. Z. Phillips says about God.

There are four related points here; I can only treat them briefly:

D. Phillips insists that God is not an object or thing. If God were an object, Phillips says, then God would be like other objects and so would not be the God of religion; God would be the sort of thing that comes into being and passes away.[23]

E. Phillips also claims that the word *God* does not refer. He says of the word *God* that it is "not the name of an individual; it does not refer to anything."[24]

F. Similarly, he holds that "God exists" is not a claim or hypothesis.[25] The affirmation of God in religious experience, Phillips insists, is not theoretical.

G. Finally, he says that to try to prove that "God exists" is to treat God as if God were one of the creatures; the very idea of trying to prove that "God exists" is deeply confused; it shows that the sense of the statement has not been grasped.

Are these four points correct? Let's consider each of them in turn.

(A) Is God an object or thing? I see no problem whatsoever in allowing as much. Of course, God is not an object or thing like other objects or things, but that is another matter. Christians must always preserve the absolute distinction between God—a necessary being who is infinitely wise, knowing, powerful, and loving—and the creatures. But it is difficult to see how that distinction is threatened by calling God an object or thing or even a "being." I simply do not detect anything in the grammar of these words that requires that all objects, things, or beings be contingent. As long as one ensures in what one says about God that God's transcendence in not endangered, there is no theological danger here.

(B) Does the term *God* refer? I certainly think so. Obviously, the term does not refer to anything real if God does not exist. When pressed on this point by religious realists, Phillips is inclined to say that even if it is allowed that the term *God* refers to something, no clarifying work whatsoever has been done showing what sort of thing the term refers to. How are we grammatically to distinguish the something that the term *God* refers to from other sorts of things, like physical objects?[26] We still do not know the grammar of the statement, "God is an existing, transcendent thing." There is certainly truth here. People who insist that the term *God* refers must go on to explain God's nature. Still, something philosophically worthwhile has been accomplished when it is allowed that God refers. Emotivist, nonrealist, and other nonreferential theories of religious language have been ruled out.

(C) Is "God exists" a claim or hypothesis? In some situations, certainly not. It is true that in religious experience (by which Phillips principally means worship) the existence of God is hardly a hypothesis that one weighs and tests carefully in hopes that convincing evidence will emerge. But, as noted above, religious experience is not the only context in which the existence of God emerges. Some of those other contexts involve conversations between believers in God and atheists or agnostics. And the existence of God can be and often is treated as a hypothesis in some such contexts. There is no reason why a deeply committed religious believer (one who does not for a moment doubt the reality of God) cannot, in contexts outside of worship, prayer, and religious instruction, treat "God exists" as a hypothesis or claim. Here perhaps Phillips will reply that you can't yank religious language out of its natural context of praise and worship and use the same terms in a quite different context. But why not? Both in philosophy and in science we are quite used to treating certainties as if they were doubtful, and dubious claims as if they were certain. In both philosophy and science we are used to borrowing terms from one context and using them in another, and the usual result is that there is enough overlap of meaning to make successful communication possible.

(D) Do theistic proofs treat God as a creature? I would reply: not necessarily. This charge is obviously untrue of the ontological argument. Anselm's term, "the Greatest Conceivable Being," ensures that the being who is proved to exist is transcendent above all other beings. Other theistic proofs (e.g., the design argument) do not require as much by their internal logic, and if such proofs are successful, the theistic prover must keep in mind that the proof, while compatible with the existence of God, does not strictly prove that a transcendent, all-power, and self-existent God exists.

VIII

In her book *Horrendous Evils and the Goodness of God,* Marilyn Adams argues that what she calls "expanded standard theism" has more "explanatory resourcefulness" in solving the problem of evil than the "restricted standard theism" presupposed by J. L. Mackie and others.[27] Expanded theism, as Adams understands it, is basically the existence, omnipotence, and goodness of God enhanced by Christian theological notions such as incarnation and redemption.[28] I do not aim here to explore Adams' fascinating proposals about the theodicy problem. I am instead interested in the idea that one theory or attempted solution to a problem might have more "metaphysical resources" than another. What might this mean?

It is clear that philosophers often find themselves in the business of solving intellectual problems or answering objections. And it seems that philosophy is full of obvious cases where a philosopher's efforts along those lines are assisted by certain metaphysical beliefs or assumptions. Plato's metaphysical belief in the existence of the realm of forms allowed him to avoid the notion that all of reality is in constant Heraclitean flux. Aristotle's positing of the metaphysical distinction between potentiality and actuality allowed him to conclude that not all change is "radical," that not all qualitative change in a thing amounts to numerical change. Epictetus' metaphysical belief that all events that occur in what he called "the external world" are inexorably fated and thus could not have been avoided allowed him to adopt a certain stoical attitude toward the misfortunes and tragedies of life. Descartes' belief that he had proved the existence not only of God but also of a God who is "no deceiver" allowed him to rule out the Evil Genius hypothesis. Berkeley's belief in an all-perceiving God allowed him to conclude that the world has uninterrupted existence despite the doctrine that "to be is to be perceived." The person who believes that determinism is false because some human actions are libertarianly free is, unlike a hard determinist, rationally able to hold people morally responsible for their actions.

Such cases do seem to be instances of philosophers' taking advantage of Adams-like "metaphysical resources." This is not to say that the problems solved by the philosophers just noted could not have been solved in other more metaphysically economical ways. It is even possible that some of the philosophical problems I have mentioned are "pseudoproblems." I only insist that certain metaphysical beliefs held by certain philosophers are used by them as resources to solve certain philosophical problems.

The philosophers whom we have been discussing would surely insist that the metaphysical beliefs in question are true beliefs. Similarly, religious beliefs and certain metaphysical claims like (7), (8), and (9) are held by believers to be true.

IX

What follows if I am correct in the main claims that I have made in this chapter? Four conclusions seem to me to follow.

First, metaphysics is allowed; it is not essentially impossible, meaningless, or confused. Metaphysical arguments may indeed be difficult rationally to assess, and metaphysical beliefs may be difficult or even impossible to verify or falsify. Some metaphysical statements may even turn out to be incoherent ("The 'not' negates itself nonnegatively"); we will have to examine each case to see. But metaphysics *tout court* is not ruled out.

Second, if religion is important, then metaphysics is important, because religion (or certainly theistic religions like Christianity) essentially contains metaphysical statements. Accordingly, items like Anselm's theory of the atonement, Aquinas' Third Way, Hume's critique of the Argument from Design, and Swinburne's defense of the Christian Trinity will continue to be important points of discussion among philosophers of religion and philosophical theologians.

Third, religious statements, or the coherent ones in any case, are either true or false. Accordingly, it constitutes an important task in theology and the philosophy of religion to try as best we can—difficult as it may be in cases—to see which are true and which false. As for (7), (8), and (9), they strike me as perfectly coherent statements. Theists will consider them true and atheists will consider them false.

Fourth, to return to the question asked in this chapter's title, religious belief or nonbelief, at least in the case of some beliefs, is indeed a metaphysical choice.[29]

15

Has the Ontological Argument Been Refuted?

I

The so-called ontological argument for the existence of God (OA) is one of the most fascinating, as well as controversial, pieces of natural theology in the history of philosophy. Invented by Anselm[1] (1033–1109), it appears in many versions and has been attacked and defended many times. Rather than try to survey the many criticisms that have been raised against it, I have decided instead to focus on the arguments of one contemporary critic of the OA, Professor Michael Martin. His objections seem to be fairly representative of what many atheists and religious skeptics have to say about the OA.

In chapter 3 of *Atheism: A Philosophical Justification*[2] Michael Martin criticizes the ontological argument. He discusses five versions of it—those of Anselm, Malcolm, Hartshorne, Carl Kordig, and Plantinga—and finds them all wanting. He concludes by admitting that he is tempted to agree with Schopenhauer's claim that the OA is nothing but a "charming joke." That is, he finds the OA entirely unsuccessful as an attempt to prove the existence of God.

Now I should point out that it will not particularly damage theism even if Martin is correct that all versions of the argument fail as theistic proofs.[3] As Martin will agree, God might exist even if the OA is a total failure. Indeed, it is safe to say that few theists place much apologetic emphasis on the OA; perhaps most theistic scholars agree with Martin that the OA is unsuccessful.

An earlier version of the present chapter appeared in Paul Copan and Paul K. Moser, eds., The Rationality of Theism *(London: Routledge, 2003).*

But despite the fact that the soundness of the OA may not be crucial to theism, my own view is that Martin has not made his case. I do find his critiques of the OAs of Malcolm, Hartshorne, and Kordig to be convincing; I, too, reject those versions of the OA, and for many of the reasons Martin cites. But his criticisms of the OAs of Anselm and Plantinga can in my view be answered. Those versions of the OA still stand. To show that this is true is the main aim of the present chapter.

II

Let's look first at Anselm's version. But before turning to Martin's criticisms of it, let me mention two closely related points where Martin misconstrues it. First, Martin calls the OA "an attempt to prove the existence of God by simply analyzing the concept of God" (79). This oft-repeated claim is relatively harmless but nevertheless quite mistaken. It is true that Anselm's definition of God—"that being than which no greater can be conceived"—is crucial to his argument. We'll call this being the "Greatest Conceivable Being" or GCB for short. But merely analyzing that concept will get one nowhere in proving the existence of anything. One must also bring into consideration what Anselm surely took to be certain necessary truths, for example, a thing is greater if it exists both in the mind and in reality than if it exists merely in the mind, and the existence of the GCB is logically possible. These claims are essential aspects of the OA and do not follow merely from an examination of any concept of God.

Second, Martin claims that Anselm claims that the fool who says, "God does not exist," contradicts himself. But this is also slightly misleading. Again, "God does not exist" only turns out to be necessarily false in conjunction with certain necessary truths like those just listed. Anselm need not be committed to the claim that the bare sentence, "God does not exist," is self-contradictory, which it surely is not. To be sure, Anselm held that the atheist's position can be shown to be necessarily false. It is so because that position is inconsistent with the definition of God together with certain other necessary truths.

It is important that I lay out a version of Anselm's argument that I think can be defended against Martin's criticisms. I do not claim that the argument I shall express here is the only argument that can be drawn from *Proslogion* II; indeed, just about everybody who talks about Anselm's argument has her own favorite version of it. I only claim that the argument I will state is the argument that seems to me to flow from Anselm's wording in *Proslogion* II, and that this version of the OA can be defended against Martin's criticisms.

1. Things can exist in only two ways: in the mind and in reality.
2. The GCB can possibly exist in reality, that is, is not an impossible thing.
3. The GCB exists in the mind.
4. Whatever exists only in the mind and might possibly also exist in reality might have been greater than it is.
5. The GCB exists only in the mind.
6. The GCB might be greater than it is.
7. The GCB is a being than which a greater is conceivable.
8. It is false that the GCB exists only in the mind.
9. Therefore, the GCB exists both in the mind and in reality.

Obviously, much of this needs explaining. So far as premise (1) is concerned, Anselm meant the expression "X exists in the mind" to mean simply that somebody imagines X, defines X, or conceives of X. The expression "X exists in reality" means that X exists as a concrete individual thing with causal properties and exists quite independently of anyone's ideas or concepts of it. Thus there are four modes of existence: X might exist in the mind and in reality (e.g., Bill Clinton); in the mind but not in reality (e.g., unicorns, or Stephen Davis' ninth daughter); in reality but not in the mind (e.g., some undiscovered but existing chemical element); and in neither way (e.g., nuclear weapons in the year A.D. 1550).

Premise (2) simply means that there is no contradiction or other sort of incoherence in the term "Greatest Conceivable Being." If so, the GCB is a being that can possibly exist (this does not mean that it *does* exist, of course), unlike impossible things like square circles or married bachelors. Thus the GCB must have one of two modes of existence (i.e., two of the above four have been eliminated): it either exists like Bill Clinton both in the mind and in reality, or else it exists like my ninth daughter—just in the mind.

Premise (2) should be understood epistemically. It is not quite a strict proof that the GCB is a possible thing. But the only way to prove that something, say X, possibly exists is to show that it exists. But when we are talking about something about which we do not know whether it exists (as we are certainly doing when we talk about the GCB in the context of a theistic proof), the only weapon we have available to us is to examine its definition or concept of the thing. I accept that to prove that the concept X is coherent (there is no contradiction or other sort of logical infelicity in the concept) does not strictly show that X possibly exists. But it does put us in the position of being within our intellectual rights in holding that it possibly exists. The burden of proof would definitely be on the side of the person who wants to deny that X possibly exists. So—to transfer this point to the conclusion of the OA—what the OA shows if it is an otherwise logically impeccable argument is that theists are within their intellectual rights in accepting its conclusion and that the burden of proof is on critics of the OA to show why "The GCB is possible" is false.

Premise (3) simply means that someone—Anselm, you the reader, or whoever—has conceived of the GCB; the GCB exists in the mind of that conceiver.

Premise (4) is sometimes called Anselm's "hidden premise." This is because he nowhere explicitly states it in *Proslogion* II, although it is perfectly clear that his argument needs it. The basic idea is that things are greater if they exist both in the mind and in reality than if they existed merely in the mind. Paul Bunyan, the legendary woodsman, would have been greater than he actually is had he existed in reality as well as in the mind. The space shuttle would have been less great than it actually is if it were only the figment of some engineer's imagination. So in terms of our earlier discussion of "greater," Anselm should accordingly be taken as implying that things that exist both in the mind and in reality are more powerful, freer, more able to do things than they would be if they existed only in the mind.

Now premises (1), (2), (3), and (4) constitute Anselm's basic assumptions. Like any deductive argument, the soundness of the OA depends on the truth of its assumptions. If any of them is false, then the OA fails. (As indicated above, I think Anselm considered them to be not only true but necessarily true, but all that the OA strictly requires is that they be true.) Premise (5) is a premise that Anselm introduced in order to refute it by *reductio ad absurdum*. He believed that assuming the nonexistence of the GCB, together with the earlier assumptions, will lead to a contradiction.

The next three premises constitute the logical outworking of Anselm's assumptions. This is where Anselm shows that premise (5) is unacceptable because it is responsible for producing a contradiction and thus is to be negated. If premises (5), (2), and (4) are true, then premise (6) follows. If the GCB is a mere concept (like my ninth daughter) and not an existing thing (like Bill Clinton), then the GCB might have been greater than it is. Mere concepts presumably have some powers and abilities—they can sometimes help stimulate us to think more clearly or act in a certain way, for example—but not nearly so many powers and abilities as existing things. Existing things are greater than the mere concepts of them. If the GCB were a mere concept, then it would still be true that the possibly existing thing we are calling the GCB could possibly exist (just as unicorns or my ninth daughter could possibly exist); and that if it did exist, it would be greater than it (the mere concept) in fact is.

Premise (6) is at least implicitly contradictory; what it says is that "the greatest conceivable being might be greater than it is." Another way of making this same point, and one that is directly entailed by premise (6), is premise (7):

7. the GCB is a being than which a greater is conceivable.

Now since premise (7) is an explicit contradiction, by reductio ad absurdum we must search for whatever premise above it in the argument is responsible for producing the contradiction. Realistically, this means inspecting the argument's assumptions, that is, (1), (2), (3), (4), and (5). Anselm would argue that since the first four are all necessary truths (or at least truths), the culprit premise must be (5). We are allowed, then, by reductio ad absurdum, to negate premise (5).

The negation of (5) is premise (8). We know by premise 1 that things can exist in only two ways, in the mind and in reality. And we know by premise (3) that the GCB exists (at least) in the mind. And we know by premise (8) that it is false that the GCB exists only in the mind. Thus it follows that

9. the GCB exists both in the mind and in reality,

which was what we were trying to prove.

Thus far I have not tried to defend the OA against objections. I have only been trying to explicate Anselm's argument or at least a version of it that can plausibly be taken from the text of *Proslogion* II. There are very many criticisms that have been made of Anselm's argument over the centuries. Obviously, I cannot address them all. But what I can do is show that Anselm's version of the OA can be defended against the objections raised by Michael Martin.

III

Let us then go on to Martin's three criticisms of Anselm's OA.

(1) Is "exists" a predicate? Martin's version of my premise 4 is, "An entity is greater if it exists in reality than if it exists only as a mental object." He then points out that this sentence has been challenged, for example, by Kant's claim that "exists" is not a "real predicate," that is, not a real property of things.[4] Martin does not argue that Kant is correct; he merely points out that Kant's argument makes the OA controversial and thus not a "clearly sound argument." Well, if a sound argument is a valid argument whose premises are true, then I suppose a clearly sound

argument is a valid argument whose premises are clearly true. Does the mere existence of Kant's argument in the history of philosophy make the OA controversial? Well, the answer to that question is surely yes, especially given the great influence that Kant's objection has had in subsequent discussions of the OA. But the philosopher who defends the OA will not mind admitting that Anselm's argument is controversial; unless she has had her head inside a bag throughout her career, she knows that already. But does the existence of Kant's objection make the OA not clearly sound? Well, perhaps it does that too; I have no desire to deny it, in any case. So let's agree that the OA is not a clearly sound argument. But the crucial point here is that the OA does not have to be clearly sound for it to be an entirely successful theistic proof. It need only be sound.[5] Martin points out that even if defenders of the OA can show that "exists" is a property of things, that is not enough for the needs of the OA. They must also show that "exists" is a property of things *that adds to the greatness of things that have it*. And Martin is correct about that. The existence of a thing may be neutral as to its greatness, he says; it may even detract from its greatness. And so far as God is concerned, Martin says, "the assumption that God does not exist does not seem to take away from His perfection [Martin should have said "greatness"]" (81).

Is this a good objection to Anselm's version of the OA? I do not think so. But while something is clearly amiss in the neighborhood here, part of the blame lies with Anselm, not Martin. Sadly, in the *Proslogion* Anselm never tells us exactly what "great" means or what it is for one thing to be "greater" than another. That constitutes a large lacuna in Anselm's argument. And it leaves to interpreters of Anselm to ask something that Martin did not bother to ask, viz., what did Anselm mean by "greater"? That is, what notion of greatness must Anselm have had in mind in order to give the OA a chance of being a successful theistic proof?

There are at first glance a host of things that we might mean by "greater"; the term might mean "faster" or "larger" or "more red-headed," for example. But clearly the OA cannot possibly work on those meanings. This is for the obvious reason that there logically can be no such thing as the "fastest conceivable being" or the "largest conceivable being" or the "red-headedest conceivable being." Now there is some textual evidence that Anselm wanted to understand greatness in terms of goodness.[6] Now I certainly agree that goodness is a great-making property, but questions can be raised about the coherence of notions like, "Morally best conceivable being." Accordingly, let me make a quite different suggestion, one that I do not claim is Anselm's intended notion of "greater" (although it is very much in the spirit of the view of God that Anselm works with in all his writings); I merely claim that it is a coherent notion of "greater" and at least has a chance of making the OA work.

Suppose we read greatness as power, ability, freedom of action. This will accomplish several things that the OA needs. First, things will be comparable with respect to greatness: coyotes are greater (freer, more able to do things, etc.) than stones, humans are greater than collies, the president of the United States is greater than the governor of South Dakota. This is important because some possible ways of understanding "greater" do not allow for commensurability, for example, if we understand it as meaning being more of a prime number (no prime number can be more of a prime number than another prime number). Second, greatness, understood in this way, admits of a maximal degree. All things will be less great than the GCB, where the GCB is understood to be an omnipotent or all-powerful being, and where an omnipotent being is understood to be a being that has the property of being able to bring about any state of affairs that it is not logically impossible for it to bring about. That is a degree of power, of freedom of action that logically cannot be bested. Third, greatness understood in this sense is intuitively a great-making property. Red-headedness is probably not; suppose there are two beings, exactly alike in as many of their properties as possible, except that one is red-headed and the other is blond; we would not feel that the red-headed one is greater. But this is not true of power or freedom of action. We do intuitively feel that an alarm clock is a greater thing than a tooth pick, a raccoon is a greater thing than an amoeba, a human being is a greater thing than a cow.

Is "exists" a property (or, as Kant would have it, a real predicate)? It certainly is an unusual property. As Kant correctly says, if we add "and X exists" to a list of assertions about X, this does not expand or increase our knowledge of X. (Or at least—as I will argue—this is correct in some cases.) This is clearly the point of Norman Malcolm's question in support of Kant (cited by Martin on page 81): "What could it mean to say that [my future house] will be a better house if its exists than if it does not?" If a property or a real predicate is something that appears in the predicate position of a sentence that increases our knowledge of the subject, then "exists" sometimes does fail to be a property or real predicate. But it seems to me that this will only be true in cases where the existence of the thing is already being presupposed in the conversation. And we often do limit our conversation to the set of existing things. Thus the oddity of the following conversation:

Do you own a car?

Yes, I do.

Does your car run?

Yes.

Is your car a Honda?

Yes

Do you drive your car to work?

Yes

But does your car exist?

The problem here is that the car's existence was apparently presupposed throughout the conversation; thus the strangeness of the concluding question. If the reply to it were to be, "Yes, of course my car exists," this would not (as Kant would surely say) change or expand our concept of the car. We were assuming an existing car all along. Here Kant is apparently correct.

But sometimes we broaden the ontological horizons of our language and talk about things that are, or possibly are, nonexistent—things that are, for example, mythical, extinct, legendary, dead, or fictional. And in those cases it might well add to our knowledge of a thing to say that it does (or does not) exist. In such cases, "exists" appears to be a property or real predicate. Malcolm's questions sound puzzling because they would normally be embedded in a conversation that takes for granted the future existence of Malcolm's house. But suppose we are not taking that for granted. Then his question can make perfect sense. I would certainly prefer to have a house that actually exists—will really give shelter from the weather, for example—than a nonexistent house that appears only in a novel. In linguistic situations where we are wondering whether the house is fictional or a legend, it will indeed increase our knowledge of the house if we are truthfully told and come to believe that it exists.

So my point is that "exists" (as in the statement, "God exists") is or can be a Kantian real property in contexts in which the existence of X is not assumed or presupposed in the conversation. But I should note that it has little to do with whether somebody is or is not sure that God exists. Theistic proofs like the OA are discussed in contexts in which the existence of God is not presupposed, even if both parties in the conversation believe in God (as both Anselm and Kant, as well as Gaunilo, did). Consequently, in those cases, "God exists" does add to or enlarge the concept of God (God may or may not exist in reality) that is presupposed in the conversation.

But even if this is true, Martin insists, it still needs to be shown that "exists" is a property that adds to the greatness of a thing. And Martin is correct that this is a quite separate point from showing that "exists" is a property. But here is where the definition of "greater" becomes crucial. Doubtless on some notions of "greater," to exist is not necessarily to be greater than not to exist. That is, exists is not a great-making property. But on the notion of greatness that I am defending, to exist in reality *is* to be greater than not to exist in reality. Existing things are more powerful, freer, more able to do things than those things would be if they didn't exist, than, for example, the mere concepts of them. Mere concepts, extinct animals, dead generals, mythical woodsmen, fictional islands, unachieved ideals—such things are able to do some things. As noted, they can provide examples, help tell stories, even stimulate us to act. But beyond that, their powers are strictly limited. An imaginary house can keep imaginary rain off our backs, but not real rain. A God that truly exists is far greater than that same God would be if it didn't exist.

Martin quite misleadingly fiddles with Anselm's notion of "greater," suggesting that it be replaced by such notions as "is more valued" or "is more prized" or "is more desirable." He then points out that desirability is a relative notion and that there will be many people who will not find the actual existence of God at all desirable. That is certainly true, but it has no relevance whatsoever to the success of the OA as a theistic proof. As long as there is a notion of "greater" (like the notion of power or freedom of action or ability to do things) that is coherent and makes the OA succeed (i.e., according to which it will be true that "A thing is greater if it exists in the mind and in reality than if it exists merely in the mind), it will not matter one bit whether there are folk who find the existence of God undesirable. The logic of the situation is this: it is unfair for critics of Anselm to supply their own notions of greatness that cannot possibly allow the OA to succeed; this is surely true of Martin's notion of "more desirable." Since Anselm, as noted, does not supply us with his own notion or definition of greatness, interpreters of the OA must ask what notion of greatness is consistent with Anselm's views about God and has a chance of allowing Anselm's argument to succeed.

Anselm's point, then, is that existing things are greater than the mere concepts of them. So if the fool were correct and the GCB were a mere concept (if it existed, as Anselm says, only in the mind), it would still be true that the nonexisting thing described by the concept "Greatest Conceivable Being" could possibly exist, and that if it did exist, it would be greater than it (as nonexisting) in fact is. There are surely lots of difficulties that could be and have been raised against the OA at this point.[7] But I have said enough to show that Anselm's argument can be defended against Martin's first objection.

(2) Lost islands and greatest evil beings. Martin's second main criticism of Anselm's argument is his appeal to what I will call "parallel OAs." (Martin calls them parodies of the OA.) That is, Martin follows the strategy laid out by Gaunilo centuries ago in arguing that the basic logic of the OA (a reductio ad absurdum argument based on a definition of a thing together with certain necessary truths) can be used to "prove" the existence of all sorts of bizarre entities that we know good and well do not exist. These are entities like "the greatest conceivable lost island" (Gaunilo's own example) or "the absolute evil one" (this is Martin's term; he should, of course, have said, "the Greatest Conceivable Evil Being" or perhaps "the Evilest Conceivable Being"). What you do is simply remove the term *GCB* from the OA and systematically replace it with some other term like *GCLI* or *GCEB*; what results will be a parallel OA; and if the OA is a successful argument (so it is argued), so will be the parallel OA. But we know that the parallel OA is fallacious (no GCLI exists); ergo, the OA itself must equally be fallacious. Moreover, Martin says, the GCB and the absolute evil one cannot both exist, since they are "mutually exclusive." "Clearly," he says, "something is wrong" (82).

Anselm himself replied to Gaunilo's objection. His response was brief and rather flippant, and Martin finds it unhelpful (it consists, he says, of "little more than insisting that the reasoning used in the argument can only be applied to God"). But I will argue that Anselm's reply was more incisive that Martin admits. What Anselm said was:

> Now I promise confidently that if any man shall devise anything existing either in reality or in concept alone (except that than which a greater cannot be conceived) to which he can adapt the sequence of my reasoning, I will discover that thing, and will give him his lost island, not to be lost again.[8]

In other words, Anselm wanted to argue, as Martin notices, that the OA is a sound argument and that Gaunilo's parallel OA containing the term *GCLI* is not.[9]

How might Anselm argue, and not just assert, that his own argument is sound and Gaunilo's is not? The crucial point concerns premise (2) of the OA, which says:

(2) The GCB can possibly exist in reality, that is, is not an impossible thing.

And in Gaunilo's parallel OA, the counterpart premise would be:

(2a) The GCLI can possibly exist in reality, that is, is not an impossible thing.

Now some philosophers have argued that premise (2) is false; they hold that the concept of God is contradictory or otherwise incoherent. But my own view is that these arguments have never amounted to much. Moreover, we are, strictly speaking, talking about the concept of the GCB, not God (even though Anselm, along with most readers of the OA, took them to be the same), which I am interpreting as the most powerful conceivable being. This, I would argue, is surely a possible thing. As noted above, the GCB has something like this property: it is able to bring about any state of affairs that it is logically possible for it (the GCB) to bring about.

But is premise (2a) true? That is, is the concept of the GCLI a coherent concept? Anselm apparently thought not. Much depends here on what is meant by the word "conceivable," that is, on how widely we draw the limits of conceivability. We might draw them narrowly or widely. To draw them narrowly is to say that conceivability equals logical possibility, that is, logically impossible things are inconceivable. To draw them widely is to say that conceivability is broader than logical possibility, that is, that it is possible to conceive of logically impossible things. How Anselm will respond to Gaunilo-type objections to the OA will depend on which route the objector takes.

Suppose the objector wants wide limits. We can conceive, then, of logically impossible things like square circles, married bachelors, and contingent things possessing unlimited perfections. Then there is a big problem with premise (2a): the greater we make the GCLI in conception, the less it will resemble an island. We have seen that more powerful things are greater than less powerful things; moreover (as Anselm explicitly says in *Proslogion* III), necessary things are greater than contingent things. It follows, then, that the GCLI will be a necessary and omnipotent being. It will be everlasting, will depend for its existence on nothing else, and will be able to solve equations, write poetry, and manufacture carburetors. Now, there is no problem with the GCB being an omnipotent, necessary being—that is just what we would expect. But surely islands are essentially contingent and nonomnipotent things. They depend for their existence on geological, oceanographic, and other forces. There are things that they cannot do. That is why the GCLI cannot possibly exist and why premise (2a) is false. On a wide understanding of conceivability, the greatest conceivable lost island, that is, a necessary and omnipotent island, is logically impossible.

At this point, a defender of Gaunilo will opt for retiring to the narrower notion of conceivability, where what is conceivable equals what is logically possible. If so, we will have to conceive of the GCLI in terms of the great-making properties that islands can possibly have, properties like the temperature, the beauty of the scenery, the height of the surf, the number of palm trees, the taste of the coconuts, etc. Thus the term GCLI will no longer name an impossible being. Martin grasps this point. He says: "But if one means by 'the greatest conceivable island' a perfect island, it will not have an unlimited number of cocoanut trees but only the *right* number of cocoanut trees, whatever that may be" (83).

But there is a big problem here as well, and Martin has walked right into it: there is no "way that may be" or "way that it is" here. These sorts of great-making properties have no intrinsic or objective criteria of greatness. How do we decide which of two beautiful scenes is more beautiful, or which taste of coconuts is better, or how high the surf should be? These items seem to be matters of taste—do we vote? Moreover, these sorts of great-making properties have no intrinsic maximums or discernible limits. Thus there logically can be no "great*est* conceivable lost island." Thus, again, even on the narrower way of understanding conceivability, premise (2a) is false.

It appears, then, that no matter how we understand the term "conceivable," Gaunilo's parallel OA will be unsound because it will contain at least one false premise, that is (2a). The GCLI cannot possibly exist in reality. Accordingly, Anselm was right in insisting that the term GCLI cannot be adapted to the sequence of his reasoning. The "lost island" objection to the OA accordingly fails.

Well, then, what about Martin's "absolute evil one" (the evilest conceivable being" or ECB)? Does this concept constitute a counterexample to Anselm's argument? Not at all, and for the same reason. In Martin's imagined parallel OA, the parallel premise to the OA's premise (2) would be:

(2b) the ECB can possibly exist in reality, that is, is not an impossible thing.

And, of course, all the same problems come up. There is no intrinsic maximum to the amount of heinous deeds a given being can do, nor any intrinsic maximum to their heinousness. Just as there logically can be no "tallest conceivable human being," so there logically can be no ECB.

For every evil deed that we imagine an evil being doing, we can always imagine a being who does one more evil deed. No matter how terrible the deeds we imagine an evil being doing, we can always imagine a being who does deeds even more terrible. Thus premise (2b) is false; Martin's imagined parallel OA fails; and Anselm's argument emerges unscathed from Martin's second criticism.

(3) Mackie's criticism. Finally, Martin repeats against Anselm a criticism of J. L. Mackie.[10] Mackie's basic point, which is a neighbor of a point also made by Gaunilo,[11] is that it is impossible to prove the existence of any concrete reality by an entirely a priori procedure, that is, merely by examining concepts or definitions. The fool only contradicts himself, Martin says, if the fool's concept is *a nonexistent being than which no greater can be conceived.* But the fool should only be conceiving of *a being than which no greater can be conceived.* There is no contradiction in the fool's claiming that such a being does not exist, that is, that the concept has no instantiation in the real world. Understood that way, the fool can even grant Anselm's claim that "exists" is a great-making property and thus that existence is part of the concept of the GCB. The fool will simply insist that the concept is not an instantiated concept. Definitionally, the GCB would exist (must be conceived as existing) in reality (just as the concept "an existing Loch Ness monster" must be conceived as existing). And the statement "The GCB does not exist" would indeed be contradictory. But that would not show that the GCB exists in fact, that is, that the concept *GCB* is instantiated.

But it must be insisted at this point that nowhere has Anselm defined the GCB as existing in reality or even assumed that the GCB exists in reality. It is possible to come up with an a priori theistic proof that does something like this, for example:

10. "God" is an existing omnipotent and omniscient and loving being.
11. Therefore, God exists.

But that argument, formally valid as it is, would be quite uninteresting and unworthy of serious consideration because it egregiously begs the question. It assumes in premise (10) exactly what it purports to prove in premise (11). But there is no such strategy in Anselm.

Perhaps at heart Martin's objection is to the very idea of using an a priori procedure to prove the existence in reality of something. But we certainly can prove some things about what exists or does not exist in reality by purely a priori procedures, that is, without empirically looking around or counting or experimenting. For example, it can be shown that married bachelors ("unmarried adult males who are married") and square circles ("plane four-sided geometrical figures all of whose points are equidistant from the center") cannot and thus do not exist in reality. Similarly, it can be shown by purely a priori procedures that "There exists at least one prime number between six and ten" is true. The point is not that Anselm's GCB is like a number, but that a priori procedures can prove the existence in reality of certain sorts of things.

But the most important point here is that it is question-begging simply to insist against Anselm that "you can't do that," that is, that no a priori proofs of the existence can possibly be successful. The OA itself will have to be examined to see whether it does succeed. If it does not, the precise reason that it fails will have to be shown.

Accordingly, Martin's criticisms of Anselm's *Proslogion* II OA are entirely unsuccessful in overturning it. Anselm's argument may or may not constitute a sound theistic proof, but Martin has not shown that it does not.

IV

It is now time to consider Martin's critique of Alvin Plantinga's version of the OA, what has come to be called the Modal OA (MOA). Here is Martin's version of Plantinga's argument (with the numbers of the premises changed to conform to the numbering in this chapter). Plantinga here defines maximal greatness as entailing maximal excellence in every possible world, and maximal excellence as entailing omniscience, omnipotence, and moral perfection in every possible world.

12. There is a possible world where maximal excellence is exemplified.
13. There is some possible world in which there is a being that is maximally great (from premise 12).
14. Necessarily, a being that is maximally great is maximally excellent in every possible world (by definition).
15. Necessarily, a being that is maximally excellent in every possible world is omniscient, omnipotent, and morally perfect in every possible world (by definition).
16. Therefore, there is in our world and in every world a being that is omniscient, omnipotent, and morally perfect (from premises 13, 14, and 15).

Martin correctly notes that Plantinga does not take the MOA as a conclusive demonstration of the existence of a maximally excellent being. This is because Plantinga knows that rational people can deny premise

(12). But since Plantinga thinks that premise (12) is not contrary to reason, the MOA demonstrates the rational acceptability of belief in God.

Since Martin says nothing about accessibility relations among possible worlds, let me add a few introductory remarks about the MOA.[12] The MOA is based on the modal logical system S5, whose characteristic theorem is:

17. $\Diamond\Box p \rightarrow \Box p$.

Also crucial to the S5 system is the symmetry condition on the accessibility relations between possible worlds. Let us say that one possible world X is accessible from another possible world Y if and only if X is possible in Y. And let us say that an accessibility relation R has the property of symmetry if and only if, when any possible world X is accessible to another possible world Y, it follows that Y is accessible to X.

Now take the property "unsurpassable greatness" (UG). If this property is possibly instantiated, then there exists a possible world X, in which a certain being instantiates UG. But given Plantinga's definition of UG, a being that instantiates UG is such that if it exists in any possible world, then it is necessary that it exists in this world. Ergo, it is necessary that a being instantiates UG in X. And since we are assuming that symmetry holds, it follows that a being that instantiates UG will exist in every world that is accessible to X. But since the actual world is obviously one of the worlds that is accessible to X, it follows that a being instantiates UG in the actual world as well. Thus the semantics of S5, especially the symmetry condition, allows Plantinga to postulate the existence of a being instantiating UG in a merely possible world and thereby establish that being's existence in the actual world.

Martin offers three criticisms of the MOA. First, following J. L. Mackie, he argues that the S5 system of modal logic is inappropriate. Second, he argues that the use Plantinga makes of Leibniz' Law (which I will explain below) is a poor example. Third, he argues as above with Gaunilo that Plantinga's MOA can be parodied. Let us consider these points in turn.

So far as the first point is concerned, Martin does not develop it at length. He simply says that

> Technical questions can be raised about the use of possible world semantics and modal logic in [Plantinga's] proof. In particular, it may be wondered if the system of modal logic used in Plantinga's proof is appropriate and if Plantinga has provided adequate truth conditions for modal sentences (83).

And Marin specifically refers to published arguments by Mackie and Michael Tooley. Martin's worry here is not easy to grasp, especially since nearly every philosopher who discusses the MOA agrees that the S5 modal system is entirely appropriate in this context. Indeed, Plantinga himself has answered Mackie's criticisms about S5, in my view rather decisively.[13]

What exactly is Martin's concern? Perhaps he wants to dispute premise (17). But premise (17) seems intuitively obvious to many people, including me, and powerful arguments can be suggested in its favor. Let us call the set of all possible worlds "p." Now let us arbitrarily pick any possible world within p and call it w. Question: if $\Box$p is true, what is the truth value of $\Box$p in w? Obviously, $\Box$p has the truth value of true in w. This is because in w, the proposition $\Box$p asserts that p is true both in w and in every other possible world. But whatever is true of any arbitrarily selected possible world is true of every possible world. Thus, if it is possible that p is necessarily true in some world, then p is necessarily true. And this is just what premise (17) asserts.

Here is another argument for the same point. Clearly, a proposition and its contrapositive are logically equivalent. If "If p then q" is true, then so is "If not q then not p." The contrapositive of premise 17 is:

18. $\sim\Box p \rightarrow \sim\Diamond\Box p$.

To some people, premise (18) might have even more intuitive appeal than premise (17), since, obviously, if a proposition p does not have the property of being true in all possible worlds, then it follows that it is not even possible that p be true in all possible worlds. That is, it is false that in some worlds it is true that p is true in all worlds. So if p is not necessarily true, then it is not possible that p be necessarily true. Now if this reasoning seems correct, then premise (18) is true. And if premise (18) is true, then so is its contrapositive premise (17).[14]

Now another characteristic formula of the S5 system of modal logic is:

19. $\Diamond p \rightarrow \Box\Diamond p$.

Perhaps premise (19) constitutes Martin's worry about S5. And premise (19) simply says that if p is true in at least one possible world, then the proposition "p is true in at least one possible world" is true in all possible worlds. In other words, a proposition's modal status—whatever it is—is always necessary. And maybe Martin is suspicious of premise (19).

But premise (19) seems eminently plausible. Look at the cost of denying it. To deny that $\Diamond$p implies $\Box\Diamond$p is to assert that p may have the property of being true in at least one possible world even though the assertion that it has this property is not true in every possible world (i.e., is false in at least one possible world). But this cannot be. Let p stand for the proposition

20. There will be a nuclear war within the next decade.

Now, I do not know whether premise (20) is true (I certainly hope not), but it is certainly possibly true. Thus, returning to premise (19), its antecedent is true for this particular substitution instance of p. But in order for Martin to deny premise (19), he must hold that there is a possible world in which it is false that premise (20) is logically possible. That is, he must hold that there is a possible world in which premise (20) is logically impossible. But surely there is no such world; any possible world in which premise (20) is logically impossible will itself be a logically impossible world. Accordingly, one cannot affirm the antecedent and deny the consequent of premise (19).

Again, this point seems plausible. How could some proposition q be true in some possible world and yet fail to be logically possible in some other possible world? If it is possible that q is true, then there is a possible world—call it w—in which q is true. But then it follows that "q is true in w" is true in every possible world. That is, it is necessary that it is possible that q is true in w.[15] So Martin's objection to the S5 system of modal logic does not amount to much. If we are to believe that there is a serious objection to the MOA somewhere in the neighborhood, Martin is going to have to say a great deal more.

As part of his argument for the truth of premise (12), which he admits rational people can deny, Plantinga makes reference to "Leibniz's Law" (LL). He points out that we have no proof of LL, but we are justified in accepting it. But Martin objects that the analogy between premise 12 and LL is tenuous. He identifies LL as:

> For any objects x and y and property P, if x = y, then x has P if and only if y has P.

He then says, "LL is a free English translation of a theorem of first-order predicate calculus with identity, but [premise (12)] is not a translation of a theorem of any standard logic. Disputes about LL in the history of philosophy, unlike disputes about [premise (12)], seem to be metalinguistic and not over the truth value of LL" (94).

This point seems to me to be Martin's best point against Plantinga, but in the end it goes nowhere. Plantinga might happily admit that there are disanalogies between LL and premise (12), maybe even that his example was poorly chosen, and proceed merrily on his way. Even if Martin is entirely correct, this does nothing to weaken the MOA. Plantinga might well find better examples of philosophical propositions that we rationally accept without proof. Clearly, what Plantinga has preeminently in mind is the fact that both premise (12) and LL are either necessarily true or necessarily false. Other positions in philosophy that are either necessarily true or necessarily false and which many people rationally accept without proof are realism on universals, nominalism, actualism, serious actualism, and David Lewis' modal realism.

V

Finally, Martin argues that Plantinga's OA, like Anselm's, can be refuted by parody or (as I prefer) by a parallel OA. He claims that the MOA

> can be parodied by using an argument with the same form to show the rational acceptability of fairies, ghosts, unicorns, and all manner of strange creatures. One *reductio* of this mode of argument proceeds as follows: "Let us define the property of being a special fairy so that it entails the property of being a fairy in every possible world. Let us define the property of being a fairy so that it entails the property of being a tiny woodland creature with magical powers in every possible world" (94).

Martin then goes on to state his parallel MOA, using the concept "special fairy" in place of "maximally excellent being." (Again, the numbers of Martin's premises have been changed.)

21. There is one possible world where the property of being a special fairy is exemplified.
22. There is one possible world where there is a special fairy (from premise 21).
23. Necessarily, a being that is a special fairy is a fairy in every possible world (by definition).
24. Necessarily, a being that is a fairy in every possible world is a tiny woodland creature with magical powers in every possible world (by definition).
25. Therefore, there is a tiny woodland creature with magical powers in our world and in every world.

Martin argues that premise (22) is "no more contrary to reason" than premise (12) of the MOA, and thus that premise (25) is just as acceptable as the conclusion of the MOA. The moral is supposed to be, as before with Gaunilo and Anselm, that something is clearly defective about the MOA.

But this argument collapses almost before it can even get going. Premise (22) is the culprit. It is about as clear as it could possibly be that there can be no such thing as a necessarily existent fairy. Fairies, presumably, are physical objects (or are at least essentially connected to physical objects). And no physical object can be a necessary being, since it is possible that there be no material objects at all. But since Plantinga's Maximally Excellent Being (like Anselm's GCB) is not necessarily a physical object, this objection to Martin's parallel MOA has no relevance to the MOA. Moreover, physical or not, the very idea of a necessarily existent fairy is, if not explicitly contradictory, at least deeply problematical. We saw above in our discussion of Gaunilo that no island can be a necessary being, and surely the same is true of fairies. It is difficult to imagine a tiny woodland creature with magical powers as anything other than a contingent being.

The conclusion is that Martin's criticisms not only do not refute the MOA but leave it virtually unscathed. Plantinga's version of the OA—even given its admitted limitation that rational people can deny premise (12)—still stands as a successful piece of natural theology. It shows that rational people can rationally believe in the existence of a maximally excellent being.

VI

It is not surprising that Michael Martin, an atheist, would reject the OA in all its versions. For the OA is a knockdown argument. If it is a formally and informally valid argument, and if its premises are true, then the being whose existence is being proven does indeed exist. That is, the OA is not a probabilistic argument or an argument based on making broad inferences from huge sets of data. If the OA succeeds, then God exists, and that is the end of the matter. Perhaps this is one reason that the OA has always been so disturbing to so many atheists, agnostics, and even some theists (who reject the OA but believe in God on other grounds).

This is related to a phenomenon that I have often observed in students who study the OA. Not infrequently, some of them describe themselves as being unable to refute the argument but being deeply suspicious of it. For one reason or another, they are unable to accept the conclusion of the OA, and so they say, "But something *must* be wrong with it." Well, perhaps there is something wrong with the OA. But even if so, Michael Martin has not located what it is. So far as his criticisms are concerned, the OA still stands.[16]

16

Three Views of God, Which Is Correct?

I

Nothing is more important in Christian philosophy than the concept of God. Christianity is essentially based on the notion of a God who creates and redeems us. But what is God like? What are God's attributes or properties? There is, among Christian philosophers, a large area of agreement or overlap in their explanations of God's nature, but serious disagreement too. On the question of God's attributes, Christian philosophers have written a great deal.

There is a core concept of God that the vast majority of Christian philosophers and theologians affirm. They accept it because they believe that it is taught in Scripture and in the Christian theological and confessional tradition.[1]

> Core Concept: God is ultimate reality; God necessarily exists[2]; and as the unique, omnipotent, omniscient, and perfectly good creator of the heavens and the earth, God is worthy of our worship.

Obviously, the meanings of many of these terms can be and have been disputed, and there are Christian philosophers who deny some of them. But I believe that this core concept of God can be said to be common ground among most Christian philosophers today.[3]

The present chapter is a slightly revised version of my "Three Views of God in Contemporary Christian Philosophy," in Readings in the Philosophy of Religion, *2nd ed., ed. Kelly James Clark (Orchard Park, N.Y.: Broadview, 2007).*

But beyond this core concept, there are sharp differences among Christian philosophers on the concept of God. Those differences emerge mainly as a result of two factors. There are, for example, disagreements about how to interpret those passages in the Christian Scriptures that talk about God. There are also different intuitions about the meaning and implications of such concepts as "ultimate reality," "perfect being," "worthy of worship," etc. In this essay I will focus on three views of God that are alive and well among Christian philosophers today.

II

We'll call the three views of God that I want to discuss, respectively, the Classical Theory (CT), the Neoclassical Theory (NCT) and the Openness Theory (OT). My descriptions of them will be rough and incomplete but, I hope, reasonably accurate.

CT has been held by many great Christian philosophers and theologians, notably Augustine, Aquinas, and Calvin. It is ably defended these days by Christian philosophers such as David Burrell, Brian Davies, Paul Helm, Brian Leftow, Hugh McCann, Ralph McInerny, and Eleonore Stump. CT can be defined roughly as follows:

> God is the unique, omnipotent, omniscient, and perfectly good creator of the heavens and the earth; God is a necessary being; and God is timeless, strongly immutable, impassible, and metaphysically simple.

Very roughly, let us say that a being is *timeless* if it is outside of time, if it has no temporal location or temporal extension. On CT it makes no sense to say, for example, that "God existed in A.D. 1529" or that "God existed during the entire time of the Cold War." Temporal terms such as these have no application to God. A being is *strongly immutable* if it is never true to say that at one point in time it has a certain property and at another point in time does not have it, except for purely relational changes like, "is believed in by Augustine or by Charles Colson" (to pick examples of two famous people who were adult converts to Christianity). On CT, it makes no sense to say, for example, that God's attitude toward me after I repent is different from what it was before. A being is *impassable* if it never suffers pain or is changed in attitude, emotion, or behavior by causes external to it. On CT, it makes no sense to say, for example, that God suffers with us when we suffer. And a being is *metaphysically simple* if it consists of no composite parts, that is, has no complexity of any kind, and is accordingly indivisible. It has no spatial parts nor even a set of distinct properties or attributes. Of course believers in divine simplicity can say things like, "God is good and wise," but they deny that it means God has two properties (goodness and wisdom). They say God "just is" God's properties, which is a slightly paradoxical way of expressing the doctrine. They even sometimes say God's goodness "just is" God's wisdom, and vice-versa.

NCT is the view of God that is held, I believe, by the majority of Christian philosophers who write about God today, including David Brown, Kelly Clark, William L. Craig, Alan Padgett, Alvin Plantinga, and Nicholas Wolterstorff. (The fact that a majority hold the theory does not make it true, of course.)

> God is the unique, omnipotent, omniscient, and perfectly good creator of the heavens and the earth; God is a necessary being; and God is temporal, weakly immutable, passable, and not metaphysically simple.

Again very roughly, let us say that a being is *temporal* if there is a real past, present, and future for it, if it has both temporal location and temporal duration. This is not to say, of course, that the being is temporally finite; defenders of NCT always insist that God is everlasting, has no beginning and no end. A being is *weakly immutable* if it changes in some ways but always retains its essential nature and character, is true to its word, keeps its promises, never wavers in its purposes, can always be relied upon, and is not fickle, mercurial, or moody. A being is *not metaphysically simple*, that is, is metaphysically complex, if it consists of composite parts.

OT is a view of God that has received considerable attention in Christian philosophical and theological circles in recent decades. Its hallmark is a denial of comprehensive divine foreknowledge; what God does not know about the future—so the most common version of the theory says—is the result of human free choices. What is called "Openness Theology" or the "Open View of God" is associated with people like David Basinger, Greg Boyd, William Hasker, Clark Pinnock, and John Sanders. OT can be briefly defined in this way:

> God is the unique, omnipotent, omniscient (in the sense of knowing everything that can possibly be known), and perfectly good creator of the heavens and the earth; God is a necessary being; God is temporal, weakly immutable, passable, and not metaphysically simple; and God does not know the results of future human free decisions.

Accordingly, OT holds that God does not know the entire future.

Now there are two ways that defenders of OT can develop their theory.[4] The less radical version (call it RFOT for "Real Future Open Theology") affirms that there is a real future to be known but denies that God knows all of it. God certainly knows, on this view, what will happen in the future as a result of God's own firm intentions about what to do, but God does not know future contingents, that is, events that may or may not occur in the future, especially what will or will not occur due to free human choices. Accordingly, God can be said to take risks and be surprised. The future is open, not fixed by divine foreknowledge or by anything else. If I will be free tomorrow morning to put on my left shoe either before or after my right shoe, God does not know, and has never known, which I will do.

The more radical version of OT (call it POT for "Presentist Open Theology") is based primarily on a metaphysical conviction, viz., that the future is not real. What we call "the future" does not exist and so logically cannot be known by God or anyone else, since there is literally nothing to know. What is real is the present, and that is all. But I will discuss this version of OT no further in the present paper, and for two reasons. The metaphysical reason is that Presentism (since it holds that the past is not real either) reduces reality ("the present") to nothing but an infinitely thin boundary line between the past and the future. And that cannot be the right way of looking at reality; what is real must amount to more than that. The biblical reason is that if there is now no fact of the matter about future events, then there is no fact of the matter about whether Jesus will return or whether God will win in the end. And that seems a hard conclusion for Christians to accept.

III

So which of these theories is true or closest to the truth? Although abstruse debates about God are rarely easy to settle, this will be the question I will try to answer in the present chapter. My own views will become clear as I progress, but let me announce here that while I am deeply attracted to CT, in the end I cannot make sense of it; I reject OT; and so NCT is the theory that I embrace.

Christian thinking about God—so it seems to me—must be done in tension, so to speak, between two opposite poles. God is transcendent and God is immanent. Christians must hold that both claims are true, and the neglect of one over the other leads to error. The claim that God is transcendent entails that God is infinitely greater than and superior to the whole of creation; we are quite unable to understand God or God's ways; God is not like a powerful and grand human being.[5] The claim that God is immanent follows from Christian notions like: we were created in God's image, so that in some ways we are like God (and since "being similar to" is a symmetrical relation, if we are in some ways like God, then God is in some ways like us); God reveals himself to us and acts in the created order; and in the incarnation of Christ God became one of us. Indeed, God is a *person*—not, of course, in the same way in which we are persons, but at least in the sense of having a mental life that includes knowledge, desires, and intentions, as well as being an agent, as having the ability to bring those intentions to fruition.

Some theories of God go too far in one direction or the other. The danger of going too far in the immanence direction is *anthropomorphism*. This is the tendency to suppose that nonhuman things—in this case, God—are very much like human beings. The ancient Greek pantheon, for example, was anthropomorphic; gods like Zeus, Ares, and Athena were indeed far more powerful than human beings and did not have to die, but in most other ways they were similar to human beings. But it is possible to go too far in the transcendence direction too. The gods of the ancient Epicureans, for example, were ideal exemplars of *ataraxia* (calm, serenity, imperturbability), but they lived far away from the earth and had nothing to do with human affairs. The God of seventeenth-century deism, who creates the heavens and the earth and its natural laws and processes but never interferes thereafter, also seems too transcendent. So the danger of going too far in the transcendence direction is that we arrive at a God who has little to do with us and about whom we can know little.

IV

As noted, the two theories that I wish to criticize are CT and OT. In approaching CT, I think a good way to proceed is for me to list five reasons why I think many Christian philosophers today reject it. They are: Scripture, human freedom, the origin of sin, apologetic concerns, and pastoral considerations.

Scripture. Many Christian philosophers have a hard time—as I do—reconciling the God depicted in the Bible with a God who is timeless, immutable, simple, and impassable. It seems that God does temporally interact with people, issuing commands that they must obey in the future, judging them for things they have done in the past, and forgiving them because of their acts of repentance. It also seems that God has different attributes that are not the same as each other, for example, (as before) goodness and wisdom; moreover, Christians believe that in at least some sense of the word "part" (not physical parts like arms and legs), God has three parts, that is, the Trinitarian persons. We know, of course, that there is anthropomorphism in the Bible as well as very many literary genres. Moreover, we are aware of the exceedingly clever and nuanced attempts by medieval philosophers (especially Aquinas) and some of our contemporaries to achieve a reconciliation between CT and the God of the Bible. Still, many of us are dubious that it can sensibly be done. This point constitutes a major impediment to accepting CT.

Human freedom. Those who accept CT are inevitably drawn to compatibilism vis-a-vis human freedom, and this is a theory that is unacceptable to many contemporary philosophers of religion, including me. (Compatibilism is the philosophical theory that says human moral responsibility is compatible with determinism. In theology, compatibilism says human moral responsibility is compatible with divine foreordination of all things.) That human beings are sometimes free in a libertarian sense is one of our deepest phenomenological convictions; that is, we think it is sometimes possible for a human being, under the same set of antecedent causes, to do a given act or not do it. Moreover, we do not find plausible the various efforts that have been made by defenders of CT and others to reconcile compatibilist freedom with moral responsibility. And the assertion that human beings are morally responsible for their sins is one of the most important principles of biblical religion. Again, we are aware of the thoughtful attempts in the tradition to reconcile compatibilist freedom and human moral responsibility, but we are unconvinced.

The origin of evil. Those who defend CT always insist that the reason God perfectly foreknows the future is that the future will be what it will be because, in some sense, God wills or foreordains what it will be.[6] It is crucial to CT to insist that all of God's aims or purposes will be accomplished. And the obvious problem here is that this seems to make God the author of evil, both natural and moral. How can God, who is perfectly morally good, foreordain people to sin? How can God, who is perfectly just, condemn foreordained sinners to hell? Defenders of CT, of course, respond to this charge. But despite the subtle distinctions they make at this point, many contemporary Christian philosophers see nothing but paradox in affirming both divine foreordination of all events and human responsibility for their sins.[7]

Apologetic issues. People who are committed to CT often insist that it makes no sense for Christians to try to argue that God is "morally good" in some sense similar to the way in which respected and honored human beings are morally good. I, too, wish strongly to affirm that God's goodness far transcends even the best of human goodness. Still, apologetic issues come into play here whenever we try to reply to Mackie-like objections in the area of the problem of evil.[8] Atheists certainly do pose questions about God's moral integrity. I once met a man—a veteran of World War II—who said to me, "I have seen things with my own eyes that God would never permit if God existed." In order to answer people who say things like that (more frequent, perhaps, are comments like, "I will not believe in a God who allows X, Y, and Z"), Christian philosophers have felt constrained to argue that God can still be perfectly morally good despite the occurrence of evil events. I regard that as a perfectly understandable and acceptable reaction. Does God need our apologetic interventions? Of course not. But some people apparently need them. Such folk need to be told where their thinking has led them astray. So this point constitutes a reason to question CT as an adequate view of God if CT holds—as it normally does—that all human attempts to show that God is "morally good" cannot get off the ground.

Pastoral considerations. A closely related point: when I was a young assistant pastor just out of theological seminary, a member of my parish was diagnosed with lupus, a disease for which there was then (and so far as I know, still is) no known cure. I spoke with him, and with his wife, on several occasions. A metalworker without much education, he, in effect, asked me the question, "Why did this happen to me?" His wife was even more deeply troubled. I was faced with a pastoral situation where a believer, that is, the wife, was calling into question God's moral integrity. I saw it as my pastoral responsibility to let her express her pain and anger, to suffer with her (usually in silence), and occasionally to try to get her to see that God was good and could be praised for his goodness despite what had happened to her husband. Had I been a strict defender of CT, I would not have been able to comfort either the husband or the wife, unless they found it comforting to be told, "Get used to it: God causes every event that occurs, and we must love and honor God nevertheless."[9]

What about CT's doctrine of divine impassibility? The classical theorist's objection to passibility is this: if God were to feel sorrow when we suffer, that would make God's emotional state depend on us, and so God's existence and nature would not be wholly independent of us. Despite this argument, in the past one hundred years, not just most philosophers of religion but virtually the entire Christian theological world (with the exception of those who embrace CT) has moved to the notion that God *qua* God suffers.[10] It is now virtually commonplace. (Again, that does not make it true.) The point that defenders of NCT or OT often make is this: once God creates human beings, reveals himself to them, and makes covenants with them, God gives up being wholly independent of the creatures. Of course, God does not depend in any sense on us for God's existence and essential nature. But God does respond to what we do, as literally hundreds of biblical passages imply.

In various ways, the defenders of CT want to increase the distance between God and human beings. For example, defenders of CT sometimes deny that God is a moral agent.[11] And I agree that God is not a moral agent in the same sense in which we are moral agents (i.e., morally responsible to a higher being). But I would have thought that God becomes a moral agent of a sort the moment God issues moral commands to human beings or makes covenants with them. Indeed, the moment God does that, God makes us part of God's moral community.

What about the notion of divine simplicity? This is a part of CT that I confess I only dimly understand. One problem is this: two attributes are obviously distinct from each other if it is logically possible for a substance to possess one of them but not the other. Thus *red* is not the same attribute as *tall* because it is possible for something to have one but not the other. So anything that is both red and tall is not metaphysically simple. But surely it is logically possible for a being to be *the creator of the heavens and the earth* without being *perfectly good*. Some religions have suggested this very thing. Thus if God possesses both these properties—as Christianity insists—God is not metaphysically simple.[12]

I do not think the arguments usually advanced in favor of divine simplicity are convincing. For example, it is sometimes said that whatever has parts that are distinct from it depends on them for its existence and nature.[13] But I would reply that if God is a necessary being and if God's parts are essential to God, this does not follow. No necessary being depends on *anything* for its existence. Another argument: Paul Helm claims that composite things must be caused to exist. Everything composite, he says, "is subsequent to its components and depends on them."[14] But I am unsure what "subsequent to" means in this context. Am I "subsequent to" my left foot? I certainly in some sense depend on it, but if God is composite, God cannot be separated from God's parts, as I can, and so is not dependent on them in any theologically untoward way. A similar argument: James Ross claims that denying divine simplicity entails "God's incompleteness and dependence on things *ad extra*."[15] But I do not think this notion entails God's incompleteness at all since God's parts are obviously going to be essential parts of God, who is a necessary being. God's parts are related to each other and to God because they cannot *not* be so related. Accordingly, it does not entail God's dependence on anything external to God. Nor, if God is a necessary being, is any explanation required of why the parts of God are related to each other as they are. It is simply an essential aspect of reality that God's parts are related to each other as they are.

Some defenders of CT strongly deny that God is "an item in the universe."[16] In my view, the answer to the question whether that is true depends on what is meant by "the universe." Perhaps the term refers to the huge aggregate of all creatures, that is, all the contingent things that have ever existed, now exist, or will ever exist. On that understanding of the term, God is not an item in the universe. God is not a contingent thing. But if by the term "the universe" we mean the set of all real or existing things, then—or so I would hold—God is indeed an item in the universe. Does it necessarily demean God's transcendence and sovereignty to affirm as much? I do not see why. One can still be quite clear about all the ways in which God differs from the creatures.

Some theologians and philosophers of religion have denied that God is a "being." But I have always thought that the English term *being* is almost infinite in what it ranges over. A being is just anything whose name or referring term can appear in the subject position of a coherent sentence, is a property bearer, and has an identity apart from other things. Is God a being like other beings? Of course not. Is God a being among others beings? Of course (or so I would say).

What clinches God's membership in the set of existing beings, in my opinion, is the fact of revelation. Apart from God's revealing God to us, we would know nothing of God. Thus Psalm 28:1: "To you, O Lord, I call; my rock, do not refuse to hear me, for if you are silent to me, I shall be like those who go down to the Pit." If God were silent, some sort of Epicureanism or deism would be believable. But, as the prophet Amos affirms, God does speak to us: "Lo, the one who forms the mountains, creates the wind, *reveals his thoughts to mortals,* makes the morning darkness, and treads on the heights of the earth—the Lord, the God of hosts is his name!" (Amos 4:13, emphasis added). If God reveals himself to us, and even becomes one of us in the incarnation, it is hard for me to see how sensibly to deny the claim that God is an item in the universe. Certainly, as just noted, God is not an item like all the other items, but that is another matter.

V

It is time to turn to OT. It is important to note that one central issue in relation to OT is philosophical in nature. Defenders of OT are convinced that (1) the future is open (reality is such that much of the future is not settled), (2) human beings are sometimes free in a libertarian sense in the decisions they make and the things they do, and (3) complete divine foreknowledge is logically incompatible with human libertarian freedom.

So God always knows everything that logically can be known and, as noted, knows his own intentions about what to do in the future as well as future events that can be inferred from past and present events. But results of future free decisions simply cannot be known. (Defenders of NCT, on the other hand, accept (1) and (2) but not (3).) According to OT, much of what God knows about the future is limited to possibilities. So God is in a sense vulnerable in that God must take risks in order to accomplish things that involve human beings and their free decisions; God will occasionally be surprised and so must be flexible and tactically astute. God's will is going to be frustrated on occasion, and God will experience regret and disappointment; God must adapt and change in order to accomplish God's goals.

Despite the fact that I reject OT, it must be admitted that the theory has two strong points. First, it is indeed difficult to see how divine foreknowledge and human libertarian freedom can be consistent. (I will address that issue below.) Second, OT seems to have ready answers to questions like: Why would God create and bestow libertarian freedom on those human beings who would become moral monsters like Hitler or Charles Manson? And why would God create and bestow freedom on those human beings whom he foreknew would end up condemned in hell? The obvious answer is that God was not able to foreknow those sorts of outcomes.

Although one central issue here is philosophical, there is no denying that there are important biblical and theological ramifications of OT. Biblically, defenders of OT tend to emphasize and interpret literally those biblical texts that have God ignorant of the future, changing his mind, or reworking his plans in response to human decisions and actions. For example, at the outset of the story of the great flood, Genesis 6:5-6 says:

> The Lord saw that the wickedness of humankind was great in the earth, and that every inclination of the thoughts of their hearts was only evil continually. And the Lord was sorry that he had made humankind on the earth, and it grieved him to his heart.

Open theologians will interpret these words as implying that when God originally made human beings, God did not know how rampant evil would become, and that God caused the great flood to occur as a way of dealing with his regret for having created human beings and as an effort to find a new way to achieve his ends for humankind. Whether this is the correct way to interpret this text, and others like it, is a matter of considerable dispute, but it is a debate that we can enter into here only briefly.

Suffice it to say that opponents of OT argue that the Bible is largely a collection of texts about God's actions in human history as seen from a human perspective; that it is not a textbook in theology or the philosophy of religion; and that an understandable degree of anthropomorphism affects many such biblical texts. Accordingly, the fact that God is sometimes depicted as being ignorant of how things will turn out and as later regretful when they turn out badly is a function of how God's actions appeared to human observers of the events in question or how they seemed to the biblical writers at the time they wrote. Such texts do not describe God's inner life, nor (in my opinion) are they meant to do so.[17] Since they describe God's actions in the world, they describe not God as God is in himself but God as seen in God's work.[18]

Let me raise three objections to OT (again, we are speaking here only of RFOT).

What did God know at creation? I would personally find it repugnant to admit, as Open theorists must, that at the moment of creation, God did not know whether even a single human being would ever freely respond positively to God's call and thus eventually enter heaven.[19] Of course, defenders of OT can insist that God could have made probability judgments about how many people would decide freely to love and obey God and how many would refuse to do so. Still, it is hard to resist the feeling that we are now dealing with a God who, so far as knowledge is concerned, has been demoted. I would suggest that even if (contrary to what I will argue below) we cannot adequately solve the problem of reconciling divine foreknowledge with human libertarian freedom, it would be better to affirm them both, and admit the paradox, than to embrace OT.[20]

Is anything left of omniscience? As we saw above, the claim that God is all-knowing is part of Christianity's core concept of God. Defenders of OT insist that the God they envision is omniscient because at all times God knows everything that can possibly be known; future contingents—so they say—logically cannot be known. This claim must mean that Open theists hold that propositions about future contingent states of affairs do not now have a truth value, that is, are (for now) neither true nor false. It does not seem possible that there could be truths that are not knowable. Take the statement "Tomorrow Stephen Davis will freely decide to wear a blue shirt." If that statement now has a truth value, surely an omniscient being must know it, that is, must know whether it is true or false. So the defenders of OT must hold that such propositions are now neither true nor false (as philosophers say, they must deny the principle of bivalence).[21]

This is fair enough: although I am not prepared to grant that future contingent propositions have no truth value, I agree that, *if* they are neither true nor false, they cannot be known, and so it is no problem for omniscience if God does not know them. But there remains a thorny problem for defenders of OT. Let's think further about how they analyze those stories in the Bible where God appears to be surprised or disappointed by what people do. In such cases, it appears that before the event actually occurred, God held a false belief (e.g., that the people would respond as God desired). For example, it appears that (at least on the literalist hermeneutic that defenders of OT deploy in such cases) before the flood, God held the erroneous belief that the people would not descend into evil to the degree that they, in fact, did. But certainly anyone who holds a false belief is not omniscient, does not "know everything that can be known." It surely seems that mental states like surprise and disappointment could have been present in God only if prior to the surprising or disappointing event, God had an expectation that in the end was not met. Now beliefs are not the same things as expectations, but it is hard to see how someone can have an expectation that an event will occur without having some sort of belief (however strongly or weakly held) that it will occur. Accordingly, if God was surprised and disappointed at what eventually occurred, then before the event occurred, God had a false belief.[22] It will hardly do for defenders of OT to insist that the surprise and disappointment that God exhibits in these texts do not really represent God's mental states; that would violate the literalist hermeneutic that defenders of OT typically deploy in such cases.

And if we consistently follow that hermeneutic, it seems that we will be led to hold that God has spatial location (God walked in the Garden of Eden at the time of the evening breeze—Gen 3:8), is forgetful (God "remembered" Noah in his ark—Genesis 8:1, and God needed a reminder for himself [the rainbow] of his promise not to destroy all flesh again by flood—Gen 9:11-17), is impatient (Exod 32:7-14), and is sardonic, vengeful, and full of rage (Deut 29:28). Now defenders of CT and NCT have hermeneutically powerful ways of understanding these texts, but there appears to be little room for anthropomorphism or even accommodation among the defenders of OT. So it would be interesting to see how they would exegete such texts.

Does God's knowledge grow as time passes? Defenders of OT will want to argue that God's knowledge grows as time passes, and that eventually, in the eschaton, there will be no more future contingents for God to be ignorant of. At that point, God will know everything. But although the basic claim being made here seems correct, there is a problem with this picture. It seems that there is a sense in which God's degree of ignorance about the future must grow as time passes. God must be unaware not only of the result of future human free decisions but of all the multitudes of effects resulting from them, which of course will grow as time passes.

Note also that as more and more time passes, human knowledge also grows, as does human technology. We are now able to do things (fly airplanes, communicate instantly with people thousands of miles away, send spaceships to Mars) that earlier generations could only dream of. And in one sense this might mean that God knows less and less as time passes. In other words, in comparing the twenty-first century with, say, the Pleistocene Age, far more of what occurs in the world now depends on free human choices than previously. Perhaps one day human beings will possess the technical ability to destroy the entire solar system, just as we now have the ability to destroy human life on earth. Does God now know that human life will survive the twenty-first century? Of course, the God of OT always knows what people are presently doing, and so could presumably interfere—at the last moment, so to speak—to prevent the manufacture or use of a bomb that could destroy the solar system. Still, the point is that as long as God does not intervene, perhaps God knows less and less about the future rather than more and more. Maybe someday virtually every future event in the solar system will be unknown to God because virtually all of them will depend on human free choices.

Accordingly, my own view is that OT proposes a view of God that errs too much on the immanence side. Its God is insufficiently transcendent and insufficiently sovereign. In the end, I reject OT because (1) I believe that divine foreknowledge and human freedom are compatible and (2) because I believe that the Bible teaches both that human beings are free and morally responsible before God and that God has complete foreknowledge of all future events.

VI

Therefore, since I reject both CT and OT, I accept NCT almost by default. But one important point remains to be considered: both defenders of CT and defenders of OT agree that complete divine foreknowledge is incompatible with human libertarian freedom. If I am to defend NCT, I must try to refute that claim. So I will try to show, in two quite distinct ways, that divine foreknowledge and human freedom are compatible. My first argument will concern what is called "simple foreknowledge." The second will concern what is called "middle knowledge."

Simple foreknowledge is the claim that God knows or "sees" the future just as we experience or see the present. No defender of this theory claims to know how God foresees future events, but of course there is much that Christians believe God does or has done that we do not understand—how God created the heavens and the earth, for example, or how God raised Jesus from the dead. But the essential claim is that God has complete and infallible knowledge of everything that will occur in the future, including future contingents.

While it is clear that divine foreordination of all future events (causing them to occur) would be incompatible with human libertarian freedom, defenders of simple foreknowledge argue that the same need not be true of divine foreknowledge of all future events. They point out that foreknowledge is not a species of causation. Suppose that today I know, of a certain person, that she will wear shoes tomorrow. Surely, my knowing today that she will wear shoes tomorrow does not *cause* her to wear shoes tomorrow (although it is logically incompatible with her not wearing shoes tomorrow).

I am unable to argue the point fully here,[23] but the basic idea is this: while no one can change the past, it is perfectly possible that what God knew a million years ago about what I will freely (via libertarian freedom) decide to eat for lunch tomorrow logically depends on what I will freely decide to eat for lunch tomorrow. People often argue that if God knows that event E is going to happen at some time in the future, then since no one can know something that is not true, it follows that E will necessarily happen. And if E necessarily happens, I am not libertarianly free.

But this argument, in my opinion, rests on a fallacy. All that follows is something about which there is no dispute whatsoever, viz. that E *will* occur. But, of course, the fact that E will occur does not rule out the possibility that I will, at the relevant moment, have it fully within my power not to do E. Now, we know that that power or ability is a power that I will not in fact exercise, but at virtually every moment we have powers that we do not exercise, and that fact does not rule out our freedom. It is within my power to insert a line of gibberish into the text at this point in the chapter, but I will not do it. From God's knowledge that I will do E, what follows is not that I *must* do E but only that I *will* do E. Moreover, it seems perfectly possible that this statement is true:

> What God knew yesterday is contingent upon what I will freely decide to do tomorrow.

Suppose it is true that I am free to decide whether or not to wear a blue shirt tomorrow; if so, then both my wearing a blue shirt and my not wearing a blue shirt are (as we might say) real options for me. That is, both are within my power; it is up to me which I will do. Then whichever option I choose, God will have known yesterday (and indeed from all eternity) which I will do.

But three objections lie close at hand. First, suppose God believed yesterday that I will not in fact choose to wear a blue shirt tomorrow, and suppose it will be within my power to wear a blue shirt tomorrow. Then (so the objection goes) it will be within my power to make it such that God had a false belief yesterday (and so is not omniscient).[24] And that surely is an unacceptable consequence. But this is too hasty. What follows is not that God held a false belief, but that it will be within my power tomorrow to do something such that if I exercise that power, then a belief that God did in fact have would have been false. But, obviously, the defender of simple foreknowledge will insist that if I will in fact exercise my power tomorrow to choose to wear a blue shirt, that will be what God will have believed yesterday.[25] Since God is omniscient, we can be sure, on these assumptions, that "Davis will wear a blue shirt tomorrow" is what God will have believed yesterday.

The crucial point here is this: it is obvious that "Davis *will not* wear a blue shirt tomorrow" and "Davis *cannot* wear a blue shirt tomorrow" are quite different statements. But it is the first statement, not the second, that is entailed by *God knew yesterday that Davis will not wear a blue shirt tomorrow*. Accordingly, even if God knew yesterday or a million years ago that I will not wear a blue shirt tomorrow, I might still have it within my power tomorrow either to wear a blue shirt or not to wear a blue shirt. Of course, if God knows that I will not wear a blue shirt tomorrow, then I will not do so (again, there is no dispute about that). But I might still be free to decide to wear a blue shirt (although I will not in fact exercise that power).

The second objection to the line of argument that I have been pursuing has to do with causality. It seems to some people that the argument that I have been giving allows or even entails that an event can be caused by something that happens after it. That is, it seems to imply that what God knew yesterday can be caused by what I will freely do tomorrow. But this notion is incoherent; as Hume claimed and as all our intuitions confirm, a cause must be temporally prior to its effect.

But the objection does not succeed. The argument that I have been pursuing does not claim or entail that what I will freely do tomorrow causes God to know something yesterday. The claim is that it is God's ability to foreknow, exercised yesterday, that caused God yesterday to know what I will do tomorrow. But even if this is so, the critic will simply change the criticism slightly and claim that my argument must hold that God's exercising yesterday his ability to foreknow is caused by what I will freely do tomorrow. And that looks like a violation of the principle that causes must precede their effects.

But the answer is this: what God foreknew yesterday is contingent upon (not caused by) what I will freely decide to do tomorrow. (I have in mind here a purely logical or explanatory notion of contingency, the sort involved in saying that in the famous syllogism, the truth of "Socrates is mortal" is contingent upon the truth of "All men are mortal" and "Socrates is a man.") And Hume's principle that causes must come before their effects does not apply to the logical relation "is contingent upon." Earlier events or states of affairs certainly can be logically contingent upon later ones. Take the state of affairs of "Stephen Davis being a great-grandfather" or rather the statement, "Stephen Davis will be, during his lifetime, a great-grandfather." I believe this statement is now either true or false. It might be true, and it might be false, but its truth value is now unknown to me and, I believe, all nonomniscient knowers. But whichever truth value it now has is clearly contingent upon certain events that will or will not occur in the future.[26]

VII

Molinism. But there is another, quite different, way of arguing that divine foreknowledge and human libertarian freedom are logically compatible. Molinism[27] is the doctrine that God possesses and uses "middle knowledge." Molina's view was that at the moment of creation, God knew three sorts of things. First, God's natural knowledge consists of everything that God knew prior to creating: all of the pure possibilities (knowledge of what could possibly be) like "It is possible that the world will have no people" or "It is possible for Steve Davis to be eight feet tall," and all necessary truths (knowledge of what *must* be) like "All triangles are three sided" and "No rocks are rational." Second, God's free knowledge obtained (knowledge of what *will* be). Accordingly, via his foreknowledge, God also knew all future actualities like "Stephen Davis will be a professor in Claremont" and "There will never exist any unicorns." Third, Molina reasoned that between God's natural knowledge (of the possible and the necessary) and his free knowledge (of the actual) lies God's middle knowledge (knowledge of what *would* be under various conditions and circumstances). Indeed, God had this knowledge logically prior to creating or issuing decrees.

Middle knowledge is also called counterfactual knowledge. It is knowledge of what would be the case if certain things that are not true were in fact true. Counterfactuals are quite common in human conversation: "If Bryant had not been injured, the Lakers would have won the game;" "If you had offered Davis a chocolate chip cookie, he would have accepted." Applied to persons, middle knowledge is knowledge of what they would do in various nonactual situations.[28]

Counterfactuals can be true or false.[29] According to the standard Lewis/Stalnaker theory, we test a counterfactual like "If Bryant had not been injured, the Lakers would have won the game" by asking whether the Lakers do win the game in the closest possible world to the actual world in which Bryant is not injured. This analysis is somewhat controversial among logicians, and matters very quickly get more complex than this. But the point is that there are procedures for deciding the truth value of counterfactual statements.

Suppose we use the word *character* to mean the sum total of all the attributes or properties that make persons who they are and what they do in various circumstances. God then presumably foreknows the characters of all soon-to-be-actual persons even before they are born. Indeed, God knows the characters of all (what I will call) possible persons, which are simply coherent combinations of attributes of persons that may or may not ever actually exist. (Those possible persons that do at some time exist are also actual persons.) Presumably, then, God's middle knowledge allows God to know precisely what any possible person would do (would, in the various possible cases, freely decide to do) in any possible circumstance in which that person could be placed.

The point then is that human beings can be libertarianly free, and God can nevertheless know, via middle knowledge, what any possible person would freely decide to do in any possible situation. Accordingly, again, divine foreknowledge and human free will are logically compatible. One advantage that middle knowledge has over simple foreknowledge is that defenders of it do not have to plead ignorance when asked how God achieves it. We have no idea how God could foresee the future, but we can understand how an omniscient being can know the character of each possible being so intimately as to be sure what he or she would do in any possible circumstance.

But it might be objected that middle knowledge, after all, ends up denying human libertarian freedom. Suppose there were a true counterfactual that involves libertarian freedom to the effect that

> *"If Steve Davis is offered a chocolate chip cookie in situation S* [where S is suitably spelled out], *Davis will accept.*

Now why is this statement true (instead of, *"If Steve Davis is offered a chocolate chip cookie in situation S, Davis will refuse"*)? The answer is that this statement is true because in every possible world in which Davis is offered the cookie and everything else is as much as possible like the actual world, Davis accepts the cookie.

But—so it might be argued—this is inconsistent with Davis' being free in a libertarian sense. Davis would only be libertarianly free in this case if the conclusion were that in situation S it is causally open to Davis to reject the cookie. Or to make the point more theologically, if God via middle knowledge knows precisely what Davis would do in any given circumstance, the very fact that God knows that Davis will exist, will exist in situation S, and will accept the cookie compromises Davis' libertarian freedom. He *will* accept the cookie.

But this argument is surely confused. Even if there logically can be no such thing as middle knowledge, it is still the case that any human being who is libertarianly free in a certain situation will, in the end, make a choice. So even if God has no middle knowledge, Davis, exercising his libertarian freedom, will choose either to accept or reject the cookie. Suppose he freely chooses to accept it. Then it could be argued with equal cogency (equal cogent, that is, to the objection that we are considering) that Davis is no longer libertarianly free because, tautologically, he *will* accept the cookie. I believe the two arguments are exactly analogous. So the objection to middle knowledge that we are considering goes nowhere. It reduces to the triviality that Davis *will* make a choice.

VIII

It appears, then, that NCT can be defended. Both simple foreknowledge and middle knowledge are possible and allow us to answer the most important objection to NCT. But since CT and OT are open to damaging criticisms, NCT is the view of God that ought to be recommended to theists.[30]

Notes

Introduction

1 I need to be clear that while some of the scholars whom I discuss in this book see themselves as enemies of Christianity or at least of orthodox Christianity—e.g., Antony Flew, Michael Martin, James Robinson, Robert Funk, John Hick—other conversation partners in the present book are friends of orthodox Christianity. This would certainly include the defenders of both the classical view of God and the "Open" view of God.

Chapter 1

1 This weighty evidence for the late and secondary character of Thomas is such an embarrassment for John Dominic Crosson (one of the most famous members of the JS) that in his own writings he posits—with little argument or evidence—a proto-Thomas that dates from the 50s. This strikes many people as special pleading.

2 I would like to thank my friend and former student Professor Craig A. Evans for his helpful comments on an earlier draft of this material. I must also acknowledge the various contributors to *Jesus Under Fire: Modern Scholarship Reinvents the Historical Jesus* (Grand Rapids: Zondervan, 1995) and Luke Timothy Johnson, the author of *The Real Jesus: The Misguided Quest for the Historical Jesus and the Truth of the Traditional Gospels* (San Francisco: HarperCollins, 1996) for stimulating my thinking about the Jesus Seminar.

Chapter 2

1 I believe most scholars who go this route hold that Matthew was written first and was a source for Luke.

2 There has been much discussion of this point in the scholarly literature; in this paragraph I am oversimplifying matters considerably.

3 There are quotations of Jesus (without any particular Gospel being named) in Clement of Rome, Ignatius, Polycarp, and the Epistle of Barnabas. See Alexander Roberts and James Donaldson, eds., *The Ante-Nicene Fathers* (Grand Rapids: Eerdmans, 1989), 1:8, 17–18, 33–35, 87, 139.

4 Helmut Koester, *Ancient Christian Gospels: Their History and Development* (London: SCM Press, 1990), 273, 324, 315.

5 Robinson seems to admit as much: "The IQP has indeed refrained from entering into the never-ending discussion over the existence of Q, and has preferred to concentrate its energy . . . on seeking to reconstruct the text of Q, *on the assumption that this may in the end be a more compelling and useful argument for its existence*." James M. Robinson, *The Sayings Gospel Q* in Greek and English (Minneapolis: Fortress, 2002), 65 n. 160, emphasis added.

6 These points are made clearly by both Nicholas Perrin (in his "The Limits of a Reconstructed Q") and Mark Goodacre (in his "When Is a Text Not a Text? The Quasi-Textual Approach of the International Q Project") in *Questioning Q: A Multidimensional Critique*, ed. Mark Goodacre and Nicholas Perrin (Downers Grove, Ill.: InterVarsity, 2004), 74–75, 116–22.

7 Most literature is produced by individuals.

8 There is another assumption made by many Q scholars that is not worth spending much time on because the issue is mainly terminological: *Q is a Gospel*. There has been a great deal of scholarly debate in recent years over the meaning of the term *Gospel*. The only point I wish to make here is that I am not impressed when I find it argued that Q must be a Gospel because Thomas (also mainly a list of sayings) is a Gospel, and that (usually in a different essay) Thomas must be a Gospel because, after all, Q is.

9 John Meier's comment is apt. Q scholars, he says, should stand before a mirror every day and repeat, "Q is only a hypothesis." *A Marginal Jew: Rethinking the Historical Jesus*, vol. 2 (New York: Doubleday, 1991), 178.

Chapter 3

1 MacDonald's paper was written for a conference called "Truth: Interdisciplinary Dialogues in a Pluralist Age" at the Claremont School of Theology in March, 2002. At the conference I was asked to respond to MacDonald's paper, and the present essay is a slightly revised version of that response.

2 Of course this sequence of events occurs in the lives of many people, so order may not count for much here. But sometimes (61, 80) MacDonald claims that the criterion of order is satisfied in cases where it seems that almost any other sequence of events would have made the account incoherent.

3 Not all "borrowing" is inconsistent with historicity, of course. New Testament authors used Old Testament texts to guide the selection and shaping of their narratives. See N. T. Wright's comparison of Luke and 1 Samuel in his *The New Testament and the People of God* (Philadelphia: Fortress, 1996), 378–82.

4 Notice also the parallels between Rom 13:7 and Mark 12:17; Rom 13:9 and Mark 12:31; Rom 14:10 and Matt 7:1-2a; Rom 14:14 and Luke 11:41 and Mark 7:19b; Rom 16:19 and Matt 10:16b; 1 Cor 13:2 and Mark 11:23; and 1 Thess 2:14-16 and Matt 23:29-38.

5 A powerful case is made, however, by Martin Hengel in various of his works. See his *Acts and the History of Earliest Christianity* (Philadelphia: Fortress, 1979), *Between Jesus and Paul* (Philadelphia: Fortress, 1983), and *The Pre-Christian Paul* (Trinity, 1991).

6 Moreover, many Greek novels mimetically borrowed from Homer by placing unmarked but unmistakable allusions to or even citations from Homer in their narratives. Notice for example, Chariton's *Chaereas and Callirhoe*, 1.1, 1.4, 2.3, and 2.9. If THT is true, why did not Mark do the same?

7 I have so argued in my *Risen Indeed: Making Sense of the Resurrection* (Grand Rapids: Eerdmans, 1993), 1–21.

8 See Raymond Brown, *An Introduction to the New Testament* (New York: Doubleday, 1997), 321.

9 I would like to thank Gordon Fee, Bruce Fisk, Christoff Landmesser, Dennis MacDonald, and Susan Peppers-Bates for their helpful comments.

Chapter 4

1 This is a point that is emphasized by Jeffrie Murphy in Jeffrie G. Murphy and Jean Hampton, *Forgiveness and Mercy* (Cambridge: Cambridge University Press, 1988), 17.

2 See Richard Swinburne, *Responsibility and Atonement* (Oxford: Oxford University Press, 1989), 73–92.

3 Murphy and Hampton, *Forgiveness and Mercy*, 40–42, 83.

4 Anna C. Minas, "God and Forgiveness," in *Philosophy and Faith: A Philosophy of Religion Reader*, ed. David Shatz, 25–34 (New York: McGraw-Hill, 2002).

5 Minas also raises the question of the apparent injustice of God's forgiving some sinners but not others. Her discussion of this point (29) turns into an implicit argument for universalism, the theory that all sins will be forgiven and all people will enjoy eternal bliss. But since this point, while important in itself, is quite separate from Minas' main argument that a perfect being cannot forgive at all, I will ignore it.

6 Minas burlesques the idea of divine forgiveness by saying, "He did the actions all right, but after God's forgiveness, they are no longer wrong" (33). No, the evil deeds of evildoers remain evil; they are just no longer counted against them.

7 Following Rudolf Bultmann (*The History of the Synoptic Tradition,* 2nd ed. [Oxford: Blackwell, 1966 (1921)], 12–14, 227), Vincent Taylor reviews the various arguments of the critics and concludes that Mark 2:1-12 is a compilation of various sources. See his *The Gospel According to St. Mark* (London: Macmillan, 1963), 191–201.

8 See, *inter alia*, Robert H. Gundry, *Matthew: A Commentary on His Literary and Theological Art* (Grand Rapids: Eerdmans, 1982), 161–65.
9 There are also several fascinating and controversial theological points in relation to this text that I will not discuss: the relationship between sin and sickness in first-century Judaism and in Jesus' teachings, the healing of one person because of the faith of other people, the clairvoyance and healing power exhibited by Jesus, and the meaning of "Son of Man." I am only interested in Jesus' apparent ability to forgive sins.
10 See Robert H. Gundry, *Mark: A Commentary on His Apology for the Cross* (Grand Rapids: Eerdmans, 1993), 112–15.
11 Thomas C. Oden and Christopher A. Hall, eds., *Mark, Ancient Christian Commentary on Scripture* (Downers Grove, Ill.: InterVarsity, 1998), 28 (*Against Heresies*, 5.17).
12 Oden and Hall, *Mark*, 28 (*The Trinity*, 13).
13 C. S. Mann, *Mark: A New Translation with Introduction and Commentary* (Garden City, N.Y.: Doubleday, 1986), 224.
14 Robert A. Guelich, *Mark 1–8:26*, Word Bible Commentary 34a (Dallas: Word, 1989), 87.
15 John Hick, *The Metaphor of God Incarnate* (Louisville, Ky.: Westminster John Knox, 1993), 32. See also E. P. Sanders, *Jesus and Judaism* (Philadelphia: Fortress, 1985), 240.
16 Robert W. Funk, et al., eds., *The Five Gospels* (New York: Macmillan, 1993), 44.
17 Had the Seminar argued that Jesus was passing on the authority to forgive sins not to all human beings but to a specific group of people, they would have been on firmer ground. Unfortunately, I do not have the space on this occasion to discuss the "keys of the kingdom" and the binding and loosing authority that Jesus passed on to Peter and the church (Matt 16:19) or the power to forgive or retain sins that Jesus gave to the disciples in John 20:23 and (apparently) Matthew 9:8.
18 Joaquim Jeremias, *New Testament Theology: The Proclamation of Jesus* (New York: SCM Press, 1971), 114.
19 Oden and Hall, *Mark*, 28–29 (*On the Incomprehensible Nature of God*, Homily 10.19).
20 Gary S. Shogren, "Forgiveness (NT)," in *The Anchor Bible Dictionary*, vol. 2, ed. David Noel Freedman, 835 (New York: Doubleday, 1992).
21 Guelich, *Mark 1–8:26*, 87.
22 I relegate to a note a final point: this chapter in effect argues against the idea that any attempt to fix the meaning of a biblical text is no more than an act of politics, an exercise of power. I am claiming that it can be cogently argued that the traditional christological interpretation of Mark 2:1-12 is correct.

Chapter 5

1 I have revised a few points and corrected a few errors in response to the detailed replies to my review by all but one of the contributors to *The Empty*

Tomb that can be found at <http://theemptytomb.googlepages.com/>. One of their common complaints is along the lines of, "Davis didn't say anything about point x or point y in my original essay." But of course in my review I had to be brief and could devote at most a few paragraphs to each essay; I could hardly respond to every point, or even every important point, that they made. Another common complaint is along the lines of, "Davis raises objection x, but I addressed objection x in my original essay." That is sometimes true as well, but in such cases I was obviously not satisfied with what they had said.

2 Yes, the title is a bit misleading. Perhaps some of the faithful will form an initial impression that the book is a defense of resurrection. Whether something to that effect was intended by the editors or the publisher, I do not know.

3 References to pages in TET will be placed in parentheses in the text.

4 Along with several articles, see Davis, *Risen Indeed.*

5 Since the term *naturalism* is used variously in philosophy today, let me define it as the view that: (1) the physical universe exhausts reality, and (2) all events can in principle be explained by methods similar to those used in the natural sciences.

6 I should point out that Richard Carrier is virtually the only contributor to TET who recognizes the controlling influence that metaphysical commitment to naturalism or supernaturalism has on one's attitude toward the resurrection of Jesus (370). On the other hand, he says, "Christian theism faces tremendous problems regarding plausibility, disconfirmation, and evidential support" (355). I just wish that Carrier had pointed out what those problems were. I would love for him to have told us what evidence, in particular, disconfirms Christian theism or even shows that it is implausible. As a professional philosopher of religion, I am of course aware of various arguments that have been suggested along those lines. I have been thinking about them for over thirty years. But none of them, in my opinion, disconfirms Christian theism.

7 These propositions claim that after his resurrection, Jesus was unable to be injured, die, age, or be sick, and that he was able instantaneously to move at will from place to place.

8 Admittedly there is a disanalogy here: Caesar's crossing the Rubicon was in no sense a miracle, as philosophers understand that term. Still, my point stands.

9 In his internet response to my original review, Richard Carrier misinterprets my meaning here. I am not necessarily arguing that it is rational to believe a proposition that you cannot prove as firmly as a proposition that you can prove, although there is no doubt that people do that very thing. My point was only that Christians might believe Cavin's propositions (8)–(12) without trying to prove them but only as a plausible (but not provable) interpretation of "God raised Jesus from the dead." In addition, Carrier

accuses me of circularity in my epistemology. Presumably he thinks I hold to something like this: the Bible is reliable because Christianity says it is reliable; and Christianity is true because the Bible reliably says it is. I am happy to report that that is not how my reasoning goes.

10 Cavin's proposition (2) says, "Jesus died and afterward he was transformed into a living supernatural body."

11 Our debate was mainly carried out on the pages of *Philo* 1, no. 1 (1998), 2, no. 1 (1999), and 3, no. 1 (2000). My concluding salvo was, "The Rationality of Christian Belief in Resurrection: A Reply to Michael Martin," *Philosophia Christi* 5, no. 2 (2003), and Martin's concluding riposte was "Davis on the Rationality of Belief in the Resurrection," which was posted in 2005 on the Secular Web. The two of us also debated the issue in Michael L. Peterson and Raymond J. VanArragon, *Contemporary Debates in Philosophy of Religion* (London: Blackwell, 2004).

12 In his summary of this argument of mine in his internet response, Martin makes two changes in it. He omits the phrase "and that includes redemption from death" in the listed second belief and he replaces my word "promised" with "permitted" in the third. These changes do not capture my meaning and change the epistemic situation considerably.

13 Some scholars reject these texts as postresurrection retrojections put into the mouth of Jesus by the evangelists. But my point is that most Christians accept them as authentic. This is one reason that for them belief in the resurrection of Jesus is not as improbable as Martin claims.

14 See, for example, Ned Block, "Mental Paint and Mental Latex," in *Philosophical Issues 7: Perception*, ed. Enrique Villanueva, 19–49 (Atascadero, Calif.: Ridgeview, 1996). Of course not all epistemologists agree with Block on this point.

15 See my "Is Belief in the Resurrection Rational," *Philo* 2, no. 1 (1999): 58.

16 I owe this illustration to William L. Craig.

17 I relegate to a note a brief point: when actual numbers are supplied, I find Swinburne's estimation of the relevant probabilities more plausible than Martin's. But there is no way to prove who is correct, so I will leave the point there.

18 See especially his *Atheism: A Philosophical Justification* (Philadelphia: Temple University Press, 1990) and *The Case Against Christianity* (Philadelphia: Temple University Press, 1991).

19 As Jeffery Lowder recognizes. TET, 265.

20 See Craig A. Evans, "Jewish Burial Traditions and the Resurrection of Jesus," *Journal of the Society of the Historical Jesus* 3, no. 2 (2005): 187–202.

21 In his internet response, Price confirms that this is exactly what he means. So presumably he would be entirely unmoved by considerations like this: I myself know or know of scores of recognized biblical scholars (they hold Ph.D. degrees from excellent institutions, have positions at various recognized colleges and universities, and do scholarly work) who affirm the res-

urrection of Jesus. Some of them are theologically to the left of me and some to the right. But to deny that they are "serious biblical critics" is both insulting and fallacious. It is an example of the "no true Englishman" fallacy. Suppose someone were to say, "No Englishman opposes the monarchy." This person is then told, "Well, what about X and Y: they are Englishmen and they oppose the monarchy?" The person then replies, "Well, no *true* Englishman opposes the monarchy." The fallacy here is to try to make a substantive claim true merely by stipulative definition.

22 Price never specifically mentions any theological implications of his thesis, although there doubtless would be some. On pages 70–71 he does briefly note that theological conclusions can depend on textual considerations.

23 The notion that those power-hungry orthodox Christians of the first two centuries persecuted those innocent, peace-loving, and marginalized heterodox dissenters and suppressed any and all texts that supported their views appears more than once in TET.

24 There are several letters that were once attributed to Ignatius that are now considered inauthentic. But seven letters, including his Epistle to the Romans, are cited as written by Ignatius by both Eusebius and Jerome and are now, despite some apparent interpolations, widely considered authentic.

25 This point does not or should not affect the argument, but I should note that I am not the kind of "fundamentalist" that Price likes to lampoon. I allow for biblical criticism, do not affirm biblical inerrancy, and am prepared to admit interpolations and contradictions in the text of the Bible where the evidence supports them.

26 Nor does 1 Corinthians 15:3 rule out the possibility that that which Paul "had received" he received directly from God and not from those who were Christians before him. On balance, however, I do not hold to this interpretation.

27 Victor Furnish makes a distinction that is helpful here—between the gospel that Paul learned directly by revelation and what he further learned *about* that gospel from the other apostles. See his *Jesus According to Paul* (Cambridge: Cambridge University Press, 1993), 29.

28 In his internet response, Price interprets me as making here a distinction between substance (what Paul taught) and form (the way it was packaged). I had no such notion in mind. I hold that some of the substance of what Paul taught he learned by private revelation and some he learned from those who were Christians before him. I made some (I hope) educated guesses as to which Pauline notions fit in which category.

29 There is indeed a slight incongruity in style because, as virtually everyone agrees, in 15:3-8 Paul is citing an early Christian credo or formula.

30 Price is particularly exercised over Craig's commitment to biblical inerrancy. Now, I suspect that William Craig does affirm biblical inerrancy, but appeal to it plays no role in his apologetic efforts. Craig argues for the historicity of the resurrection, so far as I can see, entirely on historical-critical grounds.

31 Price also seems miffed that Craig wants to convert people to Christ. But is that so surprising? That is one of the things Christians try to do. I, too, want to convert people to Christ.

32 See James Callahan's helpful study, *The Clarity of Scripture* (Downers Grove, Ill.: InterVarsity, 2001).

33 I am not arguing that all myth is radically unclear. The point is that if Fales is correct and the apparently historical texts in the Bible are not to be interpreted as it has seemed natural to do for two thousand years, then the Bible is radically unclear.

34 See also 1 Samuel 30:12-13, where "three days and three nights" (v. 12) seem to be equaled with "three days" (v. 13).

35 This is a point against Fales' thesis that both Paul Moser and I, quite independently, hit upon several years ago. Fales' response to it in his internet reply is not particularly strong, as he himself honestly admits.

36 I would have thought that this idea ought to have some appeal for Kirby. He says, after all, that "it is inconceivable for the author of Mark to have believed the silence [of the women] to be 'temporary' and not to have continued the narrative" (239). Maybe Mark did continue the narrative.

37 See Daniel Kendall, S.J. and Gerald O'Collins, S.J., "Mary Magdalene as Major Witness to Jesus' Resurrection," *Theological Studies* 48, no. 4 (1987): 631–46.

38 The story of Mary's encounter with Jesus in John, in which she at first thought Jesus' body had been moved (20:2), is actually an argument against the reburial thesis.

39 See my essay "The Rationality of Resurrection for Christians: A Rejoinder" in *Philo* 3, no. 1 (2000).

40 Lowder asks why—if this much is true—the early enemies of the Christian movement did not produce just any old corpse of a crucifixion victim, in order to falsify Christian claims about the resurrection. But, as I said in my original review, it would have to have been a corpse that was found in Jesus' tomb. Perhaps they did not do what Lowder suggests because there was no such corpse.

41 Although I will not discuss this point, I do not think the concept of a "body made of spirit" makes any sense at all. (Greg Cavin may agree with me; see p. 37 n. 2 in his "Is There Sufficient Historical Evidence to Establish the Resurrection of Jesus?" in *The Empty Tomb: Jesus Beyond the Grave* [Amherst, N.Y.: Prometheus, 2005], 19–42.) As we know from Plato and the Neo-Platonists, there were thoroughly dualistic theories (i.e., where "spirit" was understood as immaterial) that were alive and well in the ancient world.

42 In fact, here is something close to an argument from silence that I endorse: I think that if Paul had meant what Carrier says he meant, he would not have used the word *soma* at all. Note 1 Corinthians 15:35: "With what kind of body do they [resurrected persons] come?"

43 See Robert H. Gundry, *Sōma in Biblical Theology: With Emphasis on Pauline Anthropology* (Cambridge: Cambridge University Press, 1976). The point is also made compellingly in N. T. Wright, *The Resurrection of the Son of God* (Minneapolis: Fortress Press, 2003).

44 I can speak with a tiny bit of authority on a related point. Although I would not classify these experiences as hallucinations (they were, I suppose, mistakes in perception), in the two or three months after my wife died in March 2000, I "saw" her on three or four occasions. It was always a woman whom I saw at a distance that somehow resembled Charis, and for a split second I experienced myself as wondering what Charis was doing there. But in about a second's time I realized that the woman was not Charis. I definitely did not form the belief that my wife was alive and kicking here on earth.

45 There are a few non-Christians who support the claim that God raised Jesus from the dead, but very few.

46 Mike Martin's argument against the resurrection in TET does not depend on this point; still, it is clear from his essay and other writings of his that he considers the very concept of God to be incoherent. And this of course allows for a straightforward refutation of the resurrection: If the concept of God is incoherent, God does not exist; if God does not exist, God did not raise Jesus from the dead; and, if God did not raise Jesus from the dead, Jesus was not raised from the dead.

47 Again, nobody in TET argues for this view. It is clear, however, that Price is attracted to it (TET, 15).

48 I would like to thank William L. Craig, Gary Habermas, and Susan Peppers-Bates for their helpful comments on an earlier draft of this chapter.

Chapter 6

1 Rudolf Bultmann, "Is Exegesis Without Presuppositions Possible?," in *Existence and Faith*, ed. S. M. Ogden, 343 (London, SCM Press, 1964).

2 The distinction between presupposition and prejudice is made in a slightly different way by Graham N. Stanton, "Presuppositions of New Testament Criticism," in *New Testament Interpretation,* ed. I. Howard Marshall, 61 (Grand Rapids: Eerdmans, 1977).

3 James Barr, *The Bible in the Modern World* (London: SCM Press, 1973), 157.

4 An illustration: at my home institution, there is a course called Civilization 10 that is required of all first-year undergraduates. The textbook for the course is a made-for-the-course book of readings consisting of selected works (and excerpts from selected works) of history, literature, mathematics, science, the social sciences, philosophy, and religion from Genesis to the twentieth century. My point is that questions about its overall meaning can be asked even of a book such as this.

5 These and other related questions are explored skillfully by James Dunn in his *Unity and Diversity in the New Testament* (London: SCM Press, 2nd ed. 1990), esp. 56–57, 370. I have learned a great deal from Dunn's book and have no problem with its basic thrust. In particular, I do not hold that only a very narrow range of theological statements can be said to agree with Scripture. And I accept the claim that theological diversity is both present in the New Testament and healthy for the Christian community. I am inclined to believe, however, that many of the competing theologies that Dunn finds in the New Testament are much more complementary than he realizes.

6 Here I disagree with Dunn, who says: "Nor have I said, nor would I want to say, that the NT writings are canonical because they were *more inspired* than other and later Christian writings" (386).

7 For further discussion of this point, see my "Tradition, Scripture, and Theological Authority," in *Philosophy and Theological Discourse*, ed. Stephen T. Davis (London: Macmillan, 1997).

8 See John Hospers, "What Means this Freedom?," in *Determinism and Freedom in the Age of Modern Science,* ed. Sidney Hook (New York: Collier Books, 1961) and John Hospers, "Free Will and Psychoanalysis," in *The Problem of Free Will*, ed. Willard F. Enteman (New York: Scribner's, 1967).

9 I once came home from work expecting, as usual, to see my wife. Instead I found a note, in her handwriting, which said: "Hi Honey, My tooth has been hurting all day. I've gone to see the dentist. See you when I get home. Love, Charis." Now no one will deny that (1) the paper with marks on it, and (2) the meaning of the message, are two different things. Still, I believe I knew, reading that message, exactly what she meant. Thinking about that experience was enough to convince me that texts can have stable meanings and that communication between two minds via a text is possible.

10 I would like to thank Alan Padgett, John Stackhouse, and Susan Peppers-Bates for their helpful comments on an earlier version of this chapter.

Chapter 7

1 One excellent exception is my former student Harold Netland. See his *Dissonant Voices: Religious Pluralism and the Question of Truth* (Grand Rapids: Eerdmans, 1991) and *Encountering Religious Pluralism: The Challenge to Christian Faith and Mission* (Downers Grove: Ill: InterVarsity, 2001).

2 One much earlier effort was my "Evangelicals and the Religions of the World," *The Reformed Journal* 31 (1981): 9–13.

3 See his essays, "Anonymous Christians," "Anonymous Christianity and the Missionary Task of the Church," and "The One Christ and the Universality of Salvation," all reprinted in Karl Rahner, *Theological Investigations,* vols. 6, 12, and 16, respectively (New York: Crossroad, 1973, 1975, and 1979).

4 See especially his *An Interpretation of Religion: Human Responses to the Transcendent* (London: Macmillan, 1989).

5 Of course, as Alvin Plantinga points out, a *tu quoque* move can be made here. If the pluralist had been born in Madagascar or medieval France, he probably would not have been a pluralist. Actually, nothing at all about the truth of pluralism or naturalism or Christianity or any other religion follows from this point. See Alvin Plantinga, "Pluralism: A Defense of Religious Exclusivism," in *The Philosophical Challenge of Religious Diversity,* ed. Philip L. Quinn and Kevin Meeker, 187–88 (New York: Oxford University Press, 2000).

6 Hick, *Interpretation of Religion*, 240, 242.

7 Hick, *Interpretation of Religion*, 246.

8 Paul Eddy argues convincingly that some of the "purely formal" concepts that Hick allows to apply to the Real (e.g., "being the referent of a term" or "that which no greater can be conceived") do have substantive content. See his "Religious Pluralism and the Divine: Another Look at John Hick's Neo-Kantian Proposal," in Quinn and Meeker, *Philosophical Challenge*, 130.

9 It is one thing to claim that a loving God will not condemn you to hell because you come down on the wrong side of an unsettleable metaphysical claim; I myself accept that point. It is quite another to make the sweeping claim that having the correct metaphysical beliefs is unnecessary to salvation. Given his own epistemological principles, one wonders how Hick learned that.

10 Again, one wonders what evidence Hick has for this sweeping empirical claim.

11 Hick's pluralist theory has been chewed over considerably in books and journals; accordingly, there will be little here that is new.

12 See John Hick, *The Metaphor of God Incarnate: Christology in a Pluralistic Age* (Louisville, Ky: Westminster John Knox, 1993).

13 See Keith Ward, "Truth and the Diversity of Religions," in Quinn and Meeker, *Philosophical Challenge,* 124.

14 As Timothy O'Connor points out, the principle apparently at work here ought to make pluralists question their commitment to pluralism, since very many people disagree with pluralism. Timothy O'Connor, "Religious Pluralism," in *Reason for the Hope Within*, ed. Michael J. Murray, 174–75 (Grand Rapids: Eerdmans, 1999).

15 See the more detailed arguments in Davis, *Risen Indeed.*

16 See part 2 of my *Christian Philosophical Theology* (Oxford: Oxford University Press, 2006).

17 See chapter 8 of Davis, *Risen Indeed.*

18 This is not to deny the importance of Christian involvement in social and moral issues. After all, Jesus not only preached to people about God and counseled spiritually confused people—he also fed the hungry, healed the sick, and worked to overturn unjust social and economic practices. We cut the gospel in half if we do evangelism without social action or social action without evangelism.

19 Stephen Neill, *Crises of Belief* (London: Hodder & Stoughton, 1984), 31.
20 See part 4 of my *Christian Philosophical Theology.*
21 See especially his *Death and Eternal Life* (New York: Harper & Row, 1976) and, more recently, *The Fifth Dimension: An Exploration of the Spiritual Realm* (Oxford: One World, 1999).

Chapter 8

1 See, e.g., A. Roy Eckardt, "Contemporary Christian Theology and a Protestant Witness for the Shoah," *Shoah* 2, no. 1 (1980): 12.
2 See, e.g., John Roth's contributions to Stephen T. Davis, ed., *Encountering Evil: Live Options in Theodicy*, 2nd ed. (Lousville, Ky: Westminster John Knox, 2001).
3 See, among others, Paul M. van Buren, "Affirmation of the Jewish People: A Condition of Theological Coherence," *Journal of the American Academy of Religion* 45, no. 3 (1977): 1075–1100.
4 Franklin H. Littell, *The Crucifixion of the Jews* (New York: Harper & Row, 1975), 2, 5.
5 Craig A. Evans and Donald A. Hagner, *Anti-Semitism and Early Christianity: Issues of Polemic and Faith* (Minneapolis: Fortress, 1993), 15n.
6 In my opinion, the temple incident, recorded in Mark 11:15-19 and elsewhere, was Jesus' attempt to purify, rather than repudiate, temple worship. Notice, in Jesus' words on that occasion, the quotations from Isaiah 56:7 and Jeremiah 7:11.
7 There is even one text that asserts that "the Jews were divided" (John 10:19)—some rejected what Jesus had just said and some believed it.
8 Is it possible that in quoting the crowd as uttering the blood curse, Matthew was implying that the crowd was unknowingly saying more than they intended? Does he want us to understand that the curse was in part a prayer from the members of the crowd that Jesus' blood atone for their sins and the sins of their children?
9 The one caveat is that, according to evangelical Christians, all human beings, because of their sinfulness, are responsible for the crucifixion. All people—including Jews—are Christ-killers, but Jews no more than any other group of people.
10 Rosemary Ruether, *Faith and Fratricide: The Christian Theological Roots of Anti-Semitism* (New York: Seabury, 1974), 246.
11 Rosemary Ruether, "Antisemitism and Christian Theology," in *Auschwitz: Beginning of a New Era? Reflections on the Holocaust,* ed. Eva Fleischner, 79 (New York: Ktav, 1977).
12 I do not at all reject historical-critical biblical scholarship. I just want to see it practiced sensibly.
13 Consider the admittedly extreme but infinitely depressing case of those German biblical scholars during the 1930s and 1940s who supported National

Socialism. (I am not, of course, suggesting that all who accept the conclusions of radical biblical criticism are anti-Semites.)

14 There are, of course, Christian thinkers whom I cannot exonerate from the charge of making anti-Semitic statements, most notably some of the church fathers and Luther. Whatever their authority elsewhere, at this point, in my opinion, they were not practicing Christianity.

15 Elie Wiesel, *A Jew Today* (New York: Vintage Books, 1979), 13, 14.

16 Jacob Bronowski, *The Ascent of Man* (Boston: Little, Brown, 1973), 370, 374.

Chapter 9

1 See Stephen T. Davis, ed., *Encountering Evil,* 1st ed. (Atlanta, Ga.: John Knox Press, 1981), 118.

2 It emerges clearly, I believe, in discussions of David Griffin's theodicy in Davis, ed., *Encountering Evil,* 1st ed.

3 This David Griffin: "The doctrine of omnipotence is not based upon historical revelation, but upon imaginative flights designed to fulfill egocentric wishes." Davis, *Encountering Evil,* 1st ed., 132.

4 Aristotle's metaphysical theories bring with them certain baggage that I do not want or need to carry. I could instead have chosen some such term as "Common Sense ontology"—this because I suspect that the vast majority of human beings, whether they are or are not metaphysicians, think or presuppose that reality consists ultimately of things. This does not mean that they are correct, of course.

5 These definitions reflect contemporary philosophical usage; I do not claim that they capture Whitehead's definitions of these or related terms.

6 It may be, e.g., that at the level of quantum physics, talk about events as ultimate may be more fruitful than talk about objects.

7 Some philosophers opt for a wider definition of the term *event,* e.g., as an instantiation of a property in a substance at a time. And on that view (which Process philosophers can always opt for), you cannot have things without events any more than you can have events without things. This is true enough. But I reject the suggested definition as too broad and generous. What about the property, had by some numbers but not others, of being prime? Notice that it would be true to say that this property is instantiated in the number 3 on March 8, 2007. But primeness being instantiated in the number 3 on March 8, 2007, is hardly an event. This is because the number 3 is prime no matter what time we pick. There are no everlasting events. Accordingly, there still can be things without events but not events without things.

8 See, e.g., David Griffin's arguments against the doctrine in Davis, ed., *Encountering Evil,* 2nd ed., 109–15.

9 I accept the claim that the Hebrew verb *bara* does not always mean "create out of nothing" (Isa 43:15), but in the context of Genesis 1, I believe it does imply that God created the world out of nothing.

10 I believe the point is conclusively made in Paul Copan and William Lane Craig, *Creation Out of Nothing: A Biblical, Philosophical, and Scientific Exploration* (Grand Rapids: Baker, 2004), 29–91.

11 David Griffin sees Psalm 74:12-17 and Isaiah 51:9-11 as suggesting a genuine battle with chaos on God's part. But I see in these texts no hint of any battle or struggle; the texts simply list some of the things that God did in creation and is to be praised for.

12 Davis, ed., *Encountering Evil*, 2nd ed., 116.

Chapter 10

1 The Westminster Shorter Catechism, Question 1.

Chapter 11

1 There are exceptions to this claim. For example, the Westminster Confession of 1647 speaks of human "souls which neither die nor sleep, having an immortal subsistence" (34, 1). *The Book of Confessions of the Presbyterian Church (USA)* (New York: Office of the General Assembly, 1983).

2 For two recent and masterful but quite different defenses of the resurrection of Jesus, see Wright, *Resurrection of the Son of God* and Richard Swinburne, *The Resurrection of God Incarnate* (Oxford: Oxford University Press, 2003). See also William Lane Craig, *Assessing the New Testament Evidence for the Historicity of the Resurrection of Jesus* (Lewiston, N.Y.: Edwin Mellen, 1989).

3 For this point, as well as a classic statement of temporary disembodiment, see Thomas Aquinas, *Summa Contra Gentiles* (Notre Dame, Ind.: Notre Dame University Press, 1975), 4.79.11.

4 See, e.g., the essays collected in Kevin Corcoran, ed., *Soul, Body, and Survival* (Ithaca: Cornell University Press, 2001).

5 These problems are dealt with in various ways by defenders of immediate resurrection. For example, see Kevin Corcoran, "Physical Persons and Postmortem Survival without Temporal Gaps" in *Soul, Body, and Survival*, 201–17. See also the essays in part 3 of Ted Peters, Robert John Russell, and Michael Welker, eds., *Resurrection: Theological and Scientific Assessments* (Grand Rapids: Eerdmans, 2002).

6 Oscar Cullmann, "Immortality of the Soul or Resurrection of the Dead?" reprinted (among many other places) in *Immortality*, ed. Terence Penelhum (Belmont, Calif.: Wadsworth, 1973).

7 One example, of many that could be cited, is Hans Küng, *On Being a Christian* (New York: Pocket Books, 1976), 351.

8 See especially Wright, *Resurrection of the Son of God*, 686–718. See also Davis, *Risen Indeed*, 43–84.

9 This point is argued convincingly in Gundry, *Sōma in Biblical Theology*, 159ff.

10 See St. Augustine, *The Enchiridion on Faith, Hope, and Love* (Chicago: Regnery, 1961), 88.

11 John Hick is an articulate spokesperson for the modern view. See his *Death and Eternal Life*, 278–96.

12 The objection is discussed in Davis, *Risen Indeed*, 132–46.

13 The cases typically cited involve teletransportation, split brains, or shared brains.

14 See, e.g., part 3 of Derek Parfit, *Reasons and Persons* (Oxford: Oxford University Press, 1986).

15 See Peters, Russell, and Welker, eds., *Resurrection*.

16 Peters, Russell, and Welker, eds. *Resurrection*, xiii.

17 This worry is an important theme in several of the essays in Peters, Russell, and Welker's *Resurrection*.

18 Perhaps this "seeing" will not be essentially different from the way the disciples and others saw Jesus during his lifetime. On the issues connected to their seeing Jesus after his resurrection, see Stephen T. Davis, "'Seeing' the Risen Jesus," in *The Resurrection*, ed. Stephen T. Davis, Daniel Kendall, S.J., and Gerald O'Collins, S.J., 126–47 (Oxford: Oxford University Press, 1997).

Chapter 12

1 That the term *genocide* is exceedingly difficult to define precisely—for both conceptual and political reasons—is made clear in the essays in part 1 of Carol Rittner, John K. Roth, and James M. Smith, eds., *Will Genocide Ever End?* (St. Paul, Minn.: Paragon, 2002). But since I believe the concept is clear at its core (as opposed to the margins), I will leave the definition I just provided at its present broad level.

2 Albert Camus, *The Myth of Sisyphus and Other Essays*, trans. Justin O'Brien (New York: Vintage, 1955), 89.

3 Federal Bureau of Investigation, U.S. Department of Justice, Crime in the United States 2001, Uniform Crime Reports, Table 29, p. 233; http://www.fbi.gov/ucr/cius_01/01crime4.pdf.

4 Federal Bureau of Investigation, U.S. Department of Justice, Crime in the United States 2001, Uniform Crime Reports; http://www.fbi.gov/ucr/cius_01/01crime2.pdf.

5 Bureau of Justice Statistics, U.S. Department of Justice, Felony Sentences in State Courts, 2000, Table 1, p. 2; http://www.ojp.usdoj.gov/bjs/pub/pdf/fssc00.pdf.

6 Death Penalty Information Center; http://www.deathpenaltyinfo.org/article.php?scid=8&did=145.

7 NAACP Legal Defense and Educational Fund, Inc., as reported by the Death Penalty Information Center; http://deathpenaltyinfo.org/article.php?scid=9&did=145.

8 The motivation for being a relativist seems often to be the desire to promote the moral value of tolerance. After all (so the reasoning apparently goes), if one moral view is right per se and all others false, those who hold the true view (or think they do) will be tempted to persecute those who don't. If moral relativism is true, no one has the moral right to impose his or her views on anybody else. But this ignores the possibility that moral theories that are true per se might have built into them a recommendation or even command to be tolerant of those who differ.

9 In the form in which I will use it, the argument that follows is due to Professor Douglas Geivett of Talbot Theological Seminary, and I use it with his permission. The only major difference is that while I focus on genocide, Geivett argues that anything that is genuinely evil is evidence for theism in the sense that it is a departure from the way things ought to be. See the brief discussion of the classical "Moral Argument" in my *God, Reason, and Theistic Proofs* (Grand Rapids: Eerdmans, 1997), 146–50.

10 Of course the traditional problem of evil can still be raised—why did a good and all-powerful God allow genocide to happen in the first place?—and will have to be answered. Doing so is not the project of this essay. See, however, my contributions to Davis, ed., *Encountering Evil,* 2nd ed.

Chapter 13

1 Antony Flew, "Can a Man Witness His Own Funeral?" *The Hibbert Journal* 54 (1956). Flew has widened and updated his critique of survival-of-death theories in several more recent publications, e.g., *The Logic of Mortality* (Oxford: Blackwell, 1987), but the basic line is similar.

Chapter 14

1 I will ignore the origin of the word *metaphysics* in the ancient editing and arranging of Aristotle's works. It is a story with which philosophers are familiar and will not affect the argument of this paper.

2 Or, to avoid reservations that some philosophers of religion have about applying the word *exists* to God, we could just as well say, "God is real."

3 Or, to avoid objections that some philosophers of religion raise about this point, we could just as well say, "The soul is eternal" or "After death our bodies will be raised."

4 Peter van Inwagen and Dean W. Zimmerman, eds., *Metaphysics: The Big Questions* (Malden, Mass.: Blackwell, 1998), 5.

5 Ludwig Wittgenstein, *Remarks on the Philosophy of Psychology*, vol. 1, ed. G. E. M. Anscombe and G. H. von Wright, trans. G. E. M. Anscomb (Oxford: Blackwell, 1980), sec. 949. This amounts to Wittgenstein's definition of metaphysics: treating conceptual problems as if they were factual or scientific problems.

6 People who defend Theory T do not of course deny that religious statements can be proved or disproved *within* a certain religious conceptuality.

For example, they might well admit that the statement, "God is evil," can be disproved within the Christian tradition.

7 See D. Z. Phillips, "Dislocating the Soul," in *Can Religion Be Explained Away?* ed. D. Z. Phillips, 245–51 (London: Macmillan, 1996).

8 Thus Wittgenstein famously says, "It strikes me that a religious belief could only be something like a passionate commitment to a system of reference." *Culture and Value*, eds. G. H. von Wright and H. Nyman, trans. P. Winch (Oxford: Blackwell, 1980), 64.

9 Thus Wittgenstein says, "The historical accounts in the Gospels might, historically speaking, be demonstrably false and yet belief would lose nothing by this . . . because historical proof (the historical proof game) is irrelevant to belief." *Culture and Value*, 32.

10 Support for the weaker interpretation can perhaps be found at the conclusion of Wittgenstein's lectures on religion. He imagines a friend who is going to China saying to him, "We might see one another after death." Casimir Lewy then said, "In this case, you might only mean that he expressed a certain attitude." To which Wittgenstein replied, "I would say, 'No, it isn't the same thing as saying, "I'm very fond of you"'—and may not be the same thing as saying anything else. It says what it says. Why should you be able to substitute anything else?" Ludwig Wittgenstein, *Lectures and Conversations on Aesthetics, Psychology and Religious Belief*, ed. by Cyril Barrett (Berkeley: University of California Press, 2007), 70–71. Moreover, D. Z. Phillips at one point explicitly denies that he holds that religion amounts to nothing more than having certain attitudes and engaging in certain practices. See Phillip Wainwright, *Oxford Handbook of Philosophy of Religion* (Oxford: Oxford University Press, 2004), entry on "Wittgensteinianism."

11 All beliefs are at least in part expressions of attitudes, at least on a dispositional understanding of belief, which I accept.

12 Cf. D. Z. Phillips: "Religious belief is itself the expression of a moral vision," in *Religion Without Explanation* (Oxford: Blackwell, 1976), 143–44.

13 Here are two items that lead some interpreters of Theory T to believe that the stronger interpretation is correct. First, in D. Z. Phillips, *The Concept of Prayer* (New York: Schocken, 1966), 120f. Phillips argues that prayer for forgiveness and petitionary prayer are best understood in ways that make perfect sense even if God is not real. A second example of apparent reductionism is Phillips' argument in his *Death and Immortality* (London: Macmillan, 1970), where an "alternative view" of immortality that is "radically different" is proposed. The alternative view quite apparently does not involve anybody actually living again after death, but rather involves dying to the self here and now and participating in the life of God. See 19, 41, 50, 54–55, 61.

14 D. Z. Phillips has been criticized as follows: his theory entails that statements like "God exists" or "God is to be worshiped and praised" only have sense in the context of certain attitudes and practices; therefore, his theory

entails that the object of (say) Christian worship is not God but the relevant attitudes and practices. I only wish to point out that this odd objection is no part of what I am saying against Theory T.

15 I understand religious realism as the view that claims God's existence or nonexistence is completely independent of what any human being thinks or believes. Religious nonrealism is the denial of that claim. Some religious nonrealists deny or doubt that God exists but hold that some aspects of the religious life are worth retaining.

16 "Where that practice and these views go together, the practice does not spring from the view, but both of them are there." Ludwig Wittgenstein, *Remarks on Frazer's "Golden Bough,"* ed. Rush Rhees, trans. A. C. Miles and Rush Rhees (Retford, England: Brynmill, 1979), 2.

17 See D. Z. Phillips, *Death and Immortality*, 45, as well as many other places in his writings. See also Rush Rhees, *Without Answers* (London: Routledge and Kegan Paul, 1969), 27: "To know God is to worship him."

18 Hard determinism is the theory that says determinism is true and that human beings are accordingly never morally responsible for what they do. See, for example, John Hospers, "Free Will and Psychoanalysis," in *The Problem of Free Will*, ed. Willard F. Enteman (New York: Scribners, 1967) and John Hospers, "What Means This Freedom?," in *Free Will and Determinism*, ed. Bernard Berofsky (New York: Harper & Row, 1966).

19 See D. Z. Phillips, *Religion Without Explanation* (Oxford: Blackwell, 1976), 142–43.

20 Phillips seems to have held this view at least in his early writings. There is even a hint of it in his most recent book, *Religion and Friendly Fire* (Burlington, Vt.: Ashgate: 2004), 80: "It makes no sense to ask whether a practice tallies with reality or not." For what it is worth, I do not accept this point. Astrology and alchemy seem to me to be well-established practices (alchemy once was, and astrology still is) that do not tally with reality.

21 See, e.g., the essays in Kevin Corcoran, ed., *Soul, Body, and Survival* (Ithaca: Cornell University Press, 2001).

22 The notion of linear time is neutral on the A Theory and the B Theory.

23 D. Z. Phillips, *Faith After Foundationalism* (London: Routledge, 1988), 321.

24 Phillips, *Religion Without Explanation*, 148.

25 Phillips, *Religion Without Explanation*, 181.

26 See, *inter alia*, Phillips' lecture, "At the Mercy of Method," (Claremont Graduate University, 1993), 7–8, published in *Philosophy and the Grammar of Religious Belief*, Claremont Studies in the Philosophy of Religion (New York: Palgrave Macmillan, 1995).

27 Marilyn McCord Adams, *Horrendous Evils and the Goodness of God* (Ithaca, N.Y.: Cornell University Press, 1999), 3, 158, 180. The phrase "expanded standard theism" is due to William Rowe.

28 Of course, theism can be expanded in other directions too; there is Jewish theism, Moslem theism, etc.

29 I would like to thank Professors Avery Fouts, Patrick Horn, Susan Peppers-Bates, and Nick Trakakis for their helpful comments on an earlier draft of this paper.

Chapter 15

1 It appears in chapters 2 and 3 of Anselm's *Proslogion*. See M. J. Charlesworth, ed. and trans., *St. Anselm's Proslogion* (Notre Dame, Ind.: University of Notre Dame Press, 1979).

2 Michael Martin, *Atheism: A Philosophical Justification* (Philadelphia: Temple University Press, 1990). All page numbers cited in parentheses are references to Martin's book.

3 In this way, it is also quite unlike my own previous debates with Martin on the resurrection of Jesus. See, e.g., Michael Martin, "Why the Resurrection is Initially Improbable," *Philo* 1, no. 1 (1998). See also Stephen T. Davis, "Is Belief in the Resurrection Rational? A Response to Michael Martin" and Michael Martin, "Reply to Davis," both in *Philo* 2, no 1 (1999). See also Stephen T. Davis, "The Rationality of Resurrection for Christians: A Rejoinder" and Michael Martin, "Christianity and the Rationality of Resurrection," both in *Philo* 3, no. 1 (2000). My own final contribution to the debate was, "The Rationality of Belief in Resurrection: A Reply to Michael Martin," *Philosophia Christi* 5, no. 2 (2003).

4 See Immanuel Kant, *The Critique of Pure Reason*, trans. Norman Kemp Smith (New York: St. Martin's, 1965), 500–507.

5 See the discussion of criteria for success in theistic proofs in my *God, Reason, and Theistic Proofs*, 1–14, 176–93.

6 He occasionally used the term *melius* ("better") instead of *maius* ("greater"). See also *Monologion* II and *Proslogion* V, where he said to God: "Therefore, thou art just, truthful, blessed, and whatever it is better to be than not to be."

7 Many of them are explored more fully in my *God, Reason, and Theistic Proofs*, 79–95.

8 *St. Anselm's Proslogion*, 175.

9 Anselm did follow a blind alley in responding to Gaunilo: he was at great pains to show that the CGLI is not the same thing as, and is less great than, the GCB. That much is true but need hardly bother Gaunilo. Gaunilo's point was not that the GCLI *is* the GCB; his point was rather that if the OA (containing the term *GCB*) is a sound argument, then so is his own parallel OA (containing the term *GCLI*). Surely—so he would have argued—in any valid argument substitutions can be made for the terms that appear in the argument, and if the substitutions are made carefully, the resulting argument will also be valid. Thus: (1) all men are mortal; (2) Jimmy Durante is a man; therefore, (3) Jimmy Durante is mortal.

10 It is found in J. L. Mackie, *The Miracle of Theism* (Oxford: Clarendon, 1982), 52–53.
11 See *St. Anselm's Proslogion*, 163.
12 I have been influenced here by R. Kane's essay, "The Modal Ontological Argument," *Mind* 92 (1984): 33–50.
13 Alvin Plantinga, "Is Theism Really a Miracle?" *Faith and Philosophy* 3, no. 2 (1986): 109–34. See also James F. Sennett, "Universe Indexed Properties and the Fate of the Ontological Argument," *Religious Studies* 27, no. 1 (1991): 65–79.
14 See Kane, "Modal Ontological Argument," 342.
15 For this argument, see Raymond Bradley and Norman Swartz, *Possible Worlds: An Introduction to Logic and Its Philosophy* (Indianapolis: Hackett, 1979), 223.
16 I would like to thank Susan Peppers-Bates, Alvin Plantinga, Colin Ruloff, and Daniel Wagner for their helpful suggestions on earlier versions of this chapter.

Chapter 16

1 For a good introduction to the Christian understanding of God, see Colin E. Gunton, *The Triune Creator: A Historical and Systematic Study* (Grand Rapids: Eerdmans, 1998).
2 Let us define a "necessary being" as a being that (a) cannot not exist and (b) depends for its existence on no other being. This entails, of course, that it is also (c) everlasting (there is no time when it does not exist). Some people hold that (b) is considered a separate attribute called "aseity" and that (a) alone defines a necessary being, but I prefer to say that a necessary being has both (a) and (b).
3 Process philosophers, who deny omnipotence (at least as standardly understood in the tradition), are an exception to this point. I will not discuss Process views of God in the present chapter.
4 See Dale Tuggy, "Three Roads to Open Theism," *Faith and Philosophy* 24 (2007): 28–51.
5 Cf. Isaiah 45:15: "Truly you are a God who hides himself." On God's incomprehensibility and unlikeness to human beings, see Num 23:19; 1 Sam 15:29; Isa 46:5; 55:8-9; and Hos 11:9.
6 Thus the Westminister Confession declares: "God from all eternity did by the most wise and holy council of his own will freely and unchangeably ordain whatsoever comes to pass."
7 Some defenders of CT are prepared to admit the paradoxical nature of their position at this point. See Paul Helm, "The Augustinian-Calvinist View," in *Divine Foreknowledge: Four Views*, ed. James K. Beilby and Paul R. Eddy, 165–66, 169, 177 (Downers Grove, Ill.: InterVarsity, 2001).
8 See J. L. Mackie, "Evil and Omnipotence," in *God and Evil*, ed. Nelson Pike (Englewood Cliffs, N.J.: Prentice-Hall, 1964). Mackie argued that theists

hold to a logically inconsistent position because three of their core beliefs—God is all-powerful, God is perfectly good, and evil exists—form an inconsistent triad. That is, for purely logical reasons, any two of the three may be true, but not all three.

9 I recognize that my point about pastoral considerations does not amount to a refutation of CT. It is, at best, a reason why I find the theory indefensible.

10 The expression "God *qua* God" here simply means "God apart from the incarnation." It is important to add this phrase because everybody—even the strictest defenders of CT—is prepared to admit that the Son of God suffered in his humiliation, e.g., in the Garden of Gethsemane.

11 Cf. Brian Davies in D. Z. Phillips (ed.), unpublished essay.

12 A defender of divine simplicity might reply that all I have shown is that our *concepts* of goodness and wisdom are distinct, but not that the *properties* themselves are distinct; that is, our human limitations prevent us from seeing reality as God does; if we were to see things correctly, we would see that it is logically impossible for God to possess one and lack the other. But my question would then be whether there is any good reason to hold such an obscure view.

13 See Brian Leftow, "God, concepts of," in *Routledge Encyclopedia of Philosophy*, vol. 6.

14 See Helm in Beilby and Eddy, eds., *Divine Foreknowledge.*

15 See James Ross in Beilby and Eddy, eds., *Divine Foreknowledge.*

16 Cf. David Burrell in Beilby and Eddy, eds., *Divine Foreknowledge.*

17 Moreover, the Bible itself seems to me rather clearly to deny that God changes his mind. See Num 23:19 and 1 Sam 15:29.

18 Moreover, there are texts in the Bible whose plain sense seems to imply divine foreknowledge of what look to be free human decisions. See, for example, Exod 3:19; Deut 31:16; Ps 139:16, Isa 44:28; John 6:70-71; and Acts 2:23. It would be interesting to know how defenders of OT would exegete these texts; perhaps they will say that the Bible only reports beliefs that God had about future human decisions that were, before those decisions were made, not true beliefs but only very probably true beliefs.

19 This especially in the light of texts like Revelation 13:8, which seem to imply that God knew in advance precisely who would be saved and who would not, and indeed God wrote the names of the blessed in the Lamb's book of life. See also Ephesians 1:4, where the text affirms that God "chose us in Christ before the foundation of the world."

20 As is the position of J. I. Packer in his *Evangelism and the Sovereignty of God* (Downers Grove, Ill.: InterVarsity, 1961), 21–23.

21 In the following two paragraphs, I am largely following William L. Craig. See Beilby and Eddy, eds., *Divine Foreknowledge*, 55–57. See also David Hunt in the same book, 49–52.

22 Note such texts as Jeremiah 3:7, 19-20 and especially Jeremiah 19:5, where God complains that the children of Israel built altars to Baal and burned their children on them "which I did not command or decree, nor did it enter my mind." If at a certain point in time the thought that the children of Israel would do these terrible deeds had not entered God's mind, it surely seems that at that time God had a false belief. Moreover, if some of God's plans backfire and fail to come to fruition because of God's ignorance of future contingents, that calls into question God's perfect wisdom as well as God's omniscience.

23 I have tried to do so in my "Divine Omniscience and Human Freedom," *Religious Studies* 15, no. 3 (1979).

24 This is the argument (on the assumption that God is essentially omniscient) of Nelson Pike. See his, "Divine Omniscience and Voluntary Action," in *Philosophy of Religion*, ed. Steven Cahn, 68–88 (New York: Harper & Row, 1970).

25 This argument essentially follows Alvin Plantinga, *God, Freedom, and Evil* (New York: Harper & Row, 1974), 69–73.

26 It is true that one event being contingent upon another is not a purely logical relationship. But I am not talking about events, because I believe that "God knowing what I will freely do tomorrow" is everlasting and so is not an "event." What God foreknew yesterday is not an event in the mind of God.

27 Molinism is named after the Spanish Jesuit philosopher Luis Molina (1535–1600). Alvin Plantinga introduced middle knowledge into the contemporary discussion among philosophers of religion. See his *God, Freedom, and Evil*, 34–57. The foremost contemporary defenders of Molinism are Thomas P. Flint and William Lane Craig. See Flint's *Divine Providence: The Molinist Account* (Ithaca: Cornell University Press, 1998). In his various writings to date, Craig has fruitfully applied middle knowledge to several different problems in theology and the philosophy of religion.

28 I should mention that a certain philosophical objection to the very idea of middle knowledge has been much discussed of late. It is called "the grounding objection." I do not myself find the objection convincing and so will not consider it here. For a brief discussion of it by Craig, see Beilby and Eddy, eds., *Divine Foreknowledge*, 140–43. For a sensible assessment of the arguments, see Edward Wierenga, "Providence, Middle Knowledge, and the Grounding Objection," *Philosophia Christi*, ser. 2, vol. 3, no. 2 (2001): 447–57.

29 See David Lewis, *Counterfactuals* (Cambridge, Mass.: Harvard University Press, 1973) and Robert Stalnaker, *Inquiry* (Cambridge, Mass.: MIT Press, 1984).

30 I would like to thank Kelly James Clark, David Hunt, Alan Padgett, Susan Peppers-Bates, and Dale Tuggy for their helpful comments on an earlier draft of this chapter. They do not agree with everything I've said here.

Index